classic
Vegetarian
recipes

classic
Vegetarian
recipes

Sue Ashworth

Carole Handslip

Kathryn Hawkins

Cara Hobday

Jenny Stacey

Rosemary Wadey

Pamela Westland

SIENA

A Siena Book
Siena is an imprint of Parragon

First published in Great Britain in 1998 by
Parragon
13 Whiteladies Road
Clifton
Bristol BS8 1PB

ISBN: 0-75252-746-0

Printed in Italy

Edited, designed and produced by Haldane Mason, London

Acknowledgements
Editor: Jo-Anne Cox
Editorial Assistant: Elizabeth Towers
Design: dap ltd
Photographers: Karl Adamson, Sue Atkinson, Iain Bagwell, Amanda Heywood,
Joff Lee, Patrick McLeavey, Clive Streeter, Andrew Sydenham
Home Economists: Sue Ashworth, Sue Atkinson, Carole Handslip, Kathryn Hawkins,
Cara Hobday, Louise Pickford, Rosemary Wadey

Note
Cup measurements in this book are for American cups.
Tablespoons are assumed to be 15 ml. Unless otherwise stated, milk is
assumed to be full-fat, eggs are medium and pepper is freshly ground black pepper.

Contents

Introduction 8

Soups & Starters 20

Light Meals 60

Pasta Dishes 98

Grains & Pulses 118

Stir-fries & Sautés 144

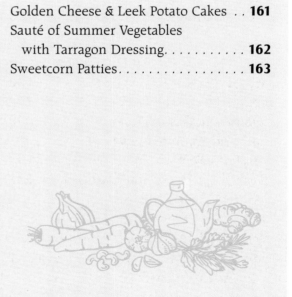

Bakes & Roasts 164

Side Dishes & Salads 190

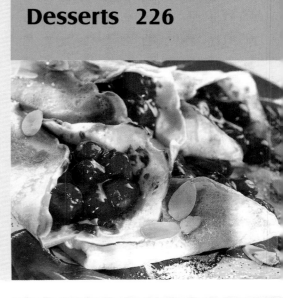

Desserts 226

Index 252

Introduction

People choose to eat vegetarian food for all sorts of different reasons, whether on moral grounds, for health reasons, for economy or simply because they prefer the flavour. Whatever the motive, one thing is certain – everyone enjoys good food, and vegetarian food can be as good as, and indeed often better than, traditional meat and fish dishes. Vegetarian meals are perfect for entertaining or just for the family to enjoy, and can be easily adapted to suit all tastes.

This inspirational cookbook is designed to appeal to vegetarians and vegans alike as it contains a wide range of recipes which will appeal to all. Another aim is to dispel the myth that vegetarian food is brown, stodgy and bland. When browsing through the recipes you will discover just how versatile, colourful and flavourful a vegetarian diet can be. It makes perfect sense when you consider the natural foods used and the wide range of produce available all year round, all of which are suitable for the vegetarian diet.

With the advent of refrigerated transport, fresh produce is now shipped from all over the world to give us a whole array of fresh fruit and vegetables with which to create delicious recipes. The use of exotic spices, fresh herbs and garlic, sauces and relishes makes for an exciting and healthy diet.

Eating a balanced, healthy diet is very important. This can be easily achieved by combining the different recipes in this book when planning your meal, to include protein, carbohydrate, vitamins, minerals and some fats. It is very important in any diet, but especially a vegetarian diet, that a good balance is achieved and that sufficient protein is eaten, and you should bear this in mind when deciding which of the wonderful recipes to try in the chapters that follow.

When it comes to recipes, there are dishes from far and wide, including the Orient, Middle East and the Mediterranean. The diets in these regions are healthy and the native ingredients and flavourings are exciting and delicious. The book also contains more familiar recipes and variations on themes, such as Vegetable Toad-in-the-Hole, a quick, tasty family meal in which I guarantee that the meat won't be missed. Indeed, this can be said for all of the recipes in this book. Many could be served to meat-eating guests without them missing the 'meat factor' in any way. It is the perfect way to introduce your friends to this healthy and delicious diet.

When cooking the following recipes, feel free to substitute some of the ingredients to suit specific diets, using soya milk, for example, instead of cow's milk, cream substitute instead of the dairy cream and vegetarian margarine instead of butter. In this way you will enjoy a whole range of super starters, tasty light meals and snacks, wonderful main meals and accompaniments, and delicious desserts. This cookbook will allow you to discover or reaffim that the vegetarian diet has progressed greatly from the nut cutlet to a colourful and imaginative way of eating. Enjoy!

VEGETARIAN NUTRITION

Vegetarian food is extremely healthy, and can provide all the important vitamins, minerals, proteins, carbohydrates and fats that make up a nutritious, well-balanced diet. And because more fruit, vegetables, grains and pulses (legumes) tend to be eaten, the diet is rich in complex carbohydrates, the primary source of energy and fibre, which helps to keep the body vibrant and healthy.

Protein

Obtaining sufficient protein is not a problem in a vegetarian diet as there are plenty of foods from which to choose. Eggs, cheese, milk, nuts, beans and soya products, such as TVP (texturized vegetable protein), soya milk, tofu (bean curd), Quorn or mycoprotein, are all excellent sources. Make sure that you eat a wide variety of these foods to get the full range of protein that your body needs.

Fat

Another additional benefit of following a vegetarian diet is that it can be quite low in fat. The main sources of fat in your diet will be from vegetable, nut and olive oils, dairy foods, nuts and any products containing these ingredients. So slimmers can succeed in losing weight following a vegetarian diet, provided they keep an eye on their overall fat intake.

Carbohydrates

A vegetarian diet is rich in complex carbohydrates, found in starchy foods, such as brown rice, oats, and wholewheat pasta and bread. These are particularly useful to dieters, as they ensure a steady release of energy and a stable blood sugar level.

Vitamins

Fruit and vegetables are packed with important vitamins, essential for our general well-being and the healthy functioning of our bodies. If you follow a vegetarian diet, you can't go far wrong.

The best sources of vitamin A are yellow fruits and vegetables and some green vegetables – apricots, peaches, spinach and carrots, for example. It is also present in butter and added to margarines. Vitamin A helps us to resist infections and keeps the skin, hair, eyes and body tissues in healthy condition.

The B group vitamins act as a catalyst in the releasing of energy from food. They are also vital for the maintenance of a healthy nervous system and red blood cells. Apart from vitamin B12, all the B vitamins can be found in yeast and wholegrain cereals, especially wheat flour and wheatgerm. Vegetarians eating a wide variety of foods should therefore have no problem in obtaining enough B vitamins, although vegans (who do not eat dairy products) need to include some sort of B12 supplement in their diet.

Vitamin C is well known for helping to prevent infections and is firmly believed by many to assist in warding off, as well as curing, winter colds and 'flu. Eat foods rich in vitamin C with iron-rich foods, as it helps to increase the absorption of iron. Fresh fruit, leafy vegetables, tomatoes, (bell) peppers and potatoes are all good sources. Avoid drinking tea, coffee and certain soft drinks with foods that contain vitamin C, as the caffeine can actually decrease the amount of vitamin C your body subsequently absorbs. Since vitamin C is easily destroyed during cooking, only use a small amount of water when boiling vegetables to cook them as quickly as possible. This will minimize the risk of the vitamin leaching into the cooking water.

The other important vitamin for good health is vitamin D, which enables the body to absorb calcium, thus providing strong bones and teeth. Vitamin D is often known as the 'sunshine vitamin', as the body can manufacture its own supply from exposure to sunlight. Good food sources include eggs, cheese, margarine and butter.

Minerals

Minerals are another group of vital nutrients that are needed by the human body. Although only minute amounts are required, minerals need to be supplied on a regular basis. It makes sense to get to know which foods contain them, and make sure you are getting plenty of these in your diet. There should be no problem as long as you eat a wide variety of foods.

Calcium is found in milk, cheese, yogurt and other dairy products, leafy green vegetables, bread, nuts, seeds and dried fruits. Iron is found in beans, seeds, nuts, eggs, cocoa, chocolate, wholemeal (whole wheat) bread, leafy green vegetables and dried fruits (especially apricots and figs). Other important minerals include magnesium, phosphorus, potassium and zinc.

THE VEGETARIAN SHOPPING BASKET

When shopping for vegetarian foods, make sure that you are not buying animal products unawares. Choose cheese that is made from vegetarian rennet; buy agar-agar or gelozone instead of gelatine; select a vegetarian suet instead of beef suet – no, you won't have to forego delicious dumplings!

Be aware of what you are spreading on your bread too. Some margarines are not suitable as they contain both fish oils and animal fats, so check that you are buying a brand made entirely of vegetable oil. Butter is perfect, unless, of course, you are a vegan.

The Vegetarian Store-cupboard

A well-stocked store-cupboard forms the backbone of any good cook's kitchen, and it is always useful to have plenty of basic foods ready to hand. Use the following information as a checklist when you need to replenish your stocks.

Flour

You will need to keep a selection of flours: plain (all-purpose) and self-raising flour if you want to make your own bread, and wholemeal (whole wheat) flour, either for using on its own or for combining with white flour for cakes and pastries. You may also like to keep some rice flour and cornflour (cornstarch) for thickening sauces and to add to cakes, biscuits and puddings. Buckwheat, chick-pea (garbanzo bean) and soya flours can also be bought. These are useful for pancakes and for combining with other flours to add different flavours and textures.

Grains

A good variety of grains is essential. For rice, choose from long-grain, basmati, Italian arborio for making risotto, short-grain for puddings, and wild rice to add flavour and interest. Look out for fragrant Thai rice, jasmine rice and combinations of different varieties to add colour and texture to your dishes. When choosing your rice, remember that brown rice is a much better source of vitamin B1 and fibre.

Other grains add variety to the diet. Try to include some barley (whole grain or pearl), millet, bulgar wheat, polenta (made from maize), oats (oatmeal, oatflakes or oatbran), semolina – including cous-cous (from which it is made), sago and tapioca.

Pasta

Pasta has become much more popular recently, and there are many types and shapes to choose from. Keep a good selection, and always make sure you have the basic lasagne sheets, tagliatelle or fettuccine (flat ribbons) and spaghetti. Try spinach- or tomato-flavoured varieties for a change, and sample some of the many fresh pastas now available. Better still, make your own – handrolling pasta, while undoubtedly time-consuming, can be very satisfying, but you can buy a special machine for rolling the dough and cutting certain shapes. You could also buy a wooden 'pasta tree' on which to hang the pasta to dry, in which case you might find you get enthusiastic help especially if you have small children!

Pulses (Legumes)

Pulses (legumes) are very important in a vegetarian diet as they are a valuable source of protein, vitamins and minerals. Stock up on soya beans, haricot (navy) beans, red kidney beans, cannellini beans, chick-peas (garbanzo beans), all types of lentils, split peas and butter beans. Buy dried pulses (legumes) for soaking and cooking yourself, or canned varieties for speed and convenience.

It is important to cook dried red and black kidney beans in plenty of vigorously boiling water for 15 minutes to destroy harmful toxins in the outer skin. Drain and rinse the beans, and then continue to simmer until the beans are tender. Soya beans should be boiled for 1 hour, as they contain a substance that inhibits protein absorption.

Spices and Herbs

A good selection of spices and herbs is important for adding variety and interest to your cooking – add to your range each time you try a new recipe. There are some good spice mixtures available – try Cajun, Chinese five-spice powder, Indonesian piri-piri and the different curry blends. Try grinding your own spices with a mortar and pestle, or in a coffee mill (wash well after using!), to make your own blends, or just experiment with those that you can buy. Although spices will keep well, don't leave them in the cupboard for too long, as they may lose some of their strength. Buy small amounts as you need them.

Fresh herbs are always preferable to dried, but it is essential to have dried ones in stock as a useful back-up. Keep the basics such as thyme, rosemary, bay leaves and some good Mediterranean mixtures for Italian and French cooking.

Chillies

These come both fresh and dried and in colours from green through yellow, orange and red to brown. The 'hotness' varies so use with caution, but as a guide the smaller they are the hotter they will be. The seeds are hottest and are usually discarded. When cutting chillies with bare hands do not touch your eyes; the juices will cause severe irritation.

Chilli powder should also be used sparingly. Check whether the powder is pure chilli or a chilli seasoning or blend, which should be milder. Chilli sauces are also used widely in oriental cookery, but again they vary in strength from hot to exceedingly hot, as well as in sweetness.

Nuts and Seeds

As well as adding protein, vitamins and useful fats to the diet, nuts and seeds add important flavour and texture to vegetarian meals. To bring out the flavour of nuts and seeds, grill (broil) or roast them until lightly browned. Make sure that you keep a good supply of almonds, brazils, cashews, chestnuts (dried or canned), hazelnuts, peanuts, pecans, pistachios, pine kernels (nuts) and walnuts. Coconut – either creamed or desiccated (shredded) – is useful too.

For your seed collection, sesame, sunflower, pumpkin and poppy seeds are a good choice. Pumpkin seeds in particular are an excellent source of zinc.

Dried Fruits

Currants, raisins, sultanas (golden raisins), dates, apples, apricots, figs, pears, peaches, prunes, paw-paws (papayas), mangoes, figs, bananas and pineapples can all be purchased dried and can be used in lots of different recipes. When buying dried fruits, look for untreated varieties: for example, buy figs that have not been rolled in sugar, and choose unsulphured apricots, if they are available.

Though dried fruits are a healthier alternative to biscuits (cookies) and sweets (candies), they are still high in calories, being a natural source of sugar.

Oils and Fats

Oils are useful for adding subtle flavourings to foods, so it is a good idea to have a selection in your store-cupboard. Use a light olive oil for cooking and extra-virgin olive oil for salad dressings. Use sunflower oil as a good general-purpose oil and select one or two speciality oils to add character to different dishes. Sesame oil is wonderful in stir-fries; hazelnut and walnut oils are superb in salad dressings.

Oils and fats add flavour to foods, and contain the important fat-soluble vitamins A, D, E and K. Remember all fats and oils are high in calories, and that oils are higher in calories than butter or margarine – one tablespoon of oil contains 134 calories, whereas one tablespoon of butter or margarine contains 110 calories. When you are using oil in dressings or adding it to a wok or frying pan (skillet), it is a good idea to measure it – it's easy to use twice as much without realizing.

Vinegars

Choose three or four vinegars – red or white wine, cider, light malt, tarragon, sherry or balsamic vinegar, to name just a few. Each will add its own character to your recipes.

Mustards

Mustards are made from black, brown or white mustard seeds which are ground, mixed with spices and then, usually, mixed with vinegar.

Meaux mustard is made from mixed mustard seeds and has a grainy texture with a warm, spicy taste.

Dijon mustard, made from husked and ground mustard seeds, is medium-hot and has a sharp flavour. Its versatility in salads and with barbecues makes it an ideal mustard for the vegetarian. It is made in Dijon, France, and only mustard made there can be labelled as such.

German mustard is mild sweet/sour and is best used in Scandinavian and German dishes.

Bottled Sauces

Soy sauce is widely used in all Eastern cookery and is made from fermented yellow soya beans mixed with wheat, salt, yeast and sugar. It comes in both light and dark varieties. Light soy sauce tends to be rather salty, whereas dark soy sauce tends to be sweeter and is more often used in dips and sauces.

Teriyaki sauce gives an authentic Japanese flavouring to stir-fries. Thick and dark brown, it contains soy sauce, vinegar, sesame oil and spices as main ingredients.

Black bean and yellow bean sauces add an instant authentic Chinese flavour to stir-fries. Black bean sauce is the stronger; the yellow bean variety is milder and is excellent with vegetables.

USEFUL EXTRAS

Tahini (sesame seed paste), yeast extract, sea salt, black and green peppercorns, tomato and garlic purées (pastes), vegetable stock (bouillon) cubes, dried yeast, gelozone or agar-agar are all useful store-cupboard additions.

THE VEGETARIAN FRIDGE AND FREEZER

Thankfully, food manufacturers have wised up to the fact that lots of us love to eat vegetarian food, so it is now possible to choose from a huge range of prepared meals from the chilled or frozen food cabinets. These are excellent standbys for when you want a meal in a hurry, and they add variety and choice to the diet. Pasta dishes, vegetable bakes and burgers, curries, flans and quiches are just some of the dishes to choose from.

Besides stocking a selection of ready-made meals, freeze other basics such as frozen pastries (shortcrust, filo or puff pastry); a selection of breads, such as pitta, French bread, rolls or part-baked bread; pre-cooked pasta dishes, pasta sauces, vegetable stock, breadcrumbs, home-made soups and sauces, flan cases, pancakes, pizza bases, and so on. All these will be useful when you are short of time.

THE SECRET OF SUCCESS

As with any cooking, the choice of ingredients is of paramount importance. If they are fresh and of good quality, you are well on your way to achieving delicious food. Not only will the flavours be better, but so will the colours, textures and nutritious value. Fresh fruit and vegetables lose their vitamin content very quickly if stored for too long, so buy from the freshest possible source, and use soon after buying.

Basic Recipes

Vegetarian stocks and sauces are invaluable for many recipes. Here are a few basics.

Fresh Vegetable Stock

This can be kept chilled for up to three days or frozen for up to three months. Salt is not added when cooking the stock: it is better to season it according to the dish in which it is to be used. Makes 1.5 litres/2½ pints/6¼ cups.

250 g/9 oz shallots
1 large carrot, diced
1 celery stalk, chopped
½ fennel bulb
1 garlic clove
1 bay leaf
a few fresh parsley and tarragon sprigs
2 litres/3½ pints/8¾ cups water
pepper

1 Put all the ingredients in a large saucepan and bring to the boil. Skim off the surface scum with a flat spoon and reduce to a gentle simmer. Partially cover and cook for 45 minutes. Leave to cool.

2 Line a sieve (strainer) with clean muslin (cheesecloth) and put over a large jug or bowl. Pour the stock through the sieve (strainer). Discard the herbs and vegetables. Cover and store in small quantities in the refrigerator for up to three days.

Tahini Cream

Tahini is a paste made from sesame seeds. This nutty-flavoured sauce is good served with Kofta Kebabs (see page 135) and other Middle Eastern dishes, such as Falafel (see page 76). Makes 150 ml/¼ pint/⅔ cup.

3 tbsp tahini (sesame seed paste)
6 tbsp water
2 tsp lemon juice
1 garlic clove, crushed
salt and pepper

1 Blend together the tahini (sesame seed paste) and water. Stir in the lemon juice and garlic. Season with salt and freshly ground black pepper.

Béchamel Sauce

This basic white sauce can be used in all kinds of dishes. Flavour it with grated cheese or chopped fresh herbs if you like. Makes 600 ml/1 pint/2½ cups.

600 ml/1 pint/2½ cups milk
4 cloves
1 bay leaf
pinch of freshly grated nutmeg
25 g/1 oz/2 tbsp butter or vegetarian margarine
25 g/1 oz/¼ cup plain (all-purpose) flour
salt and pepper

1 Put the milk in a saucepan and add the cloves, bay leaf and nutmeg. Gradually bring to the boil. Remove from the heat and leave for 15 minutes.

2 Melt the butter or margarine in another saucepan and stir in the flour to form a roux. Cook, stirring, for 1 minute.

3 Remove from the heat. Strain the milk and gradually blend into the roux.

4 Return to the heat and bring to the boil, stirring, until the sauce thickens. Season and add any flavourings.

Salads

*Salads are such a versatile way of eating, and the variety of ingredients
is so great, that they can be made to suit any occasion, from a light piquant
starter to a more substantial dish to serve as a main course, or a mixture
of exotic fruits for a delicious dessert.*

SALAD INGREDIENTS

A salad is the ideal emergency meal. It is quick to 'rustle up' and there are times when you might discover that you already have a really good combination of ingredients to hand when you need to present a meal-in-a-moment. A splash of culinary inspiration, and you will find you have prepared a fantastic salad that you had no idea was lurking in your kitchen!

Salads can be fruity, eggy, cheesy, made with grains or pulses (legumes), or just fresh green – all are highly nutritious. They are also generally low in calories if you go easy on the dressing, or use a fat-free dressing. It is easy to make a salad look attractive and appetizing, thus encouraging your family to eat fruit and vegetables. It is also often a welcome dish to serve alongside richer offerings.

Supermarkets now stock many unusual ingredients, which can add interest to an ordinary salad. Experiment with new

fruits and vegetables, buying them in small quantities to lend unusual flavours to salads made from cheaper ingredients. Always use the freshest ingredients to ensure a successful salad. Try to ensure that you buy fruit and vegetables at their peak and use them within a few days of buying.

Herbs

Every salad can be turned into something special with the addition of a few carefully chosen herbs to add flavour and a delicious aroma. The recipes in this book make liberal use of fresh herbs, adding a unique 'zip' to the food. Experiment with different varieties each time you make a salad or a dressing; try marjoram, thyme, chives, basil, mint, fennel and dill as well as the ubiquitous parsley. Basil goes especially well with tomatoes, and fennel or dill are particularly good with cucumber or beetroot salads.

Flowers

For an extra-special salad, add a few edible flowers, which look particularly colourful and attractive especially when mixed with a variety of salad leaves (greens). Common sense is the best guide as to which flowers may be used whole and which should have the petals gently separated from the calyx. Borage, primroses, violas, pot marigolds, nasturtiums, violets, rock geraniums and rose petals are all suitable, imparting a sweetness and intense colour contrast to any green salad. Chive flowers have a good strong flavour – the pretty mauve flower heads should be separated into florets before sprinkling over the salad.

It is, of course, important that the flowers should look fresh and clean. If they need washing, be sure to handle with great care. Gently pat dry with paper towels and then store them in a rigid plastic container in the refrigerator until required.

It goes without saying that flowers which have been sprayed with insecticide should not be used.

Nuts

In addition to colour and flavour, salads need texture, which can be achieved by combining crunchy ingredients with softer fruits and vegetables. Nuts are particularly useful in this respect, contributing a pleasant crunchiness as well as flavour. Many nuts taste even better if they are browned before use. These include almonds, hazelnuts, pine kernels (nuts) and peanuts. To brown nuts, place them on a baking sheet (cookie sheet) and place in a hot oven for 5–10 minutes until golden brown. Pine kernels (nuts) may also be browned by placing in a dry heavy-based frying pan (skillet) and shaking over a high heat until golden.

Chicory (Endive) This is available from autumn (fall) to spring and, with its slightly bitter flavour, makes an interesting addition to winter salads. Choose firm, tightly packed cones with yellow leaf tips. Avoid any with damaged leaves or leaf tips that are turning green as they will be rather too bitter. Red chicory (endive) is also available.

Chinese Leaves These are a most useful salad ingredient available in the autumn (fall) and winter months. Shred them fairly finely and use them as a base, adding bean-shoots and peppery leaves such as watercress or dandelion.

Cos (Romaine) Lettuce This is a superb variety used especially in Caesar salad. It has long, narrow, bright green leaves with a wonderfully crisp texture.

Endive (Chicory) A slightly bitter-tasting but attractive curly-leaved salad plant. There are two varieties: the curly endive (frisée) which has a mop head of light green frilly leaves and the Batavia endive (escarole) which has broader, smoother leaves. Before they mature, both varieties have their leaves tied together to blanch the centres, which produces tender, succulent leaves.

Feuille de Chêne (Oak Leaf) This red-tinged, delicately flavoured lettuce is good when mixed with other leaves, both for the contrast in flavour and the contrast in colour.

Iceberg Lettuce This has pale green, densely packed leaves. It may appear expensive, but is in fact extremely good value when compared with other lettuces by weight. It has a fresh, crisp texture and keeps well in the refrigerator.

Lamb's Lettuce (Corn Salad) This is so called because its dark green leaves resemble a lamb's tongue. It is also known as corn salad and the French call it mâche. It is well worth looking out for when it is in season both for its flavour and its appearance.

Purslane This has fleshy stalks and rosettes of succulent green leaves which have a sharp, clean flavour.

Radicchio This is a variety of chicory (endive) originating in Italy. It looks rather like a small, tightly packed red lettuce. It is quite expensive but comparatively few leaves are needed, as it has a bitter flavour. The leaves are a deep purple colour with a white contrasting rib. They add character to any green salad.

Rocket (Arugula) The young green leaves of this plant have a distinctive warm peppery flavour and are delicious in green salads.

Round or Cabbage Lettuce This is the one most familiar to us all. Try to avoid the hothouse variety as the leaves are limp and floppy.

Salad leaves (greens)

Supermarkets now stock a wonderful variety of previously-hard-to-find salad leaves (greens), so experiment with different types. The raw leaves from young leafy vegetables can also be used.

Watercress This has a fresh peppery taste which makes it a welcome addition to many salads. It is available throughout the year, though it is less good when flowering, or early in the season when the leaves are small.

Preparing salad leaves (greens)

Whichever salad leaves (greens) you choose, they should be firm and crisp with no sign of browning or wilting. They should be handled with care because salad leaves (greens) bruise easily.

To prepare, pull off and discard all damaged outer leaves and wash the remaining leaves in cold salted water to remove any insects, then dry them thoroughly. This can be done either by patting the leaves dry with paper towels, spinning them in a salad spinner, or by placing them in a clean tea towel (dish cloth), gathering up the loose ends and swinging the tea towel (dish cloth) around vigorously.

Dress the salad leaves (greens) just before serving. If you dress it any earlier the leaves will wilt.

Dressings

All salads depend on being well dressed and so it is necessary to use the best ingredients. The principal ingredients in a salad dressing are oil and vinegar, with a variety of other flavourings that can be varied to suit the particular salad.

The choice of oil is particularly important. Oils are produced from various nuts, seeds and beans and each has its own flavour. Unrefined oils, although more expensive, are worth using for their superior taste.

Olive Oil is the best oil for most salad dressings. Choose the green-tinged, fruity oil labelled 'extra virgin' or 'first pressing'. It has a distinctive taste and aroma.

Sesame Oil has a strong nutty tang and is particularly good with oriental-type salads.

Sunflower and Safflower Oil are neutral-flavoured oils and can be mixed with olive oil or used alone to produce a lighter dressing. Mayonnaise made with a combination of one of these oils and olive oil has a lighter consistency than one made from olive oil only.

Walnut and Hazelnut Oil have the most wonderful flavour and aroma, and are usually mixed with olive oil in a

French dressing. They are well worth their higher price and are especially good with slightly bitter salad plants such as chicory (endive), radicchio or spinach.

A good dressing needs a touch of acidity. Good quality vinegars such as wine, cider, sherry or herb-flavoured vinegars are ideal, but malt vinegar is far too harsh and overpowers the subtle balance of the dressing. Lemon juice may be used as a dressing and is often preferable if the salad is fruit-based.

Balsamic Vinegar is dark and mellow with a sweet/sour flavour. It is expensive but you need only a few drops or at most a teaspoonful to give a wonderful taste. It is made in the area around Modena in Italy.

Cider Vinegar is reputed to contain many healthy properties and valuable nutrients. It has a light, subtle flavour redolent of the fruit from which it is made.

Flavoured Vinegars can be made from cider and wine vinegar. To do this, steep your chosen ingredient in a small bottle of vinegar for anything up to two weeks. Particularly good additions are basil, tarragon, garlic, thyme, mint or rosemary. Raspberry wine vinegar can be made by adding about twelve raspberries to a bottle of vinegar.

Sherry Vinegar has a rich mellow flavour which blends well with walnut and hazelnut oils, but is equally good by itself.

Wine Vinegar is the one most commonly used for French dressing; either red or white will do.

SALAD DRESSINGS

Make up a large bottle of your favourite dressing. Here are some recipes for you to try:

Sesame Dressing

A piquant dressing with a rich creamy texture.

2 tbsp tahini (sesame seed paste)
2 tbsp cider vinegar
2 tbsp medium sherry
2 tbsp sesame oil
1 tbsp soy sauce
1 garlic clove, crushed

1 Put the tahini (sesame seed paste) in a bowl and gradually mix in the vinegar and sherry until smooth.

2 Add the remaining ingredients and mix together thoroughly.

Tomato Dressing

This completely fat-free dressing is ideal if you are counting calories.

125 ml/4 fl oz/1/2 cup tomato juice
1 garlic clove, crushed
2 tbsp lemon juice
1 tbsp soy sauce
1 tsp clear honey
2 tbsp chopped chives
salt and pepper

Put all the ingredients into a screw-top jar and shake vigorously until well mixed.

Apple & Cider Vinegar Dressing

2 tbsp sunflower oil
2 tbsp concentrated apple juice
2 tbsp cider vinegar
1 tbsp Meaux mustard
1 garlic clove, crushed
salt and pepper

Put the oil, apple juice, vinegar, mustard, garlic and salt and pepper to taste in a screw-top jar and shake vigorously until well mixed.

Green Herb Dressing

A pale green dressing with a fresh flavour, ideal with cauliflower or broccoli.

15 g/1/2 oz/1/4 cup parsley
15 g/1/2 oz/1/4 cup mint
15 g/1/2 oz/1/4 cup chives
1 garlic clove, crushed
150 ml/1/4 pint/2/3 cup natural yogurt
salt and pepper

1 Remove the stalks from the parsley and mint and put the leaves in a blender or food processor with the chives, garlic and yogurt.

2 Add seasoning to taste. Blend until smooth, then store in the refrigerator until needed.

Wok Cookery

Wok cookery is an excellent technique for vegetarians as it enables you to serve up delicious dishes of crisp, tasty vegetables in minutes.

PREPARING FOOD FOR THE WOK

Ensure all ingredients are to hand before you start to cook, otherwise the first ingredients will be overcooked before the others are ready to add. Although oriental cooks use a variety of cleavers for chopping, a sharp kitchen knife will do just as well. All ingredients should be cut into uniform sizes with as many cut surfaces exposed as possible, hence the practice of cutting on the slant or diagonal, or into julienne strips or matchsticks.

Stir-frying

This is the most popular method of cooking in a wok. Once the food has been prepared and you are ready to begin, add the oil to the wok and heat it, swirling it round until it is really hot. If it is sufficiently hot the ingredients added should sizzle and begin to cook.

Most recipes begin by cooking the onions, garlic and ginger, because they flavour the oil. The heat may need to be lowered a little at first but must be increased again as the other ingredients are added. Gas probably gives the best results because of the speed of controlling the heat, and the fact that the curved base of the wok fits so well into the hob. Electric and solid fuel hobs are more efficient if you are using a flat-bottomed wok.

Always add the ingredients in the order they are listed in the recipe. While the food is cooking, keep stirring. When you add a sauce or liquid at the end of a recipe, first push the cooked food to the side of the wok so the sauce heats as quickly as possible, then toss the food back into the sauce over a high heat so that it boils and thickens the sauce. Serve the cooked food as soon as possible.

Deep-frying

A wok is usually used for deep-frying battered egg-and-crumbed morsels of food or food encased in pastry. The best oil to use is groundnut, which has a high smoke point and mild flavour, so it will neither burn nor impart taste to the food.

If you have a round-bottomed wok, use a metal wok stand to keep it stable during cooking. It is not necessary to preheat the wok. Simply add the oil (about 600 ml/1 pint/2½ cups should be sufficient) and heat to 180°C–190°C/350°F–375°F or until a cube of bread browns in 30 seconds.

The cooking time is determined by the size of the ingredients to be cooked, and it is essential that the oil is hot enough to seal the batter or pastry as quickly as possible without the food absorbing any more oil than necessary. When golden brown, remove with a slotted spoon and drain on paper towels. Serve at once to retain the food's crispness.

Steaming

To steam food you need a large wok and a bamboo steamer with a lid. The wok needs a little water in the bottom but it must not reach the base of the bamboo steamer when it is in position: stand the steamer on a trivet. The steamer has several layers, which can be stacked on top of each other. This means more than one type of food can be cooked at the same time. Put the food on a plate that will just fit into the steamer and place it carefully in one of the layers. Add seasoning, herbs and flavourings, cover with the lid and steam until tender. Make sure the wok does not boil dry by adding extra water when necessary.

If you don't have a bamboo steamer, you can still steam food in the wok. Simply put a plate on a metal or wooden trivet in the wok, pour in enough water to come just below the plate and cover with a lid.

Braising/Simmering

The wok can also be used as a saucepan and is excellent for making stir-fry soups, for example. Just stir-fry the ingredients in a little oil, add the liquid seasonings and simmer either uncovered or with a lid. With this type of soup the vegetables should still have a good 'bite' to them, so the cooking time is a lot less than that of traditional soups.

Pan-frying and braising are speeded up using a wok because of the improved heat distribution. Simply fry the ingredients quickly, then add the stock or sauce, cover and simmer gently until tender. Sometimes it is better not to cover the wok so that the cooking liquid is reduced, intensifying the flavours even more. Whichever method is used, stir occasionally to prevent any possibility of sticking.

Vegetarian Barbecues

There are so many tasty and nutritious vegetarian dishes that can be cooked over hot coals – after all, barbecueing is just an alternative method of cooking by direct heat.

PLANNING YOUR BARBECUE

Barbecues always take longer to get going than you expect, so allow plenty of time. Don't be tempted to start cooking too soon, or the coals will not be ready. The flames should have died down and the coals reduced to a steady glow before you begin.

Don't attempt to cook for a large party on a small barbecue, as it could take hours to feed everyone! In this situation, it is better to cook most of the food in the kitchen, and either provide only a few barbecued items, or use the barbecue to finish partly-cooked foods. Vegetarian sausages and burgers are ideal, as they cook quickly and in large quantities.

ADVANCE PREPARATIONS

Many foods for barbecuing will benefit from being marinated, especially dishes using tofu (bean curd) or Quorn (mycoprotein), which absorb the flavour of the marinade. You can buy tofu (bean curd) in four varieties – smoked, firm, soft or silken; use smoked or firm for kebabs (kabobs), soft for adding to burgers, and silken for adding to sauces and dips.

Have your kebabs (kabobs) ready-threaded for quick cooking; if possible, choose flat metal skewers so that the food does not slide as the kebabs (kabobs) are turned. Alternatively, use bamboo sticks, but soak them in water beforehand so that they do not burn over the hot coals and ruin the food.

Control the heat by adjusting the distance of the food from the coals, or by altering the controls on a gas barbecue. Ideally, food should not be cooked too quickly, or it will blacken and char on the outside before the middle is cooked – it needs time for the distinctive barbecued taste to be imparted.

COOKING TIPS

First and foremost, treat food for barbecuing with care – it should be kept chilled in the refrigerator or in a cool box, complete with ice packs, until ready to cook.

Light the barbecue in plenty of time, remembering that you will need about 45 minutes for charcoal to heat and about 10–15 minutes for a gas barbecue to become hot enough. Food cooks best over glowing embers, not smoking fuel, so avoid putting the food over the hot coals until the smoking has subsided. Oil the barbecue rack lightly before adding the food, to help to prevent it from sticking, and oil the skewers, tongs and barbecue fork for the same reason.

Throw some fresh herbs on to the coals – they smell wonderful as they burn, and will add extra flavour to your food. Woody herbs burn slowly, so they are good choices.

COOKING VEGETABLES

For kebabs (kabobs), choose a mixture of vegetables that will all cook at the same rate, and cut into even-sized chunks. Choose from aubergines (eggplants), tomatoes, sliced corn-on-the-cob or baby corn cobs, mushrooms and courgettes (zucchini). New potatoes, onions, carrots, parsnips and Jerusalem artichokes can also be barbecued, but will need pre-cooking first.

If you are going to serve jacket potatoes, cook them first too – either conventionally or in a microwave. Wrap in foil and keep warm to one side of the barbecue, ready for filling. Or finish cooking potatoes directly on the grid over the coals, barbecueing them until the skins are crisp and brown.

Vegetables can be cooked in foil parcels as well as on kebab (kabob) skewers. Slice them roughly, sprinkle with olive oil, herbs and seasonings and wrap tightly. Cook until tender.

Soups & Starters

Soup is simple to make but produces tasty results. A wide variety of soups can be made with vegetables – they can be rich and creamy, thick and chunky, light and delicate, and hot or chilled. The secret of a good soup lies in using a well-flavoured stock as the base. Although there are some excellent vegetable stock cubes available, a homemade stock (see page 14) gives the edge to any soup. A wide range of ingredients can be used in addition to vegetables – try using pulses (legumes), grains, noodles, vegetarian cheese and yogurt.

With so many fresh ingredients available, it is easy to create delicious starters that are the perfect introduction to a vegetarian meal. The ideas in this chapter are an inspiration to cook and a treat to eat, and they give an edge to the appetite that makes the main course even more enjoyable. A balance of flavours, colours and textures will offer variety and contrast.

Red (Bell) Pepper & Chilli Soup

This soup has a real Mediterranean flavour, using sweet red (bell) peppers, tomato, chilli and basil. It is great served with a warm olive bread.

Serves 4
225 g/8 oz red (bell) peppers, seeded and sliced
1 onion, sliced
2 garlic cloves, crushed
1 green chilli, chopped
300 ml/$^1/_2$ pint/$1^1/_2$ cups passata (sieved tomatoes)
600 ml/1 pint/$2^1/_2$ cups vegetable stock
2 tbsp chopped basil
fresh basil sprigs, to garnish

1 Put the (bell) peppers in a large saucepan with the onion, garlic and chilli. Add the passata (sieved tomatoes) and stock and bring to the boil, stirring well.

2 Reduce the heat to a simmer and cook for 20 minutes or until the (bell) peppers have softened. Drain, reserving the liquid and vegetables separately.

3 Sieve the vegetables by pressing through a sieve (strainer) with the back of a spoon, or blend in a food processor until smooth.

4 Return the vegetable purée to a clean saucepan with the reserved cooking liquid. Add the basil and heat through until hot. Garnish and serve.

COOK'S VARIATION

This soup is also delicious served cold with 150 ml/$^1/_4$ pint/$^2/_3$ cup of natural yogurt swirled into it.

Avocado & Mint Soup

A rich and creamy pale green soup made with avocados and enhanced by a touch of chopped mint. Serve chilled in summer or hot in winter.

Serves 4-6

40 g/1¹/₂ oz/3 tbsp butter or vegetarian margarine

6 spring onions (scallions), sliced

1 garlic clove, crushed

25 g/1 oz/¹/₄ cup plain (all-purpose) flour

600 ml/1 pint/2¹/₂ cups Fresh Vegetable Stock (see page 14)

2 ripe avocados

2-3 tsp lemon juice

good pinch of grated lemon rind

150 ml/¹/₄ pint/²/₃ cup milk

150 ml/¹/₄ pint/²/₃ cup single (light) cream

1-1¹/₂ tbsp chopped fresh mint

salt and pepper

sprigs of fresh mint, to garnish

MINTED GARLIC BREAD

125 g/4¹/₂ oz/¹/₂ cup butter

1-2 tbsp chopped fresh mint

1-2 garlic cloves, crushed

1 wholemeal (whole wheat) or white French bread stick

1 Melt the butter or vegetarian margarine in a large saucepan. Add the spring onions (scallions) and garlic and fry gently for about 3 minutes until soft but not coloured.

2 Stir in the flour and cook for 1-2 minutes. Gradually stir in the stock then bring to the boil. Let simmer gently while preparing the avocados.

3 Peel the avocados, discard the stones (pits) and chop the flesh. Add to the soup with the lemon juice and rind and seasoning. Cover and simmer for about 10 minutes or until tender.

4 Cool the soup slightly then press through a sieve (strainer) or blend in a food processor or blender until smooth. Pour into a bowl.

5 Stir in the milk and cream, adjust the seasoning, then stir in the mint. Cover and chill thoroughly.

6 To make the garlic bread, soften the butter and beat in the mint and garlic.

Cut the loaf into slanting slices, but do not cut all the way through – leave the slices attached at the base. Spread each slice with the garlic butter and reassemble the loaf. Wrap in foil and place in a preheated oven, 180°C/350°F/Gas Mark 4, for 15 minutes.

7 Serve the soup garnished with a sprig of mint and accompanied by the minted garlic bread.

Mixed Bean Soup

This is a really hearty soup, filled with colour, flavour and goodness,
which may be adapted to any vegetables that you have to hand.

Serves 4

1 tbsp vegetable oil

1 red onion, halved and sliced

100 g/3¹/₂ oz/²/₃ cup potato, diced

1 carrot, diced

1 leek, sliced

1 green chilli, sliced

3 garlic cloves, crushed

1 tsp ground coriander

1 tsp chilli powder

1 litre/1³/₄ pints/4 cups vegetable stock

450 g/1 lb mixed canned beans,
such as red kidney, borlotti,
black eye or flageolet, drained

salt and pepper

2 tbsp chopped coriander (cilantro),
to garnish

1 Heat the oil in a large saucepan and
add the onion, potato, carrot and leek.
Sauté for 2 minutes, stirring, until
slightly softened. Add the chilli and
garlic and cook for a further 1 minute.

2 Stir in the ground coriander, chilli
powder and the stock. Bring to the
boil, reduce the heat and cook for
20 minutes or until the vegetables
are tender.

3 Stir in the beans, season well and
cook for a further 10 minutes.
Garnish with chopped coriander
(cilantro) and serve.

COOK'S TIP

Serve this soup with slices of warm
corn bread or a cheese loaf.

Noodle, Mushroom & Ginger Soup

Thai soups are very quickly and easily put together, and are cooked
so that each ingredient can still be tasted in the finished dish.

Serves 4

15 g/¹/₂ oz/¹/₄ cup dried
Chinese mushrooms
or 125 g/4¹/₂ oz/1¹/₃ cups field
or chestnut (crimini) mushrooms
1 litre/1³/₄ pints/4 cups hot Fresh
Vegetable Stock (see page 14)
125 g/4¹/₂ oz thread egg noodles
2 tsp sunflower oil
3 garlic cloves, crushed
2.5 cm/1 inch piece ginger,
shredded finely
¹/₂ tsp mushroom ketchup
1 tsp light soy sauce
125 g/4¹/₂ oz/2 cups beansprouts
fresh coriander (cilantro) leaves,
to garnish

1 Soak the dried Chinese
mushrooms, if using, in 300 ml/¹/₂
pint/1¹/₄ cups of the hot vegetable
stock for at least 30 minutes. Remove
the stalks and discard, then slice the
mushrooms. Reserve the stock.

2 Cook the noodles in a saucepan of
boiling water for 2–3 minutes. Drain,
rinse and drain again. Set aside until
required.

3 Heat the oil over a high heat in a
wok or large, heavy frying pan (skillet).
Add the garlic and ginger, stirring. Add
the mushrooms and cook over a high
heat for 2 minutes, stirring well.

4 Add the remaining vegetable stock
with the reserved hot stock and bring
to the boil. Add the mushroom
ketchup and soy sauce.

5 Stir in the beansprouts and cook
until tender.

6 Pour the soup over the noodles,
garnish and serve.

COOK'S TIP

Dried Chinese mushrooms are
available from oriental stores.

Jerusalem Artichoke Soup

Jerusalem artichokes belong to the tuber family. They are native
to North America, but are also grown in Europe. They have a delicious nutty flavour
which combines well with the orange in this soup.

Serves 4
675 g/1¹/₂ lb Jerusalem artichokes
5 tbsp orange juice
25 g/1 oz/2 tbsp butter
1 leek, chopped
1 garlic clove, crushed
300 ml/¹/₂ pint/1¹/₄ cups vegetable stock
150 ml/¹/₄ pint/²/₃ cup milk
2 tbsp chopped coriander (cilantro)
150 ml/¹/₄ pint/²/₃ cup natural yogurt
grated orange rind, to garnish

1 Rinse the Jerusalem artichokes
and place in a large saucepan with 2
tablespoons of the orange juice and
enough water to cover. Bring to the
boil, reduce the heat and cook for 20
minutes or until the artichokes are
tender. Drain the artichokes, reserving
425 ml/¾ pint/2 cups of the cooking
liquid. Leave the artichokes to cool.

2 Peel the artichokes and mash the
flesh with a potato masher.

3 Melt the butter in a large saucepan
and sauté the leek and garlic for
2–3 minutes, stirring until the leek
softens.

4 Stir in the artichoke flesh, the
reserved cooking water, the stock,
milk and remaining orange juice.
Bring the soup to the boil, reduce the
heat and simmer for 2–3 minutes.

5 Reserving a few pieces of leek,
transfer the remainder of the soup to
a food processor and blend for 1
minute until smooth.

6 Return the soup to a clean saucepan
and stir in the reserved leeks,
coriander (cilantro) and yogurt.

7 Transfer to individual soup bowls,
garnish with orange rind and serve.

COOK'S VARIATION

If Jerusalem artichokes are
unavailable, you could use
sweet potatoes instead.

Broad (Fava) Bean & Mint Soup

Fresh broad (fava) beans are best for this recipe, but if they are unavailable, use frozen beans instead. They combine well with the fresh flavour of mint.

Serves 4

2 tbsp olive oil

1 red onion, chopped

2 garlic cloves, crushed

2 potatoes, diced

450 g/1 lb/3 cups broad (fava) beans, thawed if frozen

850 ml/1½ pints/3¾ cups vegetable stock

2 tbsp freshly chopped mint

fresh mint sprigs and yogurt, to garnish

1 Heat the oil in a large saucepan and sauté the onion and garlic for 2–3 minutes until softened.

2 Add the potatoes and cook for 5 minutes, stirring well. Stir in the beans and the stock, cover and simmer for 30 minutes or until the beans and potatoes are tender.

3 Reserving a few vegetables, place the remainder of the soup in a food processor or blender and purée until smooth.

4 Return the soup to a clean saucepan and add the reserved vegetables and mint. Serve garnished with swirls of yogurt and sprigs of fresh mint.

COOK'S VARIATION

Use fresh coriander (cilantro) and ½ tsp ground cumin as flavourings in the soup, if you prefer.

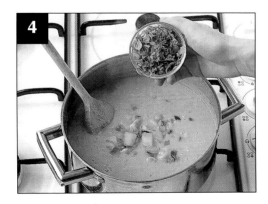

Chick-pea (Garbanzo Bean) & Tomato Soup

A thick vegetable soup which is a delicious meal in itself.
Serve the soup with thin shavings of Parmesan and warm ciabatta bread.

Serves 4
2 tbsp olive oil
2 leeks, sliced thinly
2 courgettes (zucchini), chopped
2 garlic cloves, crushed
2 × 400 g/14 oz cans chopped tomatoes
1 tbsp tomato purée (paste)
1 bay leaf
850 ml/1½ pints/3¾ cups Fresh Vegetable Stock (see page 14)
400 g/14 oz can chick-peas (garbanzo beans), drained
225 g/8 oz spinach
salt and pepper
thin shavings of Parmesan, to garnish (optional)
crusty bread, to serve

1 Heat the oil in a saucepan, add the leeks and courgettes (zucchini) and cook briskly for 5 minutes, stirring constantly.

2 Add the garlic, tomatoes, tomato purée (paste), bay leaf, stock and chick-peas (garbanzo beans). Bring to the boil and simmer for 5 minutes.

3 Shred the spinach finely, add to the soup and boil for 2 minutes. Season with salt and pepper to taste.

4 Remove the bay leaf from the soup and discard.

5 Pour the soup into a soup tureen or into individual soup bowls and sprinkle with shavings of Parmesan (if using). Serve with crusty bread.

Vegetable & Corn Chowder

This is a really filling soup, which should be served before a lighter meal.
Packed with corn and fresh vegetables it is easy to prepare and filled with flavour.

Serves 4
1 tbsp vegetable oil
1 red onion, diced
1 red (bell) pepper, diced
3 garlic cloves, crushed
1 large potato, diced
2 tbsp plain (all-purpose) flour
600 ml/1 pint/2½ cups milk
300 ml/½ pint/1¼ cups vegetable stock
50 g/1¾ oz broccoli florets
300 g/10½ oz/3 cups canned sweetcorn in brine, drained
75 g/2¾ oz/¾ cup vegetarian Cheddar cheese, grated
salt and pepper
1 tbsp chopped fresh coriander (cilantro), to garnish

COOK'S TIP

Vegetarian cheeses are made with rennets of non-animal origin, using microbial or fungal enzymes.

COOK'S TIP

Add a little double (heavy) cream to the soup after adding the milk for a really creamy flavour.

1 Heat the oil in a large saucepan and sauté the onion, (bell) peppers, garlic and potato for 2–3 minutes, stirring.

2 Stir in the flour and cook for 30 seconds. Stir in the milk and stock.

3 Add the broccoli and sweetcorn. Bring the mixture to the boil, stirring, then reduce the heat and simmer for about 20 minutes or until the vegetables are tender.

4 Stir in 50 g/1¾ oz/½ cup of the cheese until it melts.

5 Season and spoon the chowder into a warm soup tureen. Garnish with the remaining cheese and the coriander (cilantro) and serve immediately.

Gardener's Broth

This thick, hearty soup uses a variety of green vegetables with a flavouring of ground coriander. A finishing touch of thinly sliced leeks adds texture.

Serves 4
40 g/1¹/₂ oz/3 tbsp butter or vegetarian margarine
1 onion, chopped
1–2 garlic cloves, crushed
1 large leek
225 g/8 oz Brussels sprouts
125 g/4¹/₂ oz French (green) or runner beans
1.2 litres/2 pints/5 cups Fresh Vegetable Stock (see page 14)
125 g/4¹/₂ oz/³/₄ cup frozen peas
1 tbsp lemon juice
¹/₂ tsp ground coriander
4 tbsp double (heavy) cream
salt and pepper

MELBA TOAST

4–6 slices white bread

1 Melt the butter or vegetarian margarine in a saucepan, add the onion and garlic and fry very gently, stirring occasionally, until they begin to soften but not colour.

2 Slice the white part of the leek very thinly and reserve; slice the remaining leeks. Slice the Brussels sprouts and thinly slice the beans.

3 Add the green part of the leeks, the Brussels sprouts and beans to the saucepan. Add the stock and bring to the boil. Simmer for 10 minutes.

4 Add the frozen peas, seasoning, lemon juice and ground coriander and simmer for 10–15 minutes or until the vegetables are tender.

5 Cool the soup a little, then press through a sieve (strainer) or blend in a food processor or blender until smooth. Pour into a clean pan.

6 Add the reserved slices of leek to the soup, bring back to the boil and simmer for about 5 minutes until the leeks are tender. Adjust the seasoning according to taste, stir in the cream and reheat gently.

7 To make the melba toast, toast the bread on both sides under a preheated grill (broiler). Cut horizontally through the slices then toast the uncooked sides until they curl up. Serve immediately with the soup.

Gazpacho

This Spanish soup is full of chopped and grated vegetables with a puréed tomato base.
Serve with extra chopped vegetables and croûtons.

Serves 4
¹/₂ small cucumber
¹/₂ small green (bell) pepper, chopped very finely
500 g/1 lb 2 oz ripe tomatoes, peeled or 400 g/14 oz can chopped tomatoes
¹/₂ onion, chopped coarsely
2–3 garlic cloves, crushed
3 tbsp olive oil
2 tbsp white wine vinegar
1–2 tbsp lemon or lime juice
2 tbsp tomato purée (paste)
425 ml/³/₄ pint/scant 2 cups tomato juice
salt and pepper

TO SERVE

chopped green (bell) pepper
thinly sliced onion rings
garlic croûtons

1 Coarsely grate the cucumber into a bowl and add the chopped green (bell) pepper, mixing well.

2 Blend the tomatoes, onion and garlic in a food processor or blender, then add the oil, vinegar, lemon or lime juice and tomato purée (paste) and blend until smooth. Alternatively, finely chop the tomatoes and finely grate the onion, then mix both with the garlic, oil, vinegar, lemon or lime juice and tomato purée (paste).

3 Add the tomato mixture to the cucumber and green (bell) pepper mixture and combine.

4 Add the tomato juice and mix again.

5 Season to taste, cover the bowl with cling film (plastic wrap) and chill thoroughly for at least 6 hours, but preferably longer for the flavours to combine.

6 Prepare the side dishes of green (bell) pepper, onion rings and garlic croûtons to serve and arrange in individual serving bowls.

7 Ladle the soup into bowls, preferably from a soup tureen set on the table with the side dishes around it. Hand the dishes around to allow the guests to help themselves.

Cauliflower & Broccoli Soup with Gruyère

Full of flavour, this creamy cauliflower and broccoli soup is simple to make and delicious to eat.

Serves 4
3 tbsp vegetable oil
1 red onion, chopped
2 garlic cloves, crushed
300 g/10^1/$_2$ oz cauliflower florets
300 g/10^1/$_2$ oz broccoli florets
1 tbsp plain (all-purpose) flour
600 ml/1 pint/2^1/$_2$ cups milk
300 ml/^{1}/$_2$ pint/1^1/$_4$ cups vegetable stock
75 g/2^3/$_4$ oz/^{3}/$_4$ cup vegetarian Gruyère cheese, grated
pinch of paprika
150 ml/^{1}/$_4$ pint/^{2}/$_3$ cup single (light) cream
paprika and vegetarian Gruyère cheese shavings, to garnish

1 Heat the oil in a large saucepan and sauté the onion, garlic, cauliflower and broccoli for 3–4 minutes, stirring constantly.

2 Add the flour and cook for a further 1 minute, stirring.

3 Stir in the milk and stock and bring to the boil. Reduce the heat and simmer for 20 minutes or until the vegetables are tender.

4 Remove about a quarter of the vegetable pieces with a slotted spoon, set aside and reserve until required.

5 Put the remaining soup in a food processor and blend for 30 seconds until smooth. Transfer the soup to a clean saucepan.

6 Return the reserved vegetable pieces to the soup.

7 Stir in the cheese, paprika and cream and heat gently for 2–3 minutes without boiling, or until the cheese starts to melt.

8 Transfer to warm serving bowls, garnish with shavings of Gruyère and dust with paprika.

COOK'S TIP

The soup must not start to boil after the cream has been added otherwise it will curdle. Use natural yogurt instead of the cream if preferred, but again do not allow to boil.

Beetroot Soup

Here are two variations using the same vegetable: a creamy soup made
with puréed cooked beetroot; and a traditional clear soup, Bortsch.

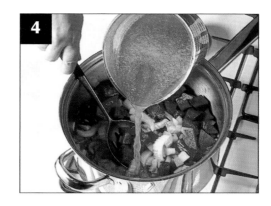

Serves 4–6
BORTSCH

500 g/1 lb 2 oz raw beetroot,
peeled and grated

2 carrots, chopped finely

1 large onion, chopped finely

1 garlic clove, crushed

1 bouquet garni

1.2 litres/2 pints/5 cups Fresh
Vegetable Stock (see page 14)

2–3 tsp lemon juice

salt and pepper

150 ml/^{1}/$_4$ pint/^{2}/$_3$ cup soured
cream, to serve

CREAMED BEETROOT SOUP

60 g/2 oz/^{1}/$_4$ cup butter or vegetarian
margarine

2 large onions, chopped finely

1–2 carrots, chopped

2 celery sticks, chopped

500 g/1 lb 2 oz cooked beetroot, diced

1–2 tbsp lemon juice

850 ml/1^1/$_2$ pints/3^1/$_2$ cups Fresh
Vegetable Stock (see page 14)

300 ml/^{1}/$_2$ pint/1^1/$_4$ cups milk

salt and pepper

TO SERVE

grated cooked beetroot or 6 tbsp soured
or double (heavy) cream, lightly whipped

1 To make bortsch, place the beetroot,
carrots, onion, garlic, bouquet garni,
stock, lemon juice and seasoning in a
saucepan. Bring to the boil, cover and
simmer for 45 minutes.

2 Press the soup through a fine sieve
(strainer) or a sieve (strainer) lined

with muslin (cheesecloth), then pour
into a clean pan. Adjust the seasoning
and add extra lemon juice if necessary.
Bring to the boil and simmer for 1–2
minutes. Serve with a spoonful of
soured cream swirled through.

3 To make creamed beetroot soup,
melt the butter or margarine in a pan
and fry the onions, carrots and celery
until just beginning to colour.

4 Add the beetroot, 1 tablespoon of
lemon juice, the stock and seasoning
and bring to the boil. Cover and
simmer for 30 minutes until tender.

5 Cool slightly, then press through a
sieve (strainer) or blend in a food
processor or blender. Pour into a clean
pan, add the milk and bring to the
boil. Adjust the seasoning and add
extra lemon juice if necessary. Serve.

Dahl Soup

Dahl is a name given to a delicious Indian lentil dish.
This soup is a variation of the theme – it is made with red lentils
and spiced with curry powder.

Serves 4

25 g/1 oz/2 tbsp butter
2 garlic cloves, crushed
1 onion, chopped
$1/2$ tsp turmeric
1 tsp garam masala
$1/4$ tsp chilli powder
1 tsp ground cumin
1 kg/2 lb 4 oz canned, chopped tomatoes, drained
175 g/6 oz/1 cup red lentils
2 tsp lemon juice
600 ml/1 pint/$2^1/2$ cups vegetable stock
300 ml/$1/2$ pint/$1^1/4$ cups coconut milk
chopped coriander (cilantro) and lemon slices, to garnish
naan bread, to serve

1 Melt the butter in a large saucepan and sauté the garlic and onion for 2–3 minutes, stirring. Add the spices and cook for a further 30 seconds.

2 Stir in the tomatoes, lentils, lemon juice, stock and coconut milk and bring to the boil. Reduce the heat and simmer for 25–30 minutes until the lentils are tender and cooked.

3 Season and spoon the soup into a warm tureen. Garnish and serve with warm naan bread.

COOK'S TIP

Add small quantities of hot water to the pan whilst the lentils are cooking if they begin to absorb too much of the liquid.

Vichyssoise

This is a classic creamy soup made from potatoes and leeks.
To achieve the delicate pale colour, be sure to use only the white parts of the leeks.

Serves 4–6
3 large leeks
45 g/1¹/₂ oz/3 tbsp butter or vegetarian margarine
1 onion, sliced thinly
500 g/1 lb 2 oz potatoes, chopped
850 ml/1¹/₂ pints/3¹/₂ cups Fresh Vegetable Stock (see page 14)
2 tsp lemon juice
pinch of ground nutmeg
¹/₄ tsp ground coriander
1 bay leaf
1 egg yolk
150 ml/¹/₄ pint/²/₃ cup single (light) cream
salt and white pepper
snipped chives, to garnish

1 Trim the leeks and remove most of the green part (it can be served as a vegetable). Slice the white part of the leeks very finely.

2 Melt the butter or margarine in a saucepan and gently fry the leeks and onion for about 5 minutes without browning, stirring from time to time.

3 Add the potatoes, stock, lemon juice, salt and white pepper to taste, ground nutmeg, ground coriander and bay leaf to the pan and bring to the boil. Cover and simmer for about 30 minutes or until all of the vegetables are very soft.

4 Leave the soup to cool a little, then discard the bay leaf. Press the soup through a sieve (strainer) or blend in a food processor or blender until smooth. Pour the soup into a clean saucepan.

5 Blend the egg yolk into the cream. Add a little of the soup to the egg and cream mixture and then whisk it all back into the soup and reheat gently without boiling. Add a little more salt and white pepper to taste, if necessary. Cool and chill thoroughly before serving.

6 Serve the soup sprinkled with freshly snipped chives.

Curried Parsnip Soup

Parsnips make a delicious soup as they have a slightly sweet flavour. In this recipe, spices are added to complement this sweetness and a dash of lemon juice adds tartness.

Serves 4
1 tbsp vegetable oil
1 tbsp butter
1 red onion, chopped
3 parsnips, chopped
2 garlic cloves, crushed
2 tsp garam masala
1/2 tsp chilli powder
1 tbsp plain (all-purpose) flour
850 ml/1 1/2 pints/3 3/4 cups vegetable stock
grated rind and juice of 1 lemon
salt and pepper
lemon zest, to garnish

1 Heat the oil and butter in a large saucepan until the butter has melted.

2 Add the onion, parsnips and garlic and sauté for 5–7 minutes, stirring, until the vegetables have softened.

3 Add the garam masala and chilli powder and cook for 30 seconds, stirring well.

4 Sprinkle in the flour, mixing well and cook for a further 30 seconds.

5 Stir in the stock, lemon rind and juice and bring to the boil. Reduce the heat and simmer for 20 minutes or until the parsnips are tender.

6 Remove some of the vegetable pieces with a slotted spoon and reserve until required. Blend the remaining soup and vegetables in a food processor for 1 minute or until smooth.

7 Return the soup to a clean saucepan and stir in the reserved vegetables. Heat the soup through for 2 minutes.

8 Transfer to soup bowls, garnish with grated lemon zest and serve.

COOK'S VARIATION

Use 1 medium orange instead of the lemon if preferred and garnish with grated orange zest.

Avocado & Vegetable Soup

Avocado has a rich flavour and colour which makes a creamy flavoured soup.
It is best served chilled, but may be eaten warm as well.

Serves 4
1 large, ripe avocado
2 tbsp lemon juice
1 tbsp vegetable oil
50 g/1³/₄ oz/¹/₂ cup canned sweetcorn, drained
2 tomatoes, peeled and seeded
1 garlic clove, crushed
1 leek, chopped
1 red chilli, chopped
425 ml/³/₄ pint/2 cups vegetable stock
150 ml/¹/₄ pint/²/₃ cup milk
shredded leeks, to garnish

1 Peel and mash the avocado with a fork, stir in the lemon juice and reserve until required.

2 Heat the oil in a pan and sauté the sweetcorn, tomatoes, garlic, leek and chilli for 2–3 minutes until softened.

3 Put half of the vegetable mixture in a food processor or blender with the avocado and blend until smooth. Transfer to a clean saucepan.

4 Add the stock and milk and reserved vegetables and cook gently for 3–4 minutes until hot. Garnish with shredded leeks and serve.

COOK'S TIP

If serving chilled, transfer from the food processor to a bowl, stir in the stock and milk, cover and chill in the refrigerator for at least 4 hours.

Soft Cheese & Fresh Herb Soup

Make the most of home-grown herbs to create this wonderfully
creamy soup with its marvellous garden-fresh fragrance.

Serves 4
25 g/1 oz/2 tbsp butter or vegetarian margarine
2 onions, chopped
850 ml/1¹/₂ pints/3¹/₂ cups Fresh Vegetable Stock (see page 14)
25 g/1 oz/2 tbsp coarsely chopped mixed fresh herbs, such as parsley, chives, thyme, basil and oregano
200 g/7 oz/1 cup full-fat soft cheese
1 tbsp cornflour (cornstarch)
1 tbsp milk
snipped fresh chives, to garnish

1 Melt the butter or margarine in a
large saucepan and add the onions.
Fry for 2 minutes, then cover and
reduce the heat to low. Allow the
onions to cook gently for 5 minutes,
then remove the lid.

2 Add the stock and herbs to the
saucepan. Bring to the boil, then
reduce the heat. Cover and simmer
gently for 20 minutes.

3 Remove the saucepan from the
heat. Blend the soup in a food
processor or blender for about 15
seconds, until smooth. Alternatively,
press it through a sieve (strainer).
Return the soup to the saucepan.

4 Spoon the soft cheese into the soup
and whisk until fully incorporated.

5 Mix the cornflour (cornstarch) with
the milk, then stir into the soup and

heat, stirring constantly, until
thickened and smooth. Pour the soup
into 4 warmed bowls. Garnish with
snipped chives and serve at once.

COOK'S TIP

Cheese is a good source of vitamins.

Celery, Stilton & Walnut Soup

This is a classic combination of ingredients all brought
together in a delicious, creamy soup.

Serves 4
50 g/1³/₄ oz/4 tbsp butter
2 shallots, chopped
3 celery sticks, chopped
1 garlic clove, crushed
2 tbsp plain (all-purpose) flour
600 ml/1 pint/2¹/₂ cups vegetable stock
300 ml/¹/₂ pint/1¹/₄ cups milk
150 g/5¹/₂ oz/1¹/₂ cups blue Stilton cheese, crumbled, plus extra to garnish
2 tbsp walnut halves, roughly chopped
150 ml/¹/₄ pint/²/₃ cup natural yogurt
salt and pepper
chopped celery leaves, to garnish

1 Melt the butter in a large saucepan
and sauté the shallots, celery and
garlic for 2–3 minutes, stirring, until
softened.

2 Add the flour and cook for
30 seconds.

3 Gradually stir in the stock and milk
and bring to the boil.

4 Reduce the heat to a gentle simmer
and add the cheese and walnuts.
Cover and leave to simmer for
20 minutes.

5 Stir in the yogurt and heat for a
further 2 minutes without boiling.

6 Transfer to a warm soup tureen or
individual serving bowls, garnish with
chopped celery leaves and extra
crumbled blue Stilton cheese and
serve at once.

COOK'S TIP

As well as adding protein, vitamins
and useful fats to the diet, nuts add
important flavour and texture to
vegetarian meals.

COOK'S VARIATION

Use an alternative blue cheese, such
as Dolcelatte or Gorgonzola, if
preferred or a strong vegetarian
Cheddar cheese, grated.

Pumpkin Soup

This is an American classic that has now become popular worldwide.
When pumpkin is out of season use butternut squash instead.

Serves 4–6
about 1 kg/2 lb 4 oz pumpkin
45 g/1¹/₂ oz/3 tbsp butter
or vegetarian margarine
1 onion, sliced thinly
1 garlic clove, crushed
850 ml/1¹/₂ pints/3¹/₂ cups
Fresh Vegetable Stock (see page 14)
¹/₂ tsp ground ginger
1 tbsp lemon juice
3–4 thinly pared strips of
orange rind (optional)
1–2 bay leaves or
1 bouquet garni
300 ml/¹/₂ pint/1¹/₄ cups milk
salt and pepper

TO GARNISH

4–6 tablespoons single (light)
or double (heavy) cream,
natural yogurt or fromage frais
snipped fresh chives

1 Peel the pumpkin, remove the seeds and then cut the flesh into 2.5 cm/1 inch cubes.

2 Melt the butter or margarine in a large saucepan, add the onion and garlic and fry gently until soft but not coloured.

3 Add the pumpkin and toss with the onion for 1–2 minutes.

4 Add the stock and bring to the boil. Add the seasoning, ginger, lemon juice, strips of orange rind, if using, and bay leaves or bouquet garni. Cover and simmer gently for about 20 minutes or until the pumpkin is very tender.

5 Discard the orange rind, if using, and the bay leaves or bouquet garni. Cool the soup a little and then press through a sieve (strainer) or blend in a food processor or blender until smooth. Pour the soup into a clean saucepan.

6 Add the milk and reheat gently. Adjust the seasoning to taste. Garnish with a swirl of cream, natural yogurt or fromage frais and snipped chives, and serve immediately.

Hot & Sour Soup

A very traditional staple of the Thai national diet, this soup is sold on street corners, at food bars and by mobile vendors all over the country.

Serves 4
1 tbsp sunflower oil
225 g/8 oz smoked tofu (bean curd), sliced
90 g/3 oz/1 cup shiitake mushrooms, sliced
2 tbsp chopped fresh coriander (cilantro)
125 g/4½ oz/2 cups watercress
1 red chilli, sliced finely, to garnish

STOCK

1 tbsp tamarind pulp
2 dried red chillies, chopped
2 kaffir lime leaves, torn in half
2.5 cm/1 inch piece ginger root, chopped
5 cm/2 inch piece galangal, chopped
1 stalk lemon grass, chopped
1 onion, quartered
1 litre/1¾ pints/4 cups cold water

1 Put all the ingredients for the stock into a saucepan and bring to the boil. Simmer for 5 minutes. Remove from the heat and strain, reserving the stock.

2 Heat the oil in a wok or large, heavy frying pan (skillet) and cook the tofu (bean curd) over a high heat for about 2 minutes, stirring constantly. Pour in the strained stock.

3 Add the mushrooms and coriander (cilantro) and boil for 3 minutes. Add the watercress and boil for 1 minute. Serve at once, garnished with chilli slices, if wished.

Spanish Tomato Soup

This Mediterranean tomato soup is thickened with bread,
as is traditional in some parts of Spain.

Serves 4
4 tbsp olive oil
1 onion, chopped
3 garlic cloves, crushed
1 green (bell) pepper, chopped
$^1\!/_2$ tsp chilli powder
450 g/1 lb tomatoes, chopped
225 g/8 oz French or Italian bread, cubed
1 litre/$1^3\!/_4$ pints/4 cups vegetable stock

GARLIC BREAD

4 slices ciabatta or French bread
4 tbsp olive oil
2 garlic cloves, crushed
25 g/1 oz/$^1\!/_4$ cup grated vegetarian Cheddar
chilli powder, to garnish

1 Heat the oil in a large frying pan (skillet) and sauté the onion, garlic and (bell) pepper for 2–3 minutes or until the onion has softened.

2 Add the chilli powder and tomatoes and cook over a medium heat until the mixture has thickened.

3 Stir in the bread and stock and cook for 10–15 minutes until the soup is thick and fairly smooth.

4 To make the garlic bread, toast the bread slices under a medium grill (broiler). Drizzle the oil over the top of the bread, rub with the garlic, sprinkle with the cheese and return to the grill (broiler) for 2–3 minutes until the cheese has melted. Sprinkle with chilli powder and serve with the soup.

Mixed Bahjis

These small bahjis are served in Indian restaurants as accompaniments to a main meal, but they are delicious as a starter with a small salad and yogurt sauce.

Serves 4
BAHJIS
175 g/6 oz/1¼ cups gram flour
1 tsp bicarbonate of soda
2 tsp ground coriander
1 tsp garam masala
1½ tsp turmeric
1½ tsp chilli powder
2 tbsp chopped coriander (cilantro)
1 small onion, halved and sliced
1 small leek, sliced
100 g/3½ oz cooked cauliflower
9–12 tbsp cold water
salt and pepper
vegetable oil, for deep-frying
SAUCE
150 ml/¼ pint/⅔ cup natural yogurt
2 tbsp chopped mint
½ tsp turmeric
1 garlic clove, crushed
fresh mint sprigs, to garnish

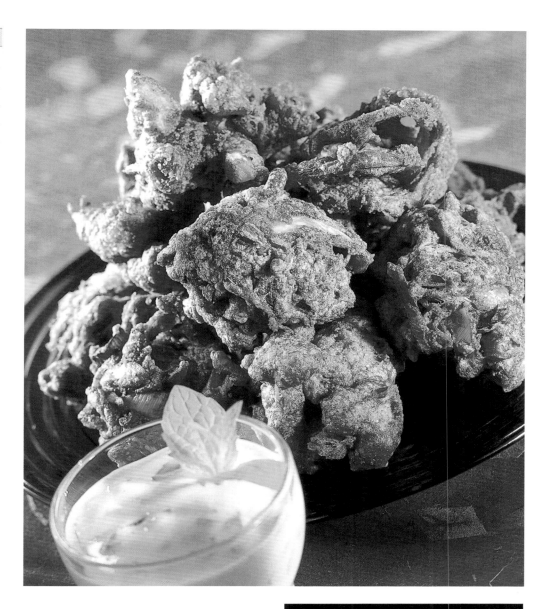

1 Sieve the flour, bicarbonate of soda and salt to taste into a mixing bowl and add the spices and fresh coriander (cilantro). Mix well.

2 Divide the mixture into 3 and place in separate bowls. Stir the onion into one bowl, the leek into another and the cauliflower into the third bowl. Add 3–4 tbsp of water to each bowl and mix each to form a smooth paste.

3 Heat the oil for deep frying in a deep fat fryer to 180°C/350°F or until a cube of bread browns in 30 seconds. Using 2 dessert spoons, form the mixture into rounds and cook each in the oil for 3–4 minutes until browned. Remove with a slotted spoon and drain on absorbent kitchen paper. Keep the bahjis warm in the oven whilst cooking the remainder.

4 Mix all of the sauce ingredients together, garnish with mint sprigs and serve with the warm bahjis.

COOK'S VARIATION

If you prefer, use cooked broccoli instead of the cauliflower or cooked, drained spinach instead of the leek for a range of different flavoured bahjis.

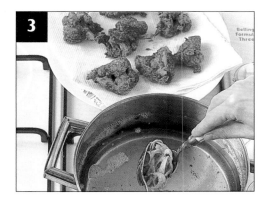

Fiery Salsa with Tortilla Chips

Make this Mexican-style salsa to perk up jaded palates.
Its lively flavours really get the tastebuds going.

Serves 6
2 small red chillies
1 tbsp lime or lemon juice
2 large ripe avocados
5 cm/2 inch piece cucumber
2 tomatoes, peeled
1 small garlic clove, crushed
few drops of Tabasco sauce
salt and pepper
lime or lemon slices, to garnish
tortilla chips, to serve

1 Remove and discard the stem and seeds from 1 chilli. Chop very finely and place in a mixing bowl. To make a chilli 'flower' for garnish, slice the remaining chilli from the stem to the tip several times without removing the stem. Place in a bowl of cold water, so that the 'petals' open out.

2 Add the lime or lemon juice to the mixing bowl. Halve, stone (pit) and peel the avocados. Add to the mixing bowl and mash with a fork. (The lime or lemon juice prevents the avocado from turning brown.)

3 Chop the cucumber and tomatoes finely and add to the avocado mixture with the crushed garlic.

4 Season the dip to taste with Tabasco sauce, salt and pepper.

5 Transfer the dip to a serving bowl. Garnish with slices of lime or lemon and the chilli flower. Put the bowl on a large plate, surround with tortilla chips and serve.

Hummus & Garlic Toasts

Hummus is a real favourite spread on these garlic toasts for a
delicious starter or as part of a light lunch.

Serves 4
HUMMUS

400 g/14 oz can chick-peas (garbanzo
beans)

juice of 1 large lemon

6 tbsp tahini (sesame seed paste)

2 tbsp olive oil

2 garlic cloves, crushed

salt and pepper

chopped fresh coriander (cilantro) and
black olives, to garnish

TOASTS

1 ciabatta loaf, sliced

2 garlic cloves, crushed

1 tbsp chopped fresh coriander (cilantro)

4 tbsp olive oil

1 To make the hummus, firstly drain
the chick-peas (garbanzo beans),
reserving a little of the liquid. Put the
chick-peas (garbanzo beans) and liquid
in a food processor and blend,
gradually adding the reserved liquid
and lemon juice. Blend well after each
addition until smooth.

2 Stir in the tahini (sesame seed
paste) and all but 1 teaspoon of the
olive oil. Add the garlic, season to
taste and blend again until smooth.
Spoon the hummus into a serving
dish. Drizzle the remaining olive oil
over the top, garnish with chopped
coriander (cilantro) and olives. Leave
to chill in the refrigerator whilst
preparing the toasts.

3 Lay the slices of ciabatta on a grill
(broiler) rack in a single layer.

4 Mix the garlic, coriander (cilantro)
and olive oil together and drizzle over
the bread slices. Cook under a hot grill
(broiler) for 2–3 minutes until golden
brown, turning once. Serve hot with
the hummus.

COOK'S TIP

Make the hummus 1 day in advance,
and chill, covered, in the refrigerator
until required. Garnish and serve.

Aubergine (Eggplant) Dipping Platter

Dipping platters are a very sociable dish, bringing together all the diners at the table.
This substantial dip is served with vegetables as an appetizer.

Serves 4
1 aubergine (eggplant), peeled and cut into 2.5 cm/1 inch cubes
3 tbsp sesame seeds, roasted in a dry pan over a low heat
1 tsp sesame oil
grated rind and juice of $\frac{1}{2}$ lime
1 small shallot, diced
$\frac{1}{2}$ tsp salt
1 tsp sugar
1 red chilli, deseeded and sliced
125 g/4$\frac{1}{2}$ oz broccoli florets
2 carrots, cut into matchsticks
125 g/4$\frac{1}{2}$ oz/8 baby corn cobs, cut in half lengthways
2 celery stalks, cut into matchsticks
1 baby red cabbage, cut into 8 wedges, the leaves of each wedge held together by the core

1 Cook the diced aubergine (eggplant) in a saucepan of boiling water for 7–8 minutes.

2 Meanwhile, grind the sesame seeds with the oil in a food processor or pestle and mortar.

3 Add the aubergine (eggplant), lime rind and juice, shallot, salt, sugar and chilli in that order to the sesame seeds. Process, or chop and mash by hand, until smooth.

4 Adjust the seasoning if necessary then spoon into a bowl. Serve the dip surrounded by the broccoli, carrots, baby corn cobs, celery and red cabbage.

Vegetable Fritters with Sweet & Sour Sauce

These mixed vegetable fritters are coated in a light batter and deep fried until golden for a deliciously crisp coating. They are ideal with the sweet and sour dipping sauce.

Serves 4

100 g/3½ oz/¾ cup wholemeal (whole wheat) flour

pinch of salt

pinch of cayenne pepper

4 tsp olive oil

12 tbsp cold water

100 g/3½ oz broccoli florets

100 g/3½ oz cauliflower florets

50 g/1¾ oz mangetout (snow peas)

1 large carrot, cut into batons

1 red (bell) pepper, sliced

2 egg whites, beaten

oil, for deep-frying

SAUCE

150 ml/¼ pint/⅔ cup pineapple juice

150 ml/¼ pint/⅔ cup vegetable stock

2 tbsp wine vinegar

2 tbsp light brown sugar

2 tsp cornflour (cornstarch)

2 spring onions (scallions), chopped

1 Sieve the flour and salt into a mixing bowl and add the cayenne pepper. Make a well in the centre and gradually beat in the oil and cold water to make a smooth batter.

2 Cook the vegetables in boiling water for 5 minutes and drain well.

3 Whisk the egg whites until peaking and fold them into the flour batter.

4 Dip the vegetables into the batter, turning to coat well. Drain off any excess batter. Heat the oil for deep-frying in a deep fat fryer to 180°C/350°F or until a cube of bread browns

in 30 seconds. Fry the vegetables for 1–2 minutes, in batches, until golden. Remove from the oil with a slotted spoon and drain on kitchen paper.

5 Place all of the sauce ingredients in a pan and bring to the boil, stirring, until thickened and clear. Serve with the vegetable fritters.

COOK'S VARIATION

Use any variety of vegetables that you have to hand for the fritters, such as cubes of potato or sweet potato, or green beans.

Cheese, Garlic & Herb Pâté

This wonderful soft cheese pâté is fragrant with the aroma of fresh herbs and garlic.
Serve with triangles of Melba toast to make the perfect starter.

Serves 4
15 g/¹/₂ oz/1 tbsp butter
1 garlic clove, crushed
3 spring onions (scallions), chopped finely
125 g/4¹/₂ oz/¹/₂ cup full-fat soft cheese
2 tbsp chopped mixed fresh herbs, such as parsley, chives, marjoram, oregano and basil
175 g/6 oz/1¹/₂ cups mature (sharp) Cheddar
4–6 slices of white bread from a medium-cut sliced loaf
pepper
mixed salad leaves (greens) and cherry tomatoes, to serve
TO GARNISH
ground paprika
sprigs of fresh herbs

1 Melt the butter in a small frying pan (skillet) and gently fry the garlic and spring onions (scallions) together for 3–4 minutes, until softened. Allow to cool.

2 Beat the soft cheese in a bowl, then add the garlic and spring onions (scallions). Stir in the herbs and season with pepper to taste, mixing well.

3 Grate the Cheddar and stir into the mixture to form a stiff paste. Cover and chill until ready to serve.

4 To make the Melba toast, toast the slices of bread on both sides, and then cut off the crusts.

5 Using a sharp bread knife, cut through the slices horizontally to make very thin slices.

6 Cut into triangles and then lightly grill (broil) the untoasted sides.

7 Arrange the mixed salad leaves on 4 serving plates with the cherry tomatoes. Pile the cheese pâté on top and sprinkle with a little paprika. Garnish with sprigs of fresh herbs and serve with the Melba toast.

Tomato, Olive & Mozzarella Bruschetta

These simple toasts are filled with colour and flavour. They are great as a speedy starter or delicious as an appetiser with a good red wine.

Serves 4
4 muffins
4 garlic cloves, crushed
2 tbsp butter
1 tbsp chopped basil
4 large, ripe tomatoes
1 tbsp tomato purée
8 pitted black olives, halved
salt and pepper
50 g/1¾ oz Mozzarella cheese, sliced
fresh basil leaves, to garnish

DRESSING

1 tbsp olive oil
2 tsp lemon juice
1 tsp clear honey

1 Cut the muffins in half to give eight thick pieces. Toast the muffin halves under a hot grill (broiler) for 2–3 minutes until golden.

2 Mix the garlic, butter and basil together and spread on to each muffin half.

3 Cut a cross shape at the base of each tomato. Plunge the tomatoes in a bowl of boiling water – this will make the skin easier to peel. After a few minutes, pick each tomato up with a fork and peel away the skin. Chop the tomato flesh and mix with the tomato purée and olives. Divide the mixture between the muffins.

4 Mix the dressing ingredients and drizzle over each muffin. Arrange the Mozzarella cheese on top and season.

5 Return the muffins to the grill (broiler) for 1–2 minutes until the cheese melts.

6 Garnish with fresh basil leaves and serve at once.

COOK'S VARIATION

Use balsamic vinegar instead of the lemon juice for an authentic Mediterranean flavour.

Mint & Cannellini Bean Dip

This dip is ideal for pre-dinner drinks or for handing around at a party, accompanied by crisps and colourful vegetable crudités.

Serves 6

175 g/6 oz/1 cup dried
cannellini beans

1 small garlic clove, crushed

1 bunch spring onions (scallions),
chopped roughly

handful of fresh mint leaves

2 tbsp tahini
(sesame seed paste)

2 tbsp olive oil

1 tsp ground cumin

1 tsp ground coriander

lemon juice

salt and pepper

sprigs of fresh mint, to garnish

TO SERVE

fresh vegetable crudités,
such as cauliflower florets,
carrots, cucumber, radishes
and (bell) peppers

1 Soak the cannellini beans overnight in plenty of cold water.

2 Rinse and drain the beans, put them into a large saucepan and cover them with cold water. Bring to the boil and boil rapidly for 10 minutes. Reduce the heat, cover and simmer until tender.

3 Drain the beans and transfer to a bowl or food processor. Add the garlic, spring onions (scallions), mint, tahini (sesame seed paste) and olive oil.

4 Blend the mixture for about 15 seconds, or mash well by hand, until smooth.

5 Transfer the mixture to a bowl and season with cumin, ground coriander, lemon juice, salt and pepper, according to taste. Mix well, cover and leave in a cool place for 30 minutes to allow the flavours to develop.

6 Spoon the dip into serving bowls, garnish with sprigs of fresh mint and surround with vegetable crudités.

Crispy Potato Skins

Potato skins are always a favourite. Prepare the skins in advance and warm through before serving with the salad fillings.

Serves 4
4 large baking potatoes
2 tbsp vegetable oil
4 tsp salt
150 ml/^{1}/$_4$ pint/^{2}/$_3$ cup soured cream and 2 tbsp chopped chives, to serve

BEANSPROUT SALAD

50 g/1^3/$_4$ oz/^{1}/$_2$ cup beansprouts
1 celery stick, sliced
1 orange, peeled and segmented
1 red dessert (eating) apple, chopped
^{1}/$_2$ red (bell) pepper, chopped
1 tbsp chopped parsley
1 tbsp light soy sauce
1 tbsp clear honey
1 small garlic clove, crushed

BEAN FILLING

100 g/3^1/$_2$ oz/1^1/$_2$ cups canned, mixed beans, drained
1 onion, halved and sliced
1 tomato, chopped
2 spring onions (scallions), chopped
2 tsp lemon juice
salt and pepper

1 Scrub the potatoes and put on a baking sheet (cookie sheet). Prick the potatoes all over with a fork and rub the oil and salt into the skin. Cook in a preheated oven at 200°C/400°F/Gas Mark 6 for 1 hour or until soft.

2 Cut the potatoes in half lengthwise and scoop out the flesh, leaving a 1 cm/^{1}/$_2$ inch thick shell. Put the shells, skin side uppermost, in the oven for 10 minutes until crisp.

3 Mix the ingredients for the beansprout salad in a bowl, tossing in the soy, honey and garlic to coat.

4 Mix the ingredients for the bean filling in a separate bowl.

5 Mix the soured cream and chives in another bowl.

6 Serve the potato skins hot, with the two salad fillings and the sour cream and chives.

Mixed Bean Pâté

This is a really quick starter to prepare if canned beans are used.
Choose a wide variety of beans for colour and flavour or use a can of mixed beans.

Serves 4
400 g/14 oz can mixed beans, drained
2 tbsp olive oil
juice of 1 lemon
2 garlic cloves, crushed
1 tbsp chopped fresh coriander (cilantro)
2 spring onions (scallions), chopped
salt and pepper
shredded spring onions (scallions), to garnish

1 Rinse the beans under cold running water and drain well.

2 Transfer the beans to a food processor or blender. Alternatively, place in a bowl and mash with a fork or potato masher.

3 Add the olive oil, lemon juice, garlic, coriander (cilantro) and spring onions (scallions) and blend until fairly smooth. Season with salt and pepper to taste.

4 Transfer the pâté to a serving bowl and chill for at least 30 minutes. Garnish with shredded spring onions (scallions) and serve.

COOK'S TIP

Serve the pâté with warm pitta bread or granary toast.

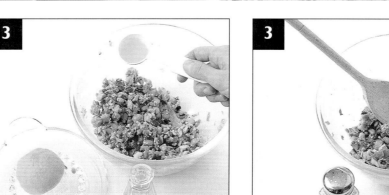

Onions à la Grecque

This is a well-known method of cooking vegetables and is perfect
with shallots or onions, served with a crisp salad.

Serves 4
450 g/1 lb shallots
3 tbsp olive oil
3 tbsp clear honey
2 tbsp garlic wine vinegar
3 tbsp dry white wine
1 tbsp tomato purée (paste)
2 celery stalks, sliced
2 tomatoes, seeded and chopped
chopped celery leaves, to garnish

1 Peel the shallots. Heat the oil in a
large saucepan and cook the shallots,
stirring, for 3–5 minutes or until they
begin to brown.

2 Add the honey and cook for a
further 30 seconds over a high heat,
then add the vinegar and wine,
stirring well.

3 Stir in the tomato purée (paste),
celery and tomatoes and bring the
mixture to the boil. Cook over a high
heat for 5–6 minutes. Season with salt
and pepper to taste and leave to cool
slightly.

4 Garnish with chopped celery leaves
and serve warm or cold from the
refrigerator.

COOK'S VARIATION

Use button mushrooms instead
of the shallots and fennel instead
of the celery for another
great starter.

(Bell) Peppers with Rosemary Baste

The flavour of grilled (broiled) or roasted (bell) peppers is very different
from when they are eaten raw, so do try them cooked in this way.

Serves 4
4 tbsp olive oil
finely grated rind of 1 lemon
4 tbsp lemon juice
1 tbsp balsamic vinegar
1 tbsp crushed fresh rosemary, or 1 tsp dried rosemary
2 red (bell) peppers, halved, cored and deseeded
2 yellow (bell) peppers, halved, cored and deseeded
2 tbsp pine kernels (nuts)
salt and pepper
sprigs of fresh rosemary, to garnish

6 Sprinkle the pine kernels over the (bell) peppers and drizzle with any remaining rosemary baste. Garnish with sprigs of fresh rosemary and serve at once.

COOK'S TIP

Rosemary contains oil of camphor, which gives an aromatic flavour.

1 Mix together the olive oil, lemon rind, lemon juice, vinegar and rosemary. Season with salt and pepper to taste.

2 Place the (bell) peppers, skin-side uppermost, on the rack of a grill (broiler) pan lined with foil. Brush the rosemary baste over the (bell) peppers.

3 Cook the (bell) peppers under a preheated grill (broiler) until the skin begins to char, basting frequently with the rosemary baste. Remove from the heat, cover with foil to trap the steam and leave for 5 minutes.

4 Meanwhile, scatter the pine kernels (nuts) on to the grill (broiler) rack and toast them lightly.

5 Peel the (bell) peppers, slice them into strips and place them in a warmed serving dish.

Lentil Pâté

Red lentils are used in this spicy recipe for speed as they do not require pre-soaking.
If you have other lentils, soak and pre-cook them and use instead of the red lentils.

Serves 4
1 tbsp vegetable oil, plus extra for greasing
1 onion, chopped
2 garlic cloves, crushed
1 tsp garam masala
$^{1}/_{2}$ tsp ground coriander
850 ml/1$^{1}/_{2}$ pints/1$^{1}/_{4}$ cups vegetable stock
175 g/6 oz/$^{2}/_{3}$ cup red lentils
1 small egg
2 tbsp milk
2 tbsp mango chutney
2 tbsp chopped parsley
chopped parsley, to garnish
salad leaves and warm toast, to serve

1 Heat the oil in a large saucepan and sauté the onion and garlic for 2–3 minutes, stirring. Add the garam masala and ground coriander and cook for a further 30 seconds.

2 Stir in the stock and lentils and bring the mixture to the boil. Reduce the heat and simmer for 20 minutes until the lentils are cooked and softened. Remove the pan from the heat and drain off any excess moisture.

3 Put the mixture in a food processor and add the egg, milk, mango chutney and parsley. Blend for 20 seconds until smooth.

4 Grease and line the base of a 450 g/1 lb loaf tin (pan) and spoon the mixture into the tin (pan), levelling the surface with the back of a spoon. Cover and cook in a preheated oven at 200°C/400°F/Gas Mark 6 for 40–45 minutes or until firm to the touch.

5 Allow the pâté to cool in the tin (pan) for 20 minutes, then transfer to the refrigerator to cool completely.

6 Turn out the pâté on to a serving plate, slice and garnish with chopped parsley. Serve with salad leaves and warm toast.

COOK'S VARIATION

Use other spices, such as chilli powder or Chinese five spice powder, to flavour the pâté and add tomato relish or chilli relish instead of the mango chutney, if you prefer.

Roasted Vegetables on Muffins

Roasted vegetables are delicious and attractive. Served on warm muffins
with a herb sauce, they are unbeatable.

Serves 4
1 red onion, cut into eight
1 aubergine (eggplant), halved and sliced
1 yellow (bell) pepper, sliced
1 courgette (zucchini), sliced
4 tbsp olive oil
1 tbsp garlic vinegar
2 tbsp vermouth
2 garlic cloves, crushed
1 tbsp chopped thyme
2 tsp light brown sugar
4 muffins, halved
salt and pepper
fresh herbs, to garnish

SAUCE
2 tbsp butter
1 tbsp flour
150 ml/$\frac{1}{4}$ pint/$\frac{2}{3}$ cup milk
85 ml/3 fl oz vegetable stock
75 g/2$\frac{3}{4}$ oz/$\frac{3}{4}$ cup vegetarian Cheddar, grated
1 tsp wholegrain mustard
3 tbsp chopped mixed herbs

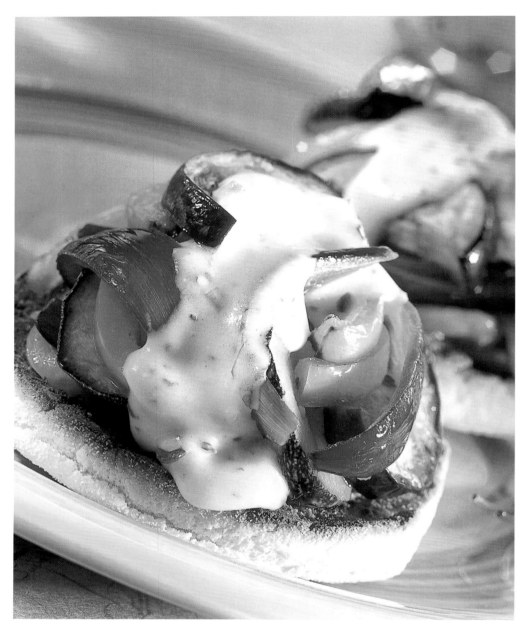

1 Arrange the vegetables in a shallow ovenproof dish. Mix the oil, vinegar, vermouth, garlic, thyme and sugar together and pour over the vegetables. Leave to marinate for 1 hour.

2 Transfer the vegetables to a baking sheet (cookie sheet). Cook in a pre-heated oven at 200°C/400°F/Gas Mark 6 for 20–25 minutes or until softened.

3 Meanwhile, make the sauce. Melt the butter in a small pan and add the flour. Cook for 1 minute and remove from the heat. Stir in the milk and stock and return the pan to the heat. Bring to the boil, stirring, until thickened. Stir in the cheese, mustard and mixed herbs and season well.

4 Preheat the grill (broiler) to high. Cut the muffins in half and grill for 2–3 minutes until golden brown, then remove and arrange on a serving plate.

5 Spoon the roasted vegetables on to the muffins and pour the sauce over the top. Garnish with fresh herbs and serve immediately.

Mushroom & Garlic Soufflés

These individual soufflés are very impressive starters, but must be cooked
just before serving to prevent them sinking.

Serves 4
50 g/1¾ oz/4 tbsp butter
75 g/2¾ oz/1 cup flat mushrooms, chopped
2 tsp lime juice
2 garlic cloves, crushed
2 tbsp chopped marjoram
25 g/1 oz/3 tbsp plain (all-purpose) flour
225 ml/8 fl oz/1 cup milk
salt and pepper
2 eggs, separated

1 Lightly grease the inside of four
150 ml/¼ pint individual soufflé
dishes with a little butter.

2 Melt 25 g/1 oz/2 tbsp of the butter
in a frying pan (skillet). Add the
mushrooms, lime juice and garlic and
sauté for 2–3 minutes. Remove the
mushroom mixture from the frying
pan (skillet) with a slotted spoon and
transfer to a mixing bowl. Stir in the
marjoram.

3 Melt the remaining butter in a pan.
Add the flour and cook for 1 minute,
then remove from the heat. Stir in the
milk and return to the heat. Bring to
the boil, stirring until thickened.

COOK'S TIP

Insert a skewer into the centre of
the soufflés to test if they are
cooked through – it should come
out clean. If not, cook for a few
minutes longer, but do not overcook
otherwise they will become rubbery.

4 Add the sauce to the mushroom
mixture, mixing well and beat in the
egg yolks.

5 Whisk the egg whites until peaking
and fold into the mushroom mixture
until fully incorporated.

6 Divide the mixture between the
soufflé dishes. Place the dishes on a
baking sheet (cookie sheet) and cook
in a preheated oven, 200°C/400°F/Gas
Mark 6, for 8–10 minutes or until the
soufflés have risen and are cooked
through. Serve immediately.

Aubergine (Eggplant) Timbale

This is a great way to serve pasta as a starter, wrapped in an aubergine (eggplant) mould (mold). It looks really impressive but it is so easy to make.

Serves 4

1 large aubergine (eggplant)
50 g/1¾ oz/½ cup macaroni
1 tbsp vegetable oil
1 onion, chopped
2 garlic cloves, crushed
2 tbsp drained canned sweetcorn
2 tbsp frozen peas, thawed
100 g/3½ oz spinach
25 g/1 oz/¼ cup vegetarian Cheddar, grated
1 egg, beaten
225 g/8 oz/3 cups canned, chopped tomatoes
1 tbsp chopped basil
salt and pepper

SAUCE

4 tbsp olive oil
2 tbsp white wine vinegar
2 garlic cloves, crushed
3 tbsp chopped basil
1 tbsp caster (superfine) sugar

1 Cut the aubergine (eggplant) lengthwise into thin strips, using a potato peeler. Place in a bowl of salted boiling water and leave to stand for 3–4 minutes. Drain well.

2 Lightly grease four 150 ml/¼ pint individual ramekin dishes and use the aubergine (eggplant) slices to line the dishes, leaving 2.5 cm/1 inch of aubergine (eggplant) overlapping.

3 Cook the pasta in a pan of boiling water for 8–10 minutes or until 'al dente'. Drain. Heat the oil in a pan and sauté the onion and garlic for 2–3 minutes. Stir in the sweetcorn and peas and remove from the heat.

4 Blanch the spinach, drain well, chop and reserve. Add the pasta to the onion mixture with the cheese, egg, tomatoes and basil. Season and mix. Half-fill each ramekin with some of the pasta. Spoon the spinach on top and then the remaining pasta mixture. Fold the aubergine (eggplant) over the pasta filling to cover. Put the ramekins in a roasting tin (pan) half-filled with boiling water, cover and cook in a preheated oven, 180°C/350°F/Gas Mark 4, for 20–25 minutes or until set. Meanwhile, heat the ingredients for the sauce in a pan. Turn out the ramekins and serve with the sauce.

Carrot, Fennel & Potato Medley

This is a colourful dish of shredded vegetables in a fresh garlic and honey dressing.
It is delicious served with crusty bread to mop up the dressing.

Serves 4
2 tbsp olive oil
1 potato, cut into thin strips
1 fennel bulb, cut into thin strips
2 carrots, grated
1 red onion, cut into thin strips
chopped chives and fennel fronds, to garnish

DRESSING

3 tbsp olive oil
1 tbsp garlic wine vinegar
1 garlic clove, crushed
1 tsp Dijon mustard
2 tsp clear honey
salt and pepper

1 Heat the oil in a frying pan (skillet) and cook the potato and fennel slices for 2–3 minutes until beginning to brown. Remove with a slotted spoon and drain on kitchen paper.

2 Arrange the carrot, red onion and potato and fennel on a serving platter.

3 Mix the dressing ingredients together and pour over the vegetables. Toss well and sprinkle with chopped chives and fennel fronds.

COOK'S VARIATION

Use mixed, grilled (bell) peppers or shredded leeks in this dish for variety, or add beansprouts and a segmented orange, if you prefer.

Light Meals

The ability to rustle up a quick light meal can be very important in our busy lives. Sometimes we may not feel like eating a full-scale meal but nevertheless want something appetizing and satisfying. Or, if lunch or dinner is going to be served late, then we may want something to tide us over.

Whatever the occasion, you're guaranteed to find a mouthwatering collection of recipes in this chapter. The recipes cater for all tastes and times of day. Many of the recipes can be prepared way

ahead of time and will not detain you in the kitchen for too long.

With such a versatile selection of recipes to choose from, using a wide range of exciting flavours and ingredients, you will easily find something to satisfy your hunger, with hardly a sandwich in sight!

Roman Focaccia

Roman focaccia makes a delicious snack on its own or
serve it with salad for a quick supper.

Makes 16 squares
7 g/¼ oz dried yeast
1 tsp sugar
300 ml/½ pint/1¼ cups hand-hot water
450 g/1 lb strong flour
2 tsp salt
3 tbsp rosemary, chopped
2 tbsp olive oil
450 g/1 lb mixed red and white onions, sliced into rings
4 garlic cloves, sliced
fresh rosemary, to garnish

1 Place the yeast and sugar in a small bowl with 100 ml/3½ fl oz/8 tbsp of the water. Leave to ferment in a warm place for 15 minutes.

2 Mix the flour with the salt in a large bowl.

3 Add the yeast mixture, half of the rosemary and the remaining water and mix to form a smooth dough. Knead the dough for 4 minutes.

4 Cover the dough with oiled cling film (plastic wrap) and leave to rise for 30 minutes or until doubled in size.

5 Meanwhile, heat the oil in a large pan. Add the onions and garlic and fry for 5 minutes or until softened. Cover the pan and continue to cook for a further 7–8 minutes or until the onions are lightly caramelized.

6 Remove the cling film (plastic wrap) from the dough and knead the dough again for 1–2 minutes.

7 Roll the dough out to form a square shape. The dough should be no more than 6 mm/¼ inch thick because it will rise during cooking.

8 Place the dough on to a large baking sheet (cookie sheet), pushing out the edges until even.

9 Spread the caramelized onions over the dough, and sprinkle with the remaining rosemary. Bake the focaccia in a preheated oven, 200°C/400°F/Gas Mark 6, for 25–30 minutes or until golden. Cut the Roman focaccia into 16 squares, garnish and serve immediately.

Vegetable Samosas

These Indian snacks are perfect for a quick or light meal.
Served with a salad they can be made in advance and frozen for ease.

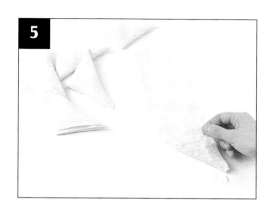

Makes 12
FILLING
2 tbsp vegetable oil
1 onion, chopped
$^1/_2$ tsp ground coriander
$^1/_2$ tsp ground cumin
pinch of turmeric
$^1/_2$ tsp ground ginger
$^1/_2$ tsp garam masala
1 garlic clove, crushed
225 g/8 oz/1$^1/_2$ cups potatoes, diced
100 g/3$^1/_2$ oz/1 cup frozen peas, thawed
150 g/5$^1/_2$ oz/2 cups spinach, chopped
PASTRY
12 sheets filo pastry
oil, for deep-frying

1 To make the filling, heat the oil in a frying pan (skillet) and sauté the onion for 1–2 minutes, stirring until softened. Stir in all of the spices and garlic and cook for 1 minute.

2 Add the potatoes and cook over a gentle heat for 5 minutes, stirring until they begin to soften.

3 Stir in the peas and spinach and cook for a further 3–4 minutes.

4 Lay the filo pastry sheets out on a clean work surface (counter) and fold each sheet in half lengthwise.

5 Place 2 tbsp of the vegetable filling at one end of each folded pastry sheet. Fold over one corner to make a triangle. Continue folding in this way to make a triangular package and seal the edges with water. Repeat with the remaining pastry and filling.

6 Heat the oil for deep-frying to 180°C/350°F or until a cube of bread browns in 30 seconds. Fry the samosas, in batches, for 1–2 minutes until golden. Drain on absorbent kitchen paper and keep warm whilst cooking the remainder. Serve.

COOK'S TIP

Serve with a yogurt sauce (see page 43) and a salad.

Tofu (Bean Curd) Stuffed Mushrooms

Use large open-capped mushrooms for this recipe
for their flavour and suitability for filling.

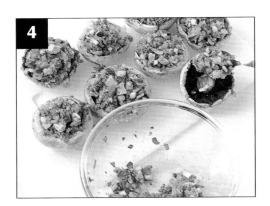

Serves 4

8 open-capped mushrooms

1 tbsp olive oil

1 small leek, chopped

1 celery stick, chopped

100 g/3½ oz firm tofu (bean curd), diced

1 courgette (zucchini), chopped

1 carrot, chopped

100 g/3½ oz/1 cup wholemeal (whole wheat) breadcrumbs

2 tbsp chopped basil

1 tbsp tomato purée

2 tbsp pine nuts

75 g/2¾ oz/¾ cup vegetarian Cheddar cheese, grated

150 ml/¼ pint/⅔ cup vegetable stock

salt and pepper

green salad, to serve

1 Remove the stalks from the mushrooms and chop finely.

2 Heat the oil in a frying pan (skillet). Add the chopped mushroom stalks, leek, celery, tofu (bean curd), courgette (zucchini) and carrot and cook for 3–4 minutes, stirring.

3 Stir in the breadcrumbs, basil, tomato purée and pine nuts. Season with salt and pepper to taste.

4 Spoon the mixture into the mushrooms and top with the cheese.

5 Place the mushrooms in a shallow ovenproof dish and pour the vegetable stock around them.

6 Cook in a preheated oven at 220°C/425°F/Gas Mark 7 for 20 minutes or until cooked through and the cheese has melted. Remove the mushrooms from the dish and serve immediately with a green salad.

COOK'S TIP

Vary the vegetables used for flavour and colour or according to those you have available.

Ricotta & Spinach Parcels

Ricotta and spinach make a great flavour combination,
especially when encased in light puff-pastry parcels.

Serves 4
350 g/12 oz/3 cups spinach, trimmed and washed thoroughly
25 g/1 oz/2 tbsp butter
1 small onion, chopped finely
1 tsp green peppercorns
450 g/1 lb puff pastry
250 g/9 oz/1 cup Ricotta
1 egg, beaten
salt
sprigs of fresh herbs, to garnish
fresh vegetables, to serve

1 Pack the spinach into a large saucepan. Add a little salt and a very small amount of water and cook until wilted. Drain well, cool and then squeeze out any excess moisture with the back of a spoon. Chop roughly.

2 Melt the butter in a small saucepan and fry the onion gently until softened, but not browned. Add the green peppercorns and cook for 2 minutes. Remove from the heat, add the spinach and mix together.

3 Roll out the puff pastry thinly on a lightly floured work surface and cut into 4 squares, each 18 cm/7 inches across. Place a quarter of the spinach mixture in the centre of each square and top with a quarter of the cheese.

4 Brush a little beaten egg around the edges of the pastry squares and bring the corners together to form parcels. Press the edges together to seal. Lift the parcels on to a greased baking sheet (cookie sheet), brush with beaten egg and bake in a preheated oven, 200°C/ 400°F/Gas Mark 6, for 20–25 minutes, until risen and golden.

5 Serve hot, garnished with sprigs of fresh herbs and accompanied by fresh vegetables.

Garlic Mushrooms on Toast

This is so simple to prepare and looks great if you use a variety of mushrooms for shape and texture. Cooked in garlic butter, they are simply irresistible.

Serves 4
75 g/2³/₄ oz/6 tbsp vegetarian margarine
2 garlic cloves, crushed
350 g/12 oz/4 cups mixed mushrooms, such as open-cap, button, oyster and shiitake, sliced
1 tbsp chopped parsley
8 slices French bread
salt and pepper

1 Melt the margarine in a frying pan (skillet). Add the garlic and cook for 30 seconds, stirring.

2 Add the mushrooms and cook for 5 minutes, turning occasionally.

3 Meanwhile, toast the French bread slices under a preheated medium grill (broiler) for 2–3 minutes, turning once. Transfer the toasts to a serving plate.

4 Toss the parsley into the mushrooms, mixing well, and spoon the mixture over the bread. Serve immediately.

COOK'S TIP

Add seasonings, such as curry powder or chilli powder, to the mushrooms for extra flavour, if liked.

Mixed Bean Pan-Fry

Fresh green beans have a wonderful flavour that is hard to beat.
If you cannot find fresh beans, use thawed, frozen beans instead.

Serves 4

350 g/12 oz/4 cups mixed green
beans, such as French (green) and
broad (fava) beans

2 tbsp vegetable oil

2 garlic cloves, crushed

1 red onion, halved and sliced

225 g/8 oz firm marinated
tofu (bean curd), diced

1 tbsp lemon juice

$1/2$ tsp turmeric

1 tsp ground mixed spice

150 ml/$1/4$ pint/$2/3$ cup vegetable stock

2 tsp sesame seeds

1 Trim and chop the French (green) beans. Set aside until required.

2 Heat the oil in a frying pan (skillet) and sauté the garlic and onion for 2 minutes, stirring well.

3 Add the tofu (bean curd) and cook for 2–3 minutes until just beginning to brown.

4 Add the French (green) beans and broad (fava) beans. Stir in the lemon juice, turmeric, mixed spice and stock and bring to the boil. Reduce the heat and simmer for 5–7 minutes or until the beans are tender. Sprinkle with sesame seeds and serve immediately.

COOK'S VARIATION

Use smoked tofu (bean curd) instead of marinated tofu (bean curd) for an alternative flavour.

Bulgar-Filled Aubergines (Eggplants)

In this recipe, aubergines (eggplants) are filled with a spicy bulgar wheat
and vegetable stuffing for a delicious light meal.

Serves 4
4 medium aubergines (eggplant)
salt
175 g/6 oz/^{3}/$_4$ cup bulgar wheat
300 ml/^{1}/$_2$ pint/1^1/$_4$ cups boiling water
3 tbsp olive oil
2 garlic cloves, crushed
2 tbsp pine nuts
^{1}/$_2$ tsp turmeric
1 tsp chilli powder
2 celery sticks, chopped
4 spring onions (scallions), chopped
1 carrot, grated
50 g/1^3/$_4$ oz/^{3}/$_4$ cup button mushrooms, chopped
2 tbsp raisins
2 tbsp chopped fresh coriander (cilantro)
green salad, to serve

1 Cut the aubergines (eggplants) in
half lengthwise and scoop out the
flesh with a teaspoon. Chop the flesh
and set aside. Rub the insides of the
aubergines (eggplants) with a little
salt and leave to stand for 20 minutes.

2 Meanwhile, put the bulgar wheat
in a mixing bowl and pour the boiling
water over the top. Leave to stand for
20 minutes or until the water has
been absorbed.

3 Heat the oil in a frying pan (skillet).
Add the garlic, nuts, turmeric, chilli
powder, celery, spring onions
(scallions), carrot, mushrooms and
raisins and cook for 2–3 minutes.

4 Stir in the reserved aubergine
(eggplant) flesh and cook for a further

2–3 minutes. Add the coriander
(cilantro), mixing well.

5 Remove the pan from the heat and
stir in the bulgar wheat. Rinse the
aubergine (eggplant) shells under cold
water and pat dry with absorbent
kitchen paper.

6 Spoon the bulgar filling into the
aubergines (eggplants) and place in a
roasting tin (pan). Pour in a little
boiling water and cook in a preheated
oven, 180°C/350°F/Gas Mark 4, for
15–20 minutes.

7 Serve hot with a green salad.

Creamy Mushroom Vol-au-Vent

A simple mixture of creamy, tender mushrooms filling a crisp, rich pastry case,
this dish will make an impression at any dinner party.

Serves 4
500 g/1 lb 2 oz puff pastry, thawed if frozen
1 egg, beaten, for glazing
FILLING
25 g/1 oz/2 tbsp butter or vegetarian margarine
750 g/1 lb 10 oz mixed mushrooms such as open-cup, field, button, chestnut, shiitake, pied de mouton, sliced
6 tbsp dry white wine
4 tbsp double (heavy) cream
2 tbsp chopped fresh chervil
salt and pepper
sprigs of fresh chervil, to garnish

1 Roll out the pastry on a lightly floured surface (counter) to form a 20 cm/8 inch square.

2 Using a sharp knife, mark a square 2.5 cm/1 inch from the pastry edge, cutting halfway through the pastry.

3 Score the top of the square in a diagonal pattern. Knock up the edges with a kitchen knife and place on a baking sheet (cookie sheet). Brush the top with beaten egg, taking care not to let the egg run into the cut edges. Bake in a preheated oven, 220°C/425°F/Gas Mark 7, for 35 minutes.

4 Cut out the central square. Scoop out the soft pastry inside the case and discard, leaving the base intact. Return to the oven, together with the central square, for about 10 minutes.

5 To make the filling, melt the butter in a frying pan (skillet) and stir-fry the mushrooms for 3 minutes.

6 Add the wine and cook for 10 minutes, stirring occasionally, until the mushrooms have softened. Stir in the cream, chervil and seasoning.

7 Spoon the filling into the pastry case. Top with the pastry square, garnish and serve.

Potato, (Bell) Pepper & Mushroom Hash

This is a quick one-pan dish which is ideal for a quick snack. Packed with colour and flavour it is very versatile and you can add any other vegetable you have to hand.

Serves 4
675 g/1¹/₂ lb potatoes, cubed
1 tbsp olive oil
2 garlic cloves, crushed
1 green (bell) pepper, cubed
1 yellow (bell) pepper, cubed
3 tomatoes, diced
75 g/2³/₄ oz/1 cup button mushrooms, halved
1 tbsp vegetarian Worcester sauce
2 tbsp chopped basil
salt and pepper
fresh basil sprigs, to garnish
warm, crusty bread, to serve

1 Cook the potatoes in a saucepan of boiling salted water for 7–8 minutes. Drain well and reserve.

2 Heat the oil in a large, heavy-based frying pan (skillet) and cook the potatoes for 8–10 minutes, stirring until browned.

3 Add the garlic and (bell) peppers and cook for 2–3 minutes. Stir in the tomatoes and mushrooms and cook, stirring, for 5–6 minutes.

4 Stir in the vegetarian Worcester sauce and basil and season well. Garnish and serve with crusty bread.

COOK'S TIP

Most brands of Worcester sauce contain anchovies so make sure you choose a vegetarian variety.

Leek & Sun-dried Tomato Timbales

Angel-hair pasta, known as cappellini, is mixed with fried leeks, sun-dried
tomatoes, fresh oregano and beaten eggs, and baked in ramekins.

Serves 4

90 g/3 oz angel-hair pasta (cappellini)
25 g/1 oz/2 tbsp butter
1 tbsp olive oil
1 large leek, sliced finely
60 g/2 oz/¹/₂ cup sun-dried tomatoes in oil, drained and chopped
1 tbsp chopped fresh oregano or 1 tsp dried oregano
2 eggs, beaten
100 ml/3¹/₂ fl oz/generous ¹/₃ cup single (light) cream
1 tbsp freshly grated Parmesan
salt and pepper
sprigs of oregano, to garnish
lettuce leaves, to serve

TOMATO SAUCE

1 small onion, chopped finely
1 small garlic clove, crushed
350 g/12 oz tomatoes, peeled and chopped
1 tsp mixed dried Italian herbs
4 tbsp dry white wine

1 Cook the pasta in a pan of boiling
salted water for about 3 minutes until
'al dente' (just tender). Drain and
rinse with cold water to cool quickly.

2 Meanwhile, heat the butter and oil
in a frying pan (skillet). Gently fry
the leek until softened, about 5–6
minutes. Add the sun-dried tomatoes
and oregano, and cook for a further
2 minutes. Remove from the heat.

3 Add the leek mixture to the pasta.
Stir in the beaten eggs, cream and
Parmesan and season.

4 Divide the mixture between 4
greased ramekins. Place in a roasting
tin (pan) with enough warm water to
come halfway up their sides. Bake in a
preheated oven, 180°C/350°F/Gas
Mark 4, for 30 minutes, or until set.

5 To make the sauce, fry the onion
and garlic until softened. Add the
tomatoes, herbs and wine. Cover and
cook for 20 minutes until pulpy. Blend
in a food processor or press through a
sieve until smooth.

6 Run a knife around the edge of the
ramekin dishes, then turn out the
timbales on to 4 serving plates. Pour
over a little sauce, garnish and serve.

Marinated Grilled Fennel

Fennel has a wonderful aniseed flavour which is ideal for grilling or barbecuing. Marinated in lime, garlic, oil and mustard, this recipe is really delicious.

Serves 4
2 fennel bulbs
1 red (bell) pepper, cut into large cubes
1 lime, cut into eight wedges

MARINADE

2 tbsp lime juice
4 tbsp olive oil
2 garlic cloves, crushed
1 tsp wholegrain mustard
1 tbsp chopped thyme
fennel fronds, to garnish
crisp salad, to serve

1 Cut each of the fennel bulbs into eight pieces and place in a shallow dish. Mix in the (bell) peppers.

2 To make the marinade, combine the lime juice, oil, garlic, mustard and thyme. Pour the marinade over the fennel and (bell) peppers and leave to marinate for 1 hour.

3 Thread the fennel and (bell) peppers on to wooden skewers with the lime wedges. Preheat a grill (broiler) to medium and grill (broil) the kebabs (kabobs) for 10 minutes, turning and basting with the marinade. Transfer to serving plates, garnish with fennel fronds and serve with a crisp salad.

COOK'S TIP

Soak the skewers in water for 20 minutes before using to prevent them from burning during cooking.

Scrambled Tofu (Bean Curd) on Toast

This is a delicious dish which would also
serve as a light lunch or supper.

Serves 4

75 g/2³/₄ oz/6 tbsp vegetarian margarine

450 g/1 lb marinated,
firm tofu (bean curd)

1 red onion, chopped

1 red (bell) pepper, chopped

4 ciabatta rolls, halved

2 tbsp chopped mixed herbs

salt and pepper

fresh herbs, to garnish

1 Melt the margarine in a frying pan (skillet) and crumble the tofu (bean curd) into the pan.

2 Add the onion and (bell) pepper and cook for 3–4 minutes, stirring occasionally.

3 Meanwhile, toast the ciabatta rolls under a hot grill (broiler) for 2–3 minutes, turning once. Remove and transfer to a serving plate.

4 Add the herbs to the tofu (bean curd) mixture, combine and season.

5 Spoon the tofu (bean curd) mixture on to the toast and garnish with fresh herbs. Serve at once.

COOK'S TIP

Marinated tofu adds extra flavour to this dish. Smoked tofu could be used in its place.

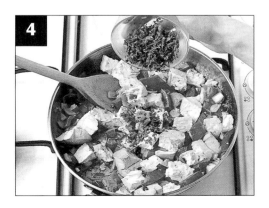

Refried Beans with Tortillas

Refried beans are a classic Mexican dish and are usually served as an accompaniment. They are, however, delicious when served with warm tortillas and a quick onion relish.

Serves 4
BEANS
2 tbsp olive oil
1 onion, finely chopped
3 garlic cloves, crushed
1 green chilli, chopped
400 g/14 oz can red kidney beans, drained
400 g/14 oz can pinto beans, drained
2 tbsp chopped coriander (cilantro)
150 ml/¼ pint/⅔ cup vegetable stock
8 wheat tortillas
25 g/1 oz/¼ cup vegetarian Cheddar cheese, grated
salt and pepper
RELISH
4 spring onions (scallions), chopped
1 red onion, chopped
1 green chilli, chopped
1 tbsp garlic wine vinegar
1 tsp caster (superfine) sugar
1 tomato, chopped

1 Heat the oil for the beans in a large frying pan (skillet). Add the onion and sauté for 3–5 minutes until softened. Add the garlic and chilli and cook for 1 minute.

2 Mash the beans with a potato masher and stir into the pan with the coriander (cilantro).

3 Stir in the stock and cook the beans, stirring, for 5 minutes until soft and pulpy.

4 Place the tortillas on a baking sheet (cookie sheet) and heat through in a warm oven for 1–2 minutes. Mix the relish ingredients together.

5 Spoon the beans into a serving dish and top with the cheese. Season well. Roll the tortillas and serve with the relish and beans.

COOK'S TIP

Add a little more liquid to the beans when they are cooking if they begin to catch on the bottom of the frying pan (skillet).

Cauliflower Roulade

A light-as-air mixture of eggs and vegetables produces a stylish vegetarian dish that can be enjoyed hot or cold.

Serves 6

1 small cauliflower, divided into florets
4 eggs, separated
90 g/3 oz/³/4 cup Cheddar, grated
60 g/2 oz/¹/4 cup cottage cheese
large pinch of grated nutmeg
¹/2 tsp mustard powder
salt and pepper

FILLING

1 bunch watercress, trimmed
60 g/2 oz/¹/4 cup butter
25 g/1 oz/¹/4 cup flour
175 ml/6 fl oz/³/4 cup natural yogurt
25 g/1 oz/¹/4 cup Cheddar, grated
60 g/2 oz/¹/4 cup cottage cheese

1 Line a Swiss roll tin (pan) with baking parchment. Steam the cauliflower until just tender, then drain. Put the cauliflower in a food processor and finely process, or chop finely and push through a sieve.

2 Beat the egg yolks, then stir in the cauliflower, 60 g/2 oz/¹/2 cup of the Cheddar and the cottage cheese. Season with nutmeg, mustard, and salt and pepper. Whisk the egg whites until stiff but not dry, then fold into the cauliflower, using a metal spoon. Spread the mixture in the prepared tin (pan) and bake in a preheated oven, 200°C/400°F/Gas Mark 6, for 20–25 minutes, until risen and golden.

3 For the filling, chop the watercress, reserving a few sprigs for garnish. Melt the butter in a small pan, add the watercress and cook for 3 minutes,

stirring, until wilted. Blend in the flour, then stir in the yogurt and simmer for 2 minutes. Stir in the cheeses.

4 Turn out the roulade on to a damp tea towel (dish cloth) covered with baking parchment. Peel off the paper and leave for 1 minute to allow the

steam to escape. Roll up the roulade, including a new sheet of paper, starting from one narrow end. Unroll the roulade, spread the filling to within 2.5 cm/1 inch of the edges, and roll up. Transfer to a baking sheet (cookie sheet), sprinkle on the Cheddar and return to the oven for 5 minutes. Serve.

Falafel

These are a very tasty, well-known Middle Eastern dish of small chick-pea (garbanzo bean) based balls, spiced and deep-fried. They are delicious hot with a crisp tomato salad.

3 Heat the oil for deep-frying to 180°C/350°F or until a cube of bread browns in 30 seconds. Fry the falafel, in batches, for 2–3 minutes until crisp and browned. Remove from the oil with a slotted spoon and dry on absorbent kitchen paper. Garnish with coriander (cilantro) and serve.

Serves 4

650 g/1 lb 7 oz/6 cups canned chick-peas (garbanzo beans), drained

1 red onion, chopped

3 garlic cloves, crushed

100 g/3¹/₂ oz wholemeal (whole wheat) bread

2 small red chillies

1 tsp ground cumin

1 tsp ground coriander

¹/₂ tsp turmeric

1 tbsp chopped coriander (cilantro), plus extra to garnish

1 egg, beaten

100 g/3¹/₂ oz/1 cup wholemeal (whole wheat) breadcrumbs

vegetable oil, for deep-frying

salt and pepper

1 Put the chick-peas (garbanzo beans), onion, garlic, bread, chillies, spices and coriander (cilantro) in a food processor and blend for 30 seconds. Stir and season well. Remove the mixture from the food processor and shape into walnut-sized balls.

2 Place the beaten egg in a shallow bowl. Dip the balls into the egg to coat and then roll them in the breadcrumbs, shaking off any excess.

COOK'S TIP

Serve the falafel with a coriander (cilantro) and yogurt sauce. Mix 150 ml/ ¹/₄ pint/²/₃ cup natural yogurt with 2 tbsp chopped coriander (cilantro) and 1 crushed garlic clove.

Ciabatta Vegetable Rolls

Sandwiches are always a welcome snack but can be quite mundane.
These crisp ciabatta rolls filled with roast (bell) peppers and cheese are irresistible
and will always be a popular light meal.

Serves 4
4 ciabatta rolls
2 tbsp olive oil
1 garlic clove crushed
FILLING
1 red (bell) pepper
1 green (bell) pepper
1 yellow (bell) pepper
4 radishes, sliced
1 bunch watercress
100 g/3½ oz/8 tbsp cream cheese

1 Halve the ciabatta rolls. Heat the oil and garlic in a pan. Pour the garlic and oil mixture over the cut surfaces of the rolls and leave to stand.

2 Halve the (bell) peppers and place, skin side uppermost, on a grill (broiler) rack. Cook under a hot grill (broiler) for 8–10 minutes until just beginning to char. Remove the (bell) peppers from the grill (broiler), peel and slice thinly.

3 Arrange the radish slices on one half of each roll with a few watercress leaves. Spoon the cream cheese on top. Pile the (bell) peppers on top of the cream cheese and top with the other half of the roll. Serve.

COOK'S TIP

Allow the (bell) peppers to cool slightly before filling the roll otherwise the cheese will melt.

Tofu (Bean Curd) & Vegetable Mini Kebabs (Kabobs)

Cubes of smoked tofu (bean curd) are speared on bamboo satay sticks with crisp vegetables, basted with lemon juice and olive oil, and then grilled.

Serves 6

300 g/10½ oz smoked tofu (bean curd), cut into cubes

1 large red and 1 large yellow (bell) pepper, deseeded and cut into small squares

175 g/6 oz button mushrooms, wiped

1 small courgette (zucchini), sliced

finely grated rind and juice of 1 lemon

3 tbsp olive oil

1 tbsp chopped fresh parsley

1 tsp caster (superfine) sugar

salt and pepper

sprigs of parsley, to garnish

SAUCE

125 g/4½ oz/1 cup cashew nuts

15 g/½ oz/1 tbsp butter

1 garlic clove, crushed

1 shallot, chopped finely

1 tsp ground coriander

1 tsp ground cumin

1 tbsp caster (superfine) sugar

1 tbsp desiccated (shredded) coconut

150 ml/¼ pint/⅔ cup natural yogurt

1 Thread the tofu (bean curd) cubes, (bell) peppers, mushrooms and courgettes (zucchini) on to bamboo satay sticks. Arrange in a shallow dish.

2 Mix together the lemon rind and juice, oil, parsley and sugar. Season with salt and pepper. Pour over the kebabs (kabobs), brushing them with the mixture. Leave for 10 minutes.

3 To make the sauce, scatter the cashew nuts on to a baking sheet (cookie sheet) and toast until browned.

4 Melt the butter in a saucepan and cook the garlic and shallot gently until softened. Transfer to a blender or food processor, add the cashew nuts, ground coriander, cumin, sugar, coconut and yogurt and blend until combined, about 15 seconds. Alternatively, chop the cashew nuts very finely by hand and mix with the remaining ingredients.

5 Place the kebabs (kabobs) under a preheated grill (broiler) and cook, turning and basting frequently with the lemon juice mixture, until lightly browned.

6 Transfer the kebabs (kabobs) to serving plates and garnish with sprigs of parsley. Serve with the cashew nut sauce.

Calzone with Sun-dried Tomatoes & Vegetables

These pizza base parcels are great for making in advance and freezing – they can be defrosted when required for a quick snack.

Makes 4
DOUGH
450 g/1 lb/3^1/$_2$ cups strong white flour
2 tsp easy-blend dried yeast
1 tsp caster (superfine) sugar
150 ml/^{1}/$_4$ pint/^{2}/$_3$ cup vegetable stock
150 ml/^{1}/$_4$ pint/^{2}/$_3$ cup passata (sieved tomatoes)
beaten egg
FILLING
1 tbsp vegetable oil
1 onion, chopped
1 garlic clove, crushed
2 tbsp chopped sun-dried tomatoes
100 g/3^1/$_2$ oz spinach, chopped
3 tbsp canned and drained sweetcorn
25 g/1 oz/^{1}/$_4$ cup French (green) beans, cut into three
1 tbsp tomato purée
1 tbsp chopped oregano
50 g/1^3/$_4$ oz Mozzarella cheese, sliced
salt and pepper

1 Sieve the flour into a bowl. Add the yeast and sugar and beat in the stock and passata (sieved tomatoes) to make a smooth dough.

2 Knead the dough on a lightly floured surface for 10 minutes. Place the dough in a clean, lightly oiled bowl and leave to rise in a warm place for 1 hour or until doubled in size.

3 Meanwhile, heat the oil for the filling in a frying pan (skillet) and sauté the onion for 2–3 minutes. Stir in the garlic, tomatoes, spinach, corn and beans and cook for a further 3–4 minutes, stirring. Add the tomato purée and oregano and season well.

4 Divide the risen dough into 4 equal portions and roll each on to a floured surface to form an 18 cm/7 inch circle. Spoon a quarter of the filling on to one half of each circle and top with cheese. Fold the dough over to encase the filling, sealing the edge with a fork. Glaze with beaten egg. Put the calzone on a lightly greased baking sheet (cookie sheet) and cook in a preheated oven, 220°C/425°F/Gas Mark 7, for 25–30 minutes until risen and golden. Serve warm.

Spinach Frittata

A frittata is another word for a large, thick omelette.
This is an Italian dish which may be made with many flavourings.
Spinach is used as the main ingredient in this recipe for colour and flavour.

Serves 4
450 g/1 lb spinach
2 tsp water
4 eggs, beaten
2 tbsp single (light) cream
2 garlic cloves, crushed
50 g/1³/₄ oz/³/₄ cup canned sweetcorn, drained
1 celery stick, chopped
1 red chilli, chopped
2 tomatoes, seeded and diced
2 tbsp olive oil
2 tbsp butter
25 g/1 oz/¹/₄ cup pecan nut halves
2 tbsp grated Pecorino cheese
25 g/1 oz/¹/₄ cup Fontina cheese, cubed
a pinch of paprika

1 Cook the spinach in 2 teaspoons of water in a covered pan for 5 minutes. Drain thoroughly and pat dry on absorbent kitchen paper.

2 Beat the eggs in a bowl and stir in the spinach, cream, garlic, sweetcorn, celery, chilli and tomato.

3 Heat the oil and butter in a 20 cm/ 8 inch heavy-based frying pan (skillet).

COOK'S TIP

Be careful not to burn the underside of the frittata during the initial cooking stage – this is why it is important to use a heavy-based frying pan (skillet). Add a little extra oil to the pan when you turn the frittata over if required.

4 Spoon the egg mixture into the frying pan (skillet) and sprinkle with the pecan nut halves, Pecorino and Fontina cheeses and paprika. Cook without stirring over a medium heat for 5–7 minutes or until the underside of the frittata is brown.

5 Put a large plate over the pan and invert to turn out the frittata. Slide it back into the frying pan (skillet) and cook the other side for a further 2–3 minutes. Serve straight from the frying pan (skillet) or transfer to a serving plate.

Aubergine (Eggplant) & Mushroom Satay

Grilled, skewered vegetables are served with a satay sauce.

Serves 4

2 aubergines (eggplants),
cut into 2.5 cm/1 inch pieces

175 g/6 oz small chestnut mushrooms

MARINADE

1 tsp cumin seeds

1 tsp coriander seeds

2.5 cm/1 inch piece ginger root, grated

2 garlic cloves, crushed lightly

$^1/_2$ stalk lemon grass, chopped roughly

4 tbsp light soy sauce

8 tbsp sunflower oil

2 tbsp lemon juice

PEANUT SAUCE

$^1/_2$ tsp cumin seeds

$^1/_2$ tsp coriander seeds

3 garlic cloves

1 small onion, quartered

1 tbsp lemon juice

1 tsp salt

$^1/_2$ red chilli, deseeded and sliced

125 ml/4 fl oz/$^1/_2$ cup coconut milk

250 g/9 oz/1 cup crunchy peanut butter

250 ml/9 fl oz/1 cup water

1 Thread the aubergines (eggplants) and mushrooms on to eight skewers.

2 To make the marinade, grind the cumin, coriander, ginger, garlic and lemon grass together. Add to a wok or a frying pan (skillet) and stir-fry over a high heat until fragrant. Remove from the heat and add the remaining marinade ingredients.

3 Place the skewers in a non-porous dish and spoon the marinade over.

Leave to marinate for a minimum of 2 hours and up to 8 hours.

4 To make the sauce, grind together the cumin, coriander and garlic. Purée the onion in a food processor, or chop finely by hand, then add to the cumin mixture. Add the remaining ingredients, except for the water.

Transfer to a pan and blend in the water. Bring to the boil and cook until thickened. Transfer to a serving bowl.

5 Place the skewers on a baking sheet (cookie sheet) and cook under a hot grill (broiler) for 15–20 minutes. Brush with the marinade and turn once. Serve with the peanut sauce.

Vegetable Burgers

These spicy vegetable burgers are delicious, especially when served with the light oven chips (fries). Serve them in a warm bun or roll with radicchio lettuce leaves and red onion relish.

Serves 4
VEGETABLE BURGERS
100 g/3¹/₂ oz spinach
1 tbsp olive oil
1 leek, chopped
2 garlic cloves, crushed
100 g/3¹/₂ oz mushrooms, chopped
300 g/10¹/₂ oz firm tofu (bean curd), chopped
1 tsp chilli powder
1 tsp curry powder
1 tbsp chopped coriander (cilantro)
75 g/2³/₄ oz fresh wholemeal (whole wheat) breadcrumbs
1 tbsp olive oil
CHIPS (FRIES)
2 large potatoes
2 tbsp flour
1 tsp chilli powder
2 tbsp olive oil
burger bap or roll and salad, to serve

1 To make the burgers, cook the spinach in a little water for 2 minutes. Drain thoroughly and pat dry with absorbent kitchen paper.

2 Heat the oil in a frying pan (skillet) and sauté the leek and garlic for 2–3 minutes. Add the remaining ingredients except for the breadcrumbs and cook for 5–7 minutes until the vegetables have softened. Toss in the spinach and cook for 1 minute.

3 Transfer the mixture to a food processor and blend for 30 seconds until almost smooth. Stir in the breadcrumbs, mixing well, and leave until cool enough to handle. Using floured hands, form the mixture into four equal-sized burgers. Leave to chill for 30 minutes.

4 To make the chips (fries), cut the potatoes into thin wedges and cook in a pan of boiling water for 10 minutes. Drain and toss in the flour and chilli.

Lay the chips on a baking sheet (cookie sheet) and sprinkle with the oil. Cook in a preheated oven, 200°C/400°F/Gas Mark 6, for 30 minutes or until golden.

5 Meanwhile, heat 1 tbsp oil in a frying pan (skillet) and cook the burgers for 8–10 minutes, turning once. Serve with salad in a bap.

Spinach Pancakes

Serve these pancakes as a light lunch or supper dish, with a tomato
and basil salad for a dramatic colour contrast.

Makes 8–12 pancakes
90 g/3 oz/³/₄ cup wholemeal (whole wheat) flour
1 egg
150 ml/¹/₄ pint/²/₃ cup natural yogurt
3 tbsp water
1 tbsp vegetable oil, plus extra for frying
200 g/7 oz frozen leaf spinach, defrosted and liquidized
pinch of grated nutmeg
salt and pepper
lemon wedges and fresh coriander (cilantro) sprigs, to garnish

FILLING

1 tbsp vegetable oil
3 spring onions (scallions), thinly sliced
250 g/9 oz/1 cup Ricotta
4 tbsp natural yogurt
90 g/3 oz/³/₄ cup Gruyère, grated
1 egg, lightly beaten
125 g/4¹/₂ oz/1 cup unsalted cashew nuts
2 tbsp chopped fresh parsley
pinch of cayenne pepper

1 Sift the flour and a pinch of salt
into a bowl. Beat together the egg,
yogurt, water and oil and gradually
pour on to the flour, beating all the
time. Stir in the spinach purée and
season with pepper and nutmeg.

2 To make the filling, heat the oil in a
pan and fry the spring onions
(scallions) until translucent. Remove
with a slotted spoon and drain on
paper towels. Beat together the Ricotta,
yogurt and half the Gruyère. Beat in
the egg and stir in the cashews and
parsley. Season with salt and cayenne.

3 Heat the oil in a frying pan (skillet).
Pour in 3–4 tbsp of the batter and tilt
the pan so that it covers the base.
Cook for 3 minutes, until bubbles
appear in the centre. Turn and cook
the other side for 2 minutes, until
lightly browned. Slide the pancake on
to a warm plate, cover with foil and
keep warm while you cook the rest.

4 Spread a little filling over each
pancake and fold in half and then half
again, envelope style. Spoon the
remaining filling into the opening.
Grease an ovenproof dish and arrange
the pancakes in a single layer. Sprinkle
with the remaining cheese and cook in a
preheated oven, 180°C/350°F/Gas Mark
4, for 15 minutes. Garnish and serve.

Mixed Vegetable Dim Sum

Dim sum are small Chinese parcels, usually served as part
of a large mixed meal. They may be filled with any variety of fillings,
steamed or fried and served with a dipping sauce.

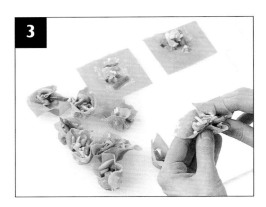

Serves 4

2 spring onions (scallions), chopped
25 g/1 oz green beans, chopped
¹/₂ small carrot, finely chopped
1 red chilli, chopped
25 g/1 oz/¹/₃ cup beansprouts, chopped
25 g/1 oz/¹/₃ cup button mushrooms, chopped
25 g/1 oz/¹/₄ cup unsalted cashew nuts, chopped
1 small egg, beaten
2 tbsp cornflour (cornstarch)
1 tsp light soy sauce
1 tsp hoi-sin sauce
1 tsp sesame oil
32 wonton wrappers
oil, for deep-frying
1 tbsp sesame seeds

1 Mix all of the vegetables together in
a bowl and stir in the nuts, egg,
cornflour (cornstarch), soy sauce, hoi-
sin sauce and sesame oil, mixing well.

2 Lay the wonton wrappers out on a
chopping board and spoon small
quantities of the mixture into the
centre of each.

3 Gather the wrapper around
the filling at the top, leaving the
top open.

4 Heat the oil for deep-frying in a
wok to 180°C/350°F or until a cube
of bread browns in 30 seconds. Fry

the wontons, in batches, for 1–2
minutes or until golden brown.
Drain on absorbent kitchen paper.

5 Sprinkle the sesame seeds over the
wontons. Serve with a soy or plum
dipping sauce.

COOK'S TIP

If preferred, arrange the wontons
on a heatproof plate and then
steam in a steamer for 5–7 minutes,
for a healthier cooking method.

Butter-crust Tartlets with Feta Cheese

These crisp-baked bread cases, filled with sliced tomatoes,
Feta cheese, black olives and quail's eggs, are quick to make and taste delicious.

Serves 4

8 slices bread from a medium-
cut large loaf

125 g/4$^{1}/_{2}$ oz/$^{1}/_{2}$ cup butter, melted

125 g/4$^{1}/_{2}$ oz Feta cheese,
cut into small cubes

4 cherry tomatoes,
cut into wedges

8 pitted black or green
olives, halved

8 quail's eggs, hard-boiled (hard-cooked)

2 tbsp olive oil

1 tbsp wine vinegar

1 tsp wholegrain mustard

pinch of caster (superfine) sugar

salt and pepper

fresh parsley sprigs, to garnish

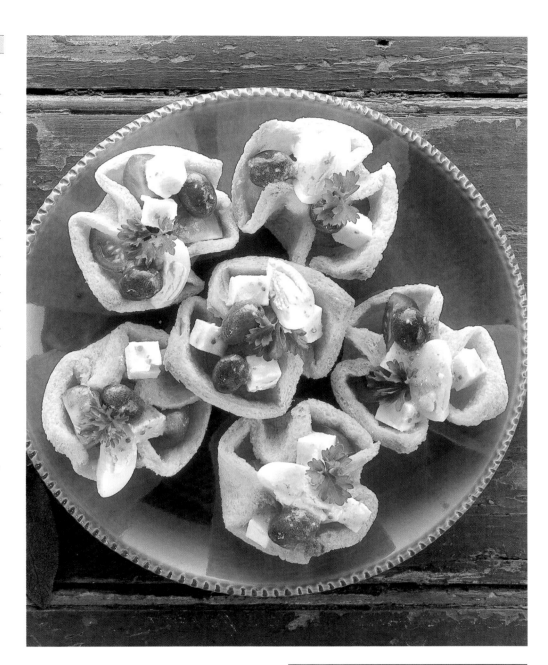

1 Remove the crusts from the bread. Trim the bread into squares and flatten each piece with a rolling pin.

2 Brush the bread with melted butter, and then arrange them in bun or muffin tins (pans). Press a piece of crumpled foil into each bread case to secure in place. Bake in a preheated oven, 190°C/375°F/Gas Mark 5, for about 10 minutes, or until crisp and browned.

3 Meanwhile, mix together the Feta cheese, tomatoes and olives. Shell the eggs and quarter them. Mix together the olive oil, vinegar, mustard and sugar. Season with salt and pepper.

4 Remove the bread cases from the oven and discard the foil. Leave to cool slightly.

5 Just before serving, fill the bread cases with the cheese and tomato mixture. Arrange the eggs on top and spoon over the mustard dressing. Garnish with parsley sprigs and serve immediately.

COOK'S TIP

Feta cheese is made from sheep or goat's milk. It is curdled naturally without the addition of rennet.

Vegetable Crêpes

Crêpes or pancakes are ideal for filling with your favourite ingredients. In this recipe they are packed with a spicy vegetable filling which may be made in advance and heated through for serving.

Serves 4
PANCAKES
100 g/3¹/₂ oz plain (all-purpose) flour
pinch of salt
1 egg, beaten
300 ml/¹/₂ pint/1¹/₄ cups milk
vegetable oil, for frying
FILLING
2 tbsp vegetable oil
1 leek, shredded
¹/₂ tsp chilli powder
¹/₂ tsp ground cumin
50 g/1³/₄ oz mangetout (snow peas)
100 g/3¹/₂ oz button mushrooms,
1 red (bell) pepper, sliced
25 g/1 oz/¹/₄ cup cashew nuts, chopped
SAUCE
25 g/1 oz/2 tbsp vegetarian margarine
25 g/1 oz/3 tbsp plain (all-purpose) flour
150 ml/¹/₄ pint/²/₃ cup vegetable stock
150 ml/¹/₄ pint/²/₃ cup milk
1 tsp Dijon mustard
75 g/2³/₄ oz Cheddar cheese, grated
2 tbsp chopped coriander (cilantro)

1 For the pancakes, sieve the flour and salt into a bowl and make a well in the centre. Beat in the egg and milk to make a batter. For the filling, heat the oil in a pan (skillet) and sauté the leek for 2–3 minutes. Add the rest of the ingredients and cook for 5 minutes, stirring. To make the sauce, melt the margarine in a pan and add the flour. Cook for 1 minute and remove from the heat. Stir in the stock and milk and return to the heat. Bring to the boil, stirring until thick. Add the mustard, half of the cheese and the coriander (cilantro); cook for 1 minute.

2 Heat 1 tbsp of oil in a non-stick 15 cm/6 inch frying pan (skillet). Pour the oil from the pan and add an eighth of the batter, swirling it around the base of the pan to cover. Cook for 2 minutes until cooked through, turn the pancake and cook on the other side for 1 minute. Repeat with the remaining batter. Spoon a little of the filling along the centre of each pancake and roll into a cigar shape. Place in a heatproof dish and pour the sauce over the top. Top with the remaining cheese and heat under a hot grill (broiler) for 3–5 minutes or until the cheese melts and turns golden.

Crisp-Fried Vegetables with Hot & Sweet Dipping Sauce

A Thai-style dipping sauce makes the perfect accompaniment
to fresh vegetables coated in a light batter and deep-fried.

Serves 4

vegetable oil, for deep-frying

500 g/1 lb 2 oz selection of vegetables,
such as cauliflower, broccoli,
mushrooms, courgettes (zucchini), (bell)
peppers and baby sweetcorn cobs, cut into
even-sized pieces

BATTER

125 g/4^1/$_2$ oz/1 cup plain (all-purpose)
flour

^{1}/$_2$ tsp salt

1 tsp caster (superfine) sugar

1 tsp baking powder

3 tbsp vegetable oil

200 ml/7 fl oz/scant 1 cup warm water

SAUCE

6 tbsp light malt vinegar

2 tbsp Thai fish sauce or light soy sauce

2 tbsp water

1 tbsp soft brown sugar

salt

2 garlic cloves, crushed

2 tsp grated ginger root

2 red chillies, deseeded and chopped finely

2 tbsp chopped fresh coriander (cilantro)

1 To make the batter, sift the flour,
salt, sugar and baking powder into a
large bowl. Add the oil and most of
the water. Whisk together to make a
smooth batter, adding extra water to
give it the consistency of single (light)
cream. Chill for 20–30 minutes.

2 Meanwhile, make the sauce. Heat the
vinegar, fish sauce or soy sauce, water,
sugar and a pinch of salt until boiling.
Remove from the heat and leave to cool.

3 Mix together the garlic, ginger,
chillies and coriander (cilantro) in a
small serving bowl. Add the cooled
vinegar mixture and stir together.

4 Heat the vegetable oil for deep-
frying in a wok or deep-fryer. Dip the

prepared vegetables in the batter and
fry them, a few at a time, until crisp
and golden – about 2 minutes. Drain
on paper towels.

5 Serve the vegetables accompanied
by the dipping sauce.

Watercress & Cheese Tartlets

These individual tartlets are great for lunchtime or for picnic food. Watercress is a good source of folic acid, which is important in early pregnancy.

Makes 4
100 g/3¹/₂ oz/³/₄ cup plain (all-purpose) flour
pinch of salt
75 g/2³/₄ oz /¹/₂ cup butter or vegetarian margarine
2–3 tbsp cold water
2 bunches watercress
2 garlic cloves, crushed
1 shallot, chopped
150 g/5¹/₂ oz Cheddar cheese, grated
4 tbsp natural yogurt
¹/₂ tsp paprika

1 Sieve the flour into a bowl and add the salt. Rub 50 g/1³/₄ oz/¹/₃ cup of the butter or margarine into the flour until the mixture resembles breadcrumbs. Stir in the cold water to make a dough.

2 Roll the dough out on a floured surface and use to line four 10 cm/ 4 inch tartlet tins. Prick the bases with a fork and leave to chill.

3 Heat the remaining butter or margarine in a frying pan (skillet). Discard the stems from the watercress and add to the pan with the garlic and shallot, cooking for 1–2 minutes until the watercress is wilted. Remove the pan from the heat and stir in the

cheese, yogurt and paprika. Spoon the mixture into the pastry cases and cook in a preheated oven, 180°C/350°F/Gas Mark 4, for 20 minutes or until the filling is firm. Turn out the tartlets and serve.

VARIATION

Use spinach instead of the watercress, making sure it is well drained before mixing with the remaining filling ingredients.

Vegetable Enchiladas

This Mexican dish uses prepared tortillas which are readily available in supermarkets. They are filled with a spicy vegetable mixture and topped with a hot tomato sauce.

Serves 4
4 flour tortillas
75 g/2³/₄ oz/³/₄ cup Cheddar, grated

FILLING
75 g/2³/₄ oz spinach
2 tbsp olive oil
8 baby sweetcorn cobs, sliced
25 g/1 oz/1 tbsp frozen peas, thawed
1 red (bell) pepper, diced
1 carrot, diced
1 leek, sliced
2 garlic cloves, crushed
1 red chilli, chopped
salt and pepper

SAUCE
300 ml/¹/₂ pint/1¹/₄ cups passata (sieved tomatoes)
2 shallots, chopped
1 garlic clove, crushed
300 ml/¹/₂ pint/1¹/₄ cups vegetable stock
1 tsp caster (superfine) sugar
1 tsp chilli powder

1 To make the filling, blanch the spinach in a pan of boiling water for 2 minutes, drain well and chop.

2 Heat the oil in a frying pan (skillet) and sauté the corn, peas, (bell) pepper, carrot, leek, garlic and chilli for 3–4 minutes. Stir in the spinach and season well.

3 Put all of the sauce ingredients in a saucepan and bring to the boil, stirring. Cook over a high heat for 20 minutes, stirring, until thickened and reduced by a third.

4 Spoon a quarter of the filling along the centre of each tortilla.

5 Roll the tortillas around the filling and place in an ovenproof dish, seam-side down.

6 Pour the sauce over the tortillas and sprinkle the cheese on top. Cook in a preheated oven, 180°C/350°F/Gas Mark 4, for 20 minutes or until the cheese has melted and browned. Serve immediately.

Mediterranean Vegetable Tart

A rich tomato pastry base topped with a mouthwatering selection of vegetables
and cheese makes a dish that's tasty as well as attractive.

Serves 6
1 aubergine (eggplant), sliced
2 tbsp salt
4 tbsp olive oil
1 garlic clove, crushed
1 large yellow (bell) pepper, deseeded and sliced
300 ml/^{1}/$_2$ pint/1^1/$_4$ cups ready-made tomato pasta sauce
125 g/4^1/$_2$ oz/^{2}/$_3$ cup sun-dried tomatoes in oil, drained and halved if necessary
175 g/6 oz Mozzarella, drained and sliced thinly
PASTRY
225 g/8 oz/2 cups plain (all-purpose) flour
pinch of celery salt
125 g/4^1/$_2$ oz/^{1}/$_2$ cup butter or vegetarian margarine
2 tbsp tomato purée (paste)
2–3 tbsp milk

1 To make the pastry, sift the flour and celery salt into a bowl. Rub in the butter or margarine until the mixture resembles fine breadcrumbs. Mix the tomato purée (paste) and milk and stir into the mixture to form a firm dough. Knead on a floured surface until smooth. Wrap and chill for 30 minutes.

2 Grease a 28 cm/11 inch loose-bottomed flan tin (pan). Roll out the pastry on a floured surface and use to line the tin (pan). Trim and prick all over with a fork. Chill for 30 minutes.

3 Layer the aubergine (eggplant) in a dish, sprinkling with the salt. Leave for 30 minutes.

4 Bake the pastry case in a preheated oven, 200°C/400°F/Gas Mark 6, for 20–25 minutes until cooked and golden. Remove from the oven and set aside. Increase the oven temperature to 230°C/450°F/Gas Mark 8.

5 Rinse the aubergine (eggplant) and pat dry. Heat 3 tbsp of the oil in a frying pan (skillet) and fry the garlic, aubergine (eggplant) and (bell) pepper for 5–6 minutes until softened. Drain well. Spread the pasta sauce over the pastry case and arrange the cooked vegetables, sun-dried tomatoes and Mozzarella on top. Brush with oil and bake for 5 minutes until the cheese is just melting. Serve.

Cheese & Garlic Mushroom Pizza

This pizza dough is flavoured with garlic and herbs and topped with mixed mushrooms and melting cheese for a really delicious pizza.

Serves 4
DOUGH
450 g/1 lb/3¹/₂ cups strong white flour
2 tsp easy-blend yeast
2 garlic cloves, crushed
2 tbsp chopped thyme
2 tbsp olive oil
300 ml/¹/₂ pint/1¹/₄ cups tepid water
TOPPING
25 g/1 oz/2 tbsp butter or vegetarian margarine
350 g/12 oz mixed mushrooms, sliced
2 garlic cloves, crushed
2 tbsp chopped parsley
2 tbsp tomato purée (paste)
6 tbsp passata (sieved tomatoes)
75 g/2³/₄ oz Mozzarella cheese, grated
salt and pepper
chopped parsley, to garnish

1 Put the flour, yeast, garlic and thyme in a mixing bowl. Make a well in the centre and gradually stir in the oil and water. Bring together to form a soft dough.

2 Turn the dough on to a floured surface and knead for 5 minutes or until smooth. Roll into a 35 cm/14 inch round and place on a greased baking sheet (cookie sheet). Leave in a

COOK'S TIP

If preferred, spread the base with a prepared cheese sauce before adding the mushrooms.

warm place for 20 minutes or until the dough puffs up.

3 Meanwhile, make the topping. Melt the margarine or butter in a frying pan (skillet) and sauté the mushrooms, garlic and parsley for 5 minutes. Mix the tomato purée (paste) and passata (sieved tomatoes) and spoon on to the

pizza base, leaving a 1 cm/¹/₂ inch edge of dough. Spoon the mushroom mixture on top. Season well and sprinkle the cheese on top. Cook the pizza in a preheated oven, 190°C/ 375°F/Gas Mark 5, for 20–25 minutes or until the base is crisp and the cheese has melted. Garnish with chopped parsley and serve.

Fried Tofu (Bean Curd) with Peanut Sauce

This is a very sociable dish if put in the centre of the table
where people can help themselves with cocktail sticks (toothpicks).

Serves 4
500 g/1 lb 2 oz marinated or plain tofu (bean curd)
1 litre/1³/₄ pints/4 cups sunflower oil
2 tbsp sesame oil

BATTER

4 tbsp plain (all-purpose) flour
2 eggs, beaten
4 tbsp milk
¹/₂ tsp baking powder
¹/₂ tsp chilli powder

PEANUT SAUCE

2 tbsp rice vinegar
2 tbsp sugar
1 tsp salt
3 tbsp smooth peanut butter
¹/₂ tsp chilli flakes
3 tbsp barbecue sauce

1 Cut the tofu (bean curd) into
2.5 cm/1 inch triangles. Set aside
until required.

2 To make the sauce, combine the
vinegar, sugar and salt in a saucepan.
Bring to the boil and then simmer for
2 minutes. Remove from the heat and
add the peanut butter, chilli flakes
and barbecue sauce, stirring to mix.

3 To make the batter, sift the flour
into a bowl. Make a well in the centre
and add the eggs. Draw in the flour,
adding the milk slowly. Add the
baking powder and chilli powder,
stirring to form a batter.

4 Heat the oils in a deep-fryer or large
wok until a light haze appears on top.
Dip the tofu (bean curd) triangles into
the batter and deep-fry until golden.
Drain and serve with the sauce.

COOK'S TIP

Tofu (bean curd) is rich in protein,
iron, calcium and B vitamins.

Baked Aubergine (Eggplant), Basil & Mozzarella Rolls

Thin slices of aubergine (eggplant) are fried in olive oil and garlic,
and then topped with pesto sauce and finely sliced Mozzarella.

Serves 4
2 aubergines (eggplants), sliced thinly lengthwise
5 tbsp olive oil
1 garlic clove, crushed
4 tbsp pesto
175 g/6 oz/1½ cups Mozzarella, grated
basil leaves, torn into pieces
salt and pepper
fresh basil leaves, to garnish

1 Sprinkle the aubergine (eggplant) slices liberally with salt and leave for 10–15 minutes to extract the bitter juices. Turn the slices over and repeat. Rinse well with cold water and drain thoroughly on paper towels.

2 Heat the olive oil in a large frying pan (skillet) and add the garlic. Add the aubergine (eggplant) slices, in batches, and fry lightly on both sides. Drain well on paper towels.

3 Spread the pesto on to one side of the aubergine (eggplant) slices.

4 Top with the grated Mozzarella and sprinkle with the torn basil leaves. Season with a little salt and pepper to taste.

5 Roll up the slices and secure with wooden cocktail sticks (toothpicks).

6 Arrange the aubergine (eggplant) rolls in a greased ovenproof baking dish and cook in a preheated oven, 180°C/350°F/Gas Mark 4, for about 8–10 minutes.

7 Transfer the baked aubergine (eggplant), basil and Mozzarella rolls to a warmed serving plate.

8 Scatter with fresh basil leaves and serve at once.

COOK'S TIP

You may find it easier to slice the Mozzarella rather than grate it yourself.

Barbecue Bean Burgers

These tasty burgers are ideal for a barbecue in the summer but they
are equally delicious cooked indoors at any time of year.

Serves 6
125 g/4¹/₂ oz/¹/₃ cup aduki beans
125 g/4¹/₂ oz/¹/₃ cup black-eye beans (peas)
6 tbsp vegetable oil
1 large onion, chopped finely
1 tsp yeast extract
125 g/4¹/₂ oz grated carrot
90 g/3 oz/1¹/₂ cups fresh wholemeal (whole wheat) breadcrumbs
2 tbsp wholemeal (whole wheat) flour
salt and pepper

BARBECUE SAUCE

¹/₃ tsp chilli powder
1 tsp celery salt
2 tbsp light muscovado sugar
2 tbsp red wine vinegar
2 tbsp vegetarian Worcestershire sauce
3 tbsp tomato purée (paste)
dash of Tabasco sauce

TO SERVE

6 wholemeal (whole wheat) baps, toasted
mixed green salad
jacket potato fries

1 Place the beans in separate saucepans, cover with water and bring to the boil. Cover and simmer the aduki beans for 40 minutes and the black-eye beans (peas) for 50 minutes, or until tender. Drain and rinse well.

2 Transfer to a mixing bowl and lightly mash together with a potato masher or fork. Set aside.

3 Heat 1 tablespoon of the oil in a frying pan (skillet) and gently fry the onion for 3–4 minutes until softened. Mix into the beans with the yeast extract, grated carrot, breadcrumbs and seasoning. Bind together well.

4 With wet hands, divide the mixture into 6 and form into burgers 8 cm/3½ inches in diameter. Put the flour on a plate and use to coat the burgers.

5 Heat the remaining oil in a large frying pan (skillet) and cook the burgers for 3–4 minutes on each side, turning carefully, until golden and crisp. Drain on paper towels.

6 Meanwhile, make the sauce. Mix all the ingredients together until well blended. Place the burgers in the toasted baps and serve with a mixed green salad, jacket potato fries and a spoonful of the barbecue sauce.

Corn-on-the-cob

Corn-on-the-cob is available nearly all the year round,
and it can be barbecued with the husk on or off.

Serves 4–6

4–6 corn-on-the-cobs

oil, for brushing

TO SERVE

butter (optional)

salt (optional)

1 Soak the corn cobs in hand-hot water for 20 minutes. Drain thoroughly.

2 If the corn cobs have no husks, brush generously with oil and cook over a hot barbecue for 30 minutes, brushing occasionally with the oil and turning often.

3 If your corn cobs have husks, tear off all but the last two layers and brush with oil.

4 Cook over a hot barbecue for 40 minutes, brushing with oil once or twice and turning occasionally.

5 Serve hot, without the husks. Add a knob of butter and salt to taste.

COOK'S TIP

Try to buy the corn cobs with the husk still on, as they will retain more moisture this way. While you are barbecuing the corn cobs, you may like to flavour them with herbs – try tucking some fresh rosemary, coriander (cilantro) or thyme inside the husk for an aromatic flavour.

Tofu (Bean Curd) & Mushroom Brochettes

These tofu (bean curd) and mushroom brochettes are marinated in a lemon, garlic and herb mixture so that they soak up a delicious flavour.

Serves 4
1 lemon
1 garlic clove, crushed
4 tbsp olive oil
4 tbsp white wine vinegar
1 tbsp chopped fresh herbs, such as rosemary, parsley and thyme
300 g/10½ oz smoked tofu (bean curd)
350 g/12 oz mushrooms, wiped
salt and pepper
fresh herbs, to garnish

TO SERVE

mixed salad leaves (greens)
cherry tomatoes, halved

1 Grate the rind from the lemon finely and squeeze out the juice.

2 Add the garlic, olive oil, vinegar and herbs to the lemon rind and juice, mixing well. Season with salt and pepper to taste.

3 Slice the tofu (bean curd) into large chunks. Thread the tofu (bean curd) on to metal or wooden skewers, alternating the tofu (bean curd) with the mushrooms.

4 Lay the kebabs (kabobs) in a shallow dish and pour over the marinade. Cover and chill for 1–2 hours, turning the kebabs (kabobs) in the marinade from time to time.

5 Cook the kebabs (kabobs) over a hot barbecue, brushing them with the marinade and turning often, for about 6 minutes.

6 Garnish with fresh herbs and serve with mixed salad leaves (greens) and cherry tomatoes.

COOK'S TIP

Soak wooden skewers in hand-hot water for 30 minutes to prevent them from burning during cooking.

Naan Bread with Curried Vegetable Kebabs (Kabobs)

Warmed Indian bread is served with barbecued vegetable kebabs (kabobs), which are brushed with a curry-spiced yogurt baste.

Serves 4

naan bread, to serve
sprigs of fresh mint, to garnish

YOGURT BASTE

150 ml/¼ pint/²/₃ cup natural yogurt
1 tbsp chopped fresh mint
or 1 tsp dried mint
1 tsp ground cumin
1 tsp ground coriander
½ tsp chilli powder
pinch of turmeric
pinch of ground ginger
salt and pepper

KEBABS (KABOBS)

8 small new potatoes
1 small aubergine (eggplant)
1 courgette (zucchini), cut into chunks
8 chestnut (crimini) or closed-
cup mushrooms
8 small tomatoes

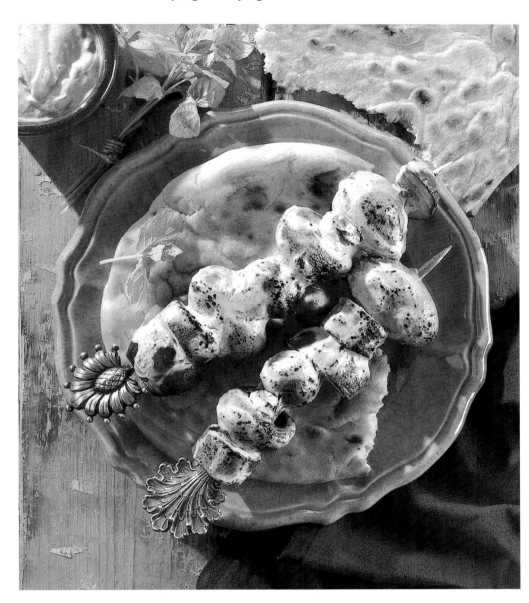

1 To make the spiced yogurt baste, mix together the yogurt, mint, cumin, coriander, chilli powder, turmeric and ginger. Season with salt and pepper, cover and chill.

2 Cook the potatoes in a saucepan of boiling water until just tender. Chop the aubergine (eggplant) into chunks and sprinkle them liberally with salt. Leave for 10–15 minutes to extract the bitter juices. Rinse and drain them well. Drain the potatoes.

3 If using wooden skewers, soak them in warm water for 30 minutes. Thread all of the vegetables on to 4 metal or wooden skewers, alternating the different types of vegetables.

4 Place the kebabs (kabobs) in a shallow dish and brush with the yogurt baste, coating them evenly. Cover and chill until ready to cook.

5 Wrap the naan bread in foil and place towards one side of the barbecue to warm through.

6 Cook the kebabs (kabobs) over the barbecue, basting with any remaining spiced yogurt, until they just begin to char slightly. Serve with the warmed naan bread, garnished with sprigs of fresh mint.

Pasta Dishes

Pasta is one of the most popular and versatile foods on sale today. Available fresh or dried, pasta is made in a wide variety of colours and flavours, shapes and sizes, each lending itself to a particular type of sauce. For instance, flat ribbons go well with cream or cheese-based sauces; tubes and shapes are ideal for trapping chunkier sauces in their crevices.

Wholewheat pastas have a chewier texture and are valuable for the additional fibre they contain. Pasta is a marvellous convenience food – both nourishing and satisfying. All types of pasta are quick to cook and provide good basic food that can be dressed up in all kinds of ways. Pasta combines very well with vegetables, herbs, nuts and cheeses, to provide scores of interesting and tasty vegetarian meals.

Spinach Gnocchi with Tomato & Basil Sauce

These gnocchi or small dumplings are made with potato and flavoured with spinach and nutmeg and served in a rich tomato sauce for an ideal light meal.

Serves 4
450 g/1 lb baking potatoes
75 g/2³/₄ oz spinach
1 tsp water
25 g/1 oz/3 tbsp butter or vegetarian margarine
1 small egg, beaten
150 g/5¹/₂ oz/³/₄ cup plain (all-purpose) flour
fresh basil sprigs, to garnish

TOMATO SAUCE
1 tbsp olive oil
1 shallot, chopped
1 tbsp tomato purée (paste)
225 g/8 oz can chopped tomatoes
2 tbsp chopped basil
85 ml/3 fl oz/6 tbsp red wine
1 tsp caster (superfine) sugar
salt and pepper

1 To make the gnocchi, cook the potatoes in their skins in a pan of boiling salted water for 20 minutes or until cooked through. Drain well and press through a sieve into a bowl.

2 Meanwhile, cook the spinach in 1 tsp water for 5 minutes until wilted. Drain and pat dry with kitchen paper. Chop and stir into the potatoes.

3 Add the butter or margarine, egg and half of the flour to the potato mixture, mixing well. Turn out on to a floured surface, gradually kneading in the remaining flour to form a soft dough. With floured hands, roll the dough into thin ropes and cut off 2 cm/³/₄ inch pieces. Press the centre

of each dumpling with your finger, drawing it towards you to curl the sides of the gnocchi. Cover and leave to chill.

4 Heat the oil for the sauce in a pan and sauté the shallots for 5 minutes. Add the tomato purée (paste), tomatoes, basil, red wine and sugar

and season well. Bring to the boil and then simmer for 20 minutes.

5 Bring a pan of salted water to the boil and cook the gnocchi for 2–3 minutes or until they rise to the top of the pan. Drain well and transfer to serving dishes. Spoon the tomato sauce over the top. Garnish and serve.

Vegetable Pasta Nests

These large pasta nests look impressive when presented filled
with grilled mixed vegetables, and taste delicious.

Serves 4
175 g/6 oz spaghetti
1 aubergine (eggplant), halved and sliced
1 courgette (zucchini), diced
1 red (bell) pepper, seeded and chopped diagonally
6 tbsp olive oil
2 garlic cloves, crushed
50 g/1³/₄ oz/4 tbsp butter or vegetarian margarine, melted
15 g/¹/₂ oz/1 tbsp dry white breadcrumbs
salt and pepper
fresh parsley sprigs, to garnish

1 Bring a large saucepan of water
to the boil and cook the spaghetti
until 'al dente' or according to the
instructions on the packet. Drain.

2 Place the aubergine (eggplant),
courgette (zucchini) and (bell) pepper
on a baking sheet (cookie sheet).

3 Mix the oil and garlic together and
pour over the vegetables, tossing
to coat.

4 Cook under a preheated hot grill
(broiler) for about 10 minutes,
turning, until tender and lightly
charred. Set aside and keep warm.

5 Divide the spaghetti among 4
lightly greased Yorkshire pudding tins
(pans). Using a fork, curl the spaghetti
to form nests.

6 Brush the pasta nests with melted
butter or margarine and sprinkle with
the breadcrumbs. Bake in a preheated

oven, at 200°C/400°F/ Gas Mark 6, for
15 minutes or until lightly golden.
Remove the pasta nests from the tins
(pans) and transfer to serving plates.
Divide the grilled vegetables between
the pasta nests, season and garnish.

COOK'S TIP

'Al dente' means 'to the bite' and
describes cooked pasta that is not
too soft, but still has a bite to it.

Spring Vegetable & Tofu (Bean Curd) Fusilli

This is a simple, clean-tasting dish of green vegetables,
tofu (bean curd) and pasta, lightly tossed in olive oil.

Serves 4
250 g/9 oz asparagus
125 g/4^{1}/$_2$ oz mangetout (snow peas)
250 g/9 oz French (green) beans
1 leek
250 g/9 oz shelled small broad (fava) beans
300 g/10^{1}/$_2$ oz dried fusilli
2 tbsp olive oil
25 g/1 oz/2 tbsp butter or vegetarian margarine
1 garlic clove, crushed
250 g/9 oz tofu (bean curd), cut into 2.5 cm/1 inch cubes
60 g/2 oz/^{1}/$_3$ cup pitted green olives in brine, drained
salt and pepper
freshly grated Parmesan, to serve

1 Cut the asparagus into 5 cm/2 inch lengths. Finely slice the mangetout (snow peas) diagonally and slice the French (green) beans into 2.5 cm/1 inch pieces. Finely slice the leek.

2 Bring a large saucepan of water to the boil and add the asparagus, green beans and broad (fava) beans. Bring back to the boil and cook for 4 minutes until just tender. Drain well and rinse in cold water. Set aside.

3 Bring a large pan of salted water to the boil and cook the fusilli for 8–9 minutes until just tender. Drain well. Toss in 1 tbsp of the oil and season.

4 Meanwhile, in a wok or large frying pan (skillet), heat the remaining oil and the butter or margarine and

gently fry the leek, garlic and tofu (bean curd) for 1–2 minutes until the vegetables have just softened.

5 Stir in the mangetout (snow peas) and cook for 1 minute.

6 Add the boiled vegetables and olives to the pan and heat through for 1 minute. Carefully stir in the pasta and seasoning. Cook for 1 minute and pile into a warmed serving dish. Serve sprinkled with Parmesan.

Fried Noodles with Bean-sprouts, Chives & Chillies

This is a simple idea to jazz up noodles which accompany
main course dishes in Thailand.

Serves 4
500 g/1 lb 2 oz medium egg noodles
60 g/2 oz/1 cup bean-sprouts
15 g/$\frac{1}{2}$ oz chives
3 tbsp sunflower oil
1 garlic clove, crushed
4 green chillies, deseeded,
sliced and soaked in
2 tbsp rice vinegar
salt

1 To cook the noodles, soak them in boiling water for 10 minutes. Drain and set aside.

2 Soak the bean-sprouts in cold water while you cut the chives into 2.5 cm/1 inch pieces. Set a few chives aside for garnish. Drain the bean-sprouts thoroughly.

3 Heat the oil in a wok or large, heavy frying pan (skillet). Add the crushed garlic and stir; then add the chillies and stir until fragrant, about 1 minute.

4 Add the bean-sprouts, stir and then add the noodles. Stir in a little salt and the chives. Using 2 spoons, lift and stir the noodles for 1 minute.

5 Garnish the finished dish with the reserved chives, and serve immediately.

Vegetable-filled Ravioli

These small parcels are very easy to make and have
the advantage of being filled with your favourite mixture of succulent mushrooms.
Serve with freshly grated cheese sprinkled on top.

Serves 4
FILLING
25 g/1 oz/3 tbsp butter or vegetarian margarine
2 garlic cloves, crushed
1 small leek, chopped
2 celery sticks, chopped
200 g/7 oz/2⅓ cups open-cup mushrooms, chopped
1 egg, beaten
2 tbsp grated Parmesan cheese
salt and pepper
RAVIOLI
4 sheets filo pastry
25 g/1 oz/3 tbsp vegetarian margarine
oil, for deep-frying

1 To make the filling, melt the butter or margarine in a frying pan (skillet) and sauté the garlic and leek for 2–3 minutes. Add the celery and mushrooms and cook for a further 4–5 minutes until all of the vegetables are tender.

2 Turn off the heat and stir in the egg and Parmesan cheese. Season with salt and pepper to taste.

3 Lay the pastry sheets on a chopping board and cut each into nine squares. Spoon a little of the filling into the centre half of the squares and brush the edges of the pastry with butter or margarine. Lay another square on top and seal the edges to make a parcel.

4 Heat the oil for deep-frying to 180°C/350°F or until a cube of bread browns in 30 seconds. Fry the ravioli, in batches, for 2–3 minutes or until golden brown. Remove from the oil with a slotted spoon and pat dry on absorbent kitchen paper. Transfer to a warm serving plate and serve.

COOK'S TIP

If time is short, boil some frozen mixed vegetables and use as a quick filling for the ravioli.

Pasta with Pine Kernels (Nuts) & Blue Cheese

Simple, quick and inexpensive, this tasty pasta dish
can be prepared in minutes.

Serves 4

60 g/2 oz/1 cup pine kernels (nuts)
350 g/12 oz dried pasta shapes
2 courgettes (zucchini), sliced
125 g/4¹/₂ oz broccoli, broken into florets
200 g/7 oz/1 cup full-fat soft cheese
150 ml/¹/₄ pint/²/₃ cup milk
1 tbsp chopped fresh basil
125 g/4¹/₂ oz button mushrooms, sliced
90 g/3 oz blue cheese, crumbled
salt and pepper
sprigs of fresh basil, to garnish
green salad, to serve

1 Scatter the pine kernels (nuts) on to
a baking sheet (cookie sheet) and cook
under a preheated grill (broiler),
turning occasionally, until lightly
browned all over. Set aside.

2 Cook the pasta in plenty of boiling
salted water for 8–10 minutes until
just tender. Meanwhile, cook the
courgettes (zucchini) and broccoli in a
small amount of boiling, lightly salted
water for about 5 minutes until tender.

3 Put the soft cheese into a saucepan
and heat gently, stirring constantly.
Add the milk and stir to mix.

COOK'S TIP

Watch the pine kernels (nuts)
carefully, otherwise they will burn.
They will toast in 2–3 minutes.

4 Add the basil and mushrooms and
cook gently for 2–3 minutes. Stir in
the blue cheese and season to taste.

5 Drain the pasta and the vegetables
and mix together. Pour the cheese and
mushroom sauce over and add the
pine kernels (nuts). Toss gently to mix.
Garnish with basil sprigs and serve
with a green salad.

Vegetable Lasagne

This colourful and tasty lasagne, with layers of vegetables in tomato sauce and aubergines (eggplants), all topped with a rich cheese sauce is simply delicious.

Serves 4
1 aubergine (eggplant), sliced
3 tbsp olive oil
2 garlic cloves, crushed
1 red onion, halved and sliced
1 green (bell) pepper, diced
1 red (bell) pepper, diced
1 yellow (bell) pepper, diced
225 g/8 oz mixed mushrooms, sliced
2 celery sticks, sliced
1 courgette (zucchini), diced
$\frac{1}{2}$ tsp chilli powder
$\frac{1}{2}$ tsp ground cumin
2 tomatoes, chopped
300 ml/$\frac{1}{2}$ pint/$1\frac{1}{4}$ cups passata
2 tbsp chopped basil
8 no pre-cook lasagne verdi sheets

CHEESE SAUCE

2 tbsp butter or vegetarian margarine
1 tbsp flour
150 ml/$\frac{1}{4}$ pint/$\frac{2}{3}$ cup vegetable stock
300 ml/$\frac{1}{2}$ pint/$1\frac{1}{4}$ cups milk
75 g/$2\frac{3}{4}$ oz/$\frac{3}{4}$ cup Cheddar, grated
1 tsp Dijon mustard
1 tbsp chopped basil
1 egg, beaten

1 Place the aubergine (eggplant) slices in a colander, sprinkle with salt and leave for 20 minutes. Rinse under cold water, drain and reserve. Heat the oil in a pan and sauté the garlic and onion for 1–2 minutes. Add the (bell) peppers, mushrooms, celery and courgette (zucchini) and cook for 3–4 minutes, stirring. Stir in the spices and cook for 1 minute. Mix the tomatoes, passata (sieved tomatoes) and basil together and season well.

2 For the sauce, melt the butter in a pan, add the flour and cook for 1 minute. Remove from the heat and stir in the stock and milk. Return to the heat and add half of the cheese and the mustard. Boil, stirring, until thickened. Stir in the basil and season. Remove the pan from the heat and stir in the egg. Place half of the lasagne sheets in an ovenproof dish. Top with half of the vegetables, then half of the tomato sauce. Cover with half the aubergines (eggplants). Repeat and spoon the cheese sauce on top. Sprinkle with cheese and cook in a preheated oven, 180°C/350°F/Gas 4, for 40 minutes.

Pasta Provençale

A Mediterranean mixture of red (bell) peppers, garlic and courgettes
(zucchini) cooked in olive oil and tossed with pasta.

Serves 4
3 tbsp olive oil
1 onion, sliced
2 garlic cloves, chopped
3 red (bell) peppers, deseeded and cut into strips
3 courgettes (zucchini), sliced
400 g/14 oz can chopped tomatoes
3 tbsp sun-dried tomato paste
2 tbsp chopped fresh basil
250 g/9 oz fresh pasta spirals
125 g/4$^{1}/_{2}$ oz/1 cup grated Gruyère cheese
salt and pepper
fresh basil sprigs, to garnish

1 Heat the oil in a heavy-based saucepan or flameproof casserole.

2 Add the onion and garlic and cook, stirring occasionally, until softened.

3 Add the (bell) peppers and courgettes (zucchini) and fry for 5 minutes, stirring occasionally.

4 Add the tomatoes, sun-dried tomato paste, basil and salt and pepper to taste, cover and cook for 5 minutes, stirring.

5 Meanwhile, bring a large saucepan of salted water to the boil and add the pasta. Stir and bring back to the boil. Reduce the heat slightly and cook, uncovered, for 3 minutes, or until just tender. Drain the pasta thoroughly.

6 Add the pasta to the vegetables and toss gently to mix well. Put the mixture into a shallow ovenproof dish and sprinkle with the cheese.

7 Cook under a preheated grill (broiler) for 5 minutes until the cheese is golden brown. Garnish with fresh basil sprigs and serve.

Tagliatelle Tricolore with Broccoli & Cheese Sauce

Some of the simplest and most satisfying dishes are made with pasta,
such as this delicious combination of tagliatelle with its two-cheese sauce.

Serves 4

300 g/10½ oz dried tagliatelle tricolore (plain, spinach-and tomato-flavoured noodles)

250 g/9 oz broccoli, broken into small florets

350g/12 oz/1½ cups Mascarpone cheese

125 g/4½ oz/1 cup blue cheese, chopped

1 tbsp chopped fresh oregano

25 g/1 oz/2 tbsp butter

salt and pepper

sprigs of fresh oregano, to garnish

freshly grated Parmesan, to serve

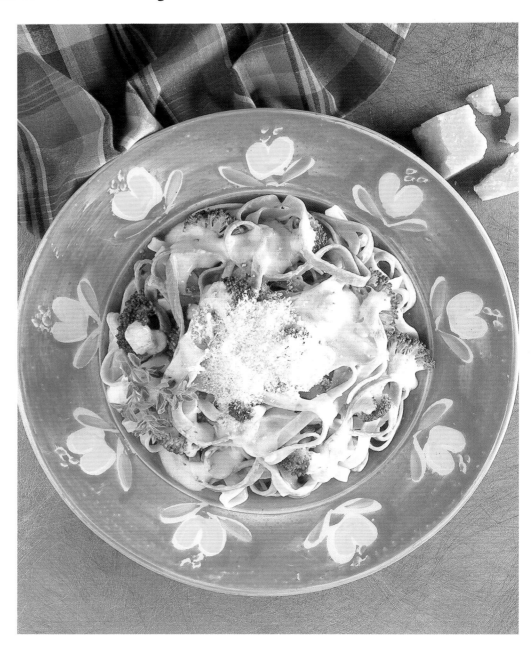

1 Cook the tagliatelle in a saucepan of boiling salted water until just tender, according to the instructions on the packet.

2 Meanwhile, cook the broccoli florets in a small amount of lightly salted, boiling water. Avoid overcooking the broccoli, so that it retains its colour and texture.

3 Heat the Mascarpone and blue cheeses together gently in a large saucepan until they are melted.

4 Stir in the oregano and season with salt and pepper to taste.

5 Drain the tagliatelle thoroughly and return to the pan. Add the cheese sauce and butter and toss to coat.

6 Drain the broccoli and add to the pasta, tossing to mix.

7 Divide the pasta between 4 warmed serving plates.

8 Garnish with sprigs of fresh oregano and serve with freshly grated Parmesan cheese.

COOK'S TIP

Choose your favourite pasta shapes as an alternative to tagliatelle, if you prefer.

Vegetable Cannelloni

This dish is made with prepared cannelloni tubes,
but may also be made by rolling ready-bought lasagne sheets.

Serves 4
1 aubergine (eggplant)
125 ml/4 fl oz/$\frac{1}{2}$ cup olive oil
225 g/8 oz spinach
2 garlic cloves, crushed
1 tsp ground cumin
75 g/2$\frac{3}{4}$ oz/1 cup mushrooms, chopped
12 cannelloni tubes
salt and pepper

TOMATO SAUCE

1 tbsp olive oil
1 onion, chopped
2 garlic cloves, crushed
2 x 400 g/14 oz cans chopped tomatoes
1 tsp caster (superfine) sugar
2 tbsp chopped basil
50 g/1$\frac{3}{4}$ oz/$\frac{1}{2}$ cup Mozzarella, sliced

1 Cut the aubergine (eggplant) into small dice.

2 Heat the oil in a frying pan (skillet) and cook the aubergine (eggplant) for 2–3 minutes.

3 Add the spinach, garlic, cumin and mushrooms. Season to taste and cook for 2–3 minutes, stirring. Spoon the mixture into the cannelloni tubes and place in an ovenproof dish in a single layer.

4 To make the sauce, heat the olive oil in a saucepan and sauté the onion and garlic for 1 minute. Add the tomatoes, caster (superfine) sugar and basil and bring to the boil. Reduce the heat and simmer for 5 minutes. Pour the sauce over the cannelloni tubes.

5 Arrange the sliced Mozzarella on top of the sauce and cook in a preheated oven, 190°C/375°F/Gas Mark 5, for 30 minutes or until the cheese is bubbling and golden brown. Serve immediately.

COOK'S TIP

You can prepare the tomato sauce in advance and store it in the refrigerator for up to 24 hours.

Three-Cheese Macaroni Bake

Based on a traditional family favourite, this pasta bake has plenty of flavour.
Serve with a crisp salad for a quick, tasty supper.

Serves 4
600 ml/1 pint/2¹/₂ cups Béchamel Sauce (see page 14)
250 g/9 oz/2 cups macaroni
1 egg, beaten
125 g/4¹/₂ oz/1 cup grated mature (sharp) Cheddar
1 tbsp wholegrain mustard
2 tbsp chopped fresh chives
4 tomatoes, sliced
125 g/4¹/₂ oz/1 cup grated Red Leicester (brick) cheese
60 g/2 oz/¹/₂ cup grated blue cheese
2 tbsp sunflower seeds
salt and pepper
snipped fresh chives, to garnish

1 Make the béchamel sauce, put into a bowl and cover with cling film (plastic wrap) to prevent a skin forming. Set aside until required.

2 Bring a saucepan of salted water to the boil and cook the macaroni for 8–10 minutes until just tender. Drain well and place in an ovenproof dish.

3 Stir the beaten egg, Cheddar, mustard, chives and salt and pepper to taste into the béchamel sauce. Spoon the sauce over the macaroni, making sure it is well covered.

4 Arrange a layer of sliced tomatoes on top of the sauce.

5 Sprinkle over the Red Leicester (brick) and blue cheeses, and the sunflower seeds.

6 Place on a baking sheet (cookie sheet) and bake in a preheated oven, 190°C/375°F/Gas Mark 5, for 25–30 minutes until bubbling and golden.

7 Garnish the macaroni bake with freshly snipped chives and serve immediately.

Tagliatelle with Courgette (Zucchini) Sauce

This is a really fresh tasting dish which is ideal with
a crisp white wine and some crusty bread.

Serves 4

650 g/1 lb 7 oz courgettes (zucchini)
6 tbsp olive oil
3 garlic cloves, crushed
3 tbsp chopped basil
2 red chillies, sliced
juice of 1 large lemon
5 tbsp single (light) cream
4 tbsp grated Parmesan cheese
225 g/8 oz tagliatelle
salt and pepper

1 Using a vegetable peeler, slice the courgettes (zucchini) into thin ribbons.

2 Heat the oil in a frying pan (skillet) and sauté the garlic for 30 seconds. Add the courgettes (zucchini) and cook over a gentle heat, stirring, for 5–7 minutes.

3 Stir in the basil, chillies, lemon juice, cream and Parmesan and season with salt and pepper to taste.

4 Meanwhile, cook the pasta in a large pan of boiling salted water for 10 minutes until 'al dente'. Drain well and put in a warm serving bowl. Pile the courgette (zucchini) mixture on top of the pasta. Serve immediately.

COOK'S VARIATION

Lime juice and zest could be
used instead of the lemon
as an alternative.

Spaghetti with Pear & Walnut Sauce

This is quite an unusual combination of ingredients in a savoury dish,
but is absolutely wonderful tossed into a fine pasta such as spaghetti.

Serves 4
225 g/8 oz spaghetti
2 small ripe pears, peeled and sliced
150 ml/¼ pint/⅔ cup vegetable stock
85 ml/3 fl oz/6 tbsp dry white wine
2 tbsp butter
1 tbsp olive oil
1 red onion, quartered and sliced
1 garlic clove, crushed
50 g/1¾ oz/½ cup walnut halves
2 tbsp chopped oregano
1 tbsp lemon juice
75 g/2¾ oz/¾ cup dolcelatte cheese
salt and pepper
fresh oregano sprigs, to garnish

1 Cook the pasta in a saucepan of boiling salted water for 8–10 minutes or until 'al dente'. Drain thoroughly.

2 Meanwhile, place the pears in a pan and pour over the stock and wine. Poach the pears over a gentle heat for 10 minutes. Drain and reserve the cooking liquid and pears.

3 Melt the butter with the oil and sauté the red onion and garlic for 2–3 minutes, stirring.

4 Add the walnuts, oregano and lemon juice, stirring.

5 Stir in the pears and 4 tablespoons of the poaching liquid.

6 Crumble the dolcelatte cheese into the pan and cook over a gentle heat, stirring occasionally, for 1–2 minutes or until the cheese just begins to melt.

Season the sauce with salt and pepper to taste.

7 Toss the pasta into the sauce, garnish and serve.

COOK'S TIP

You can use any good-flavoured blue cheese for this dish.

Olive, (Bell) Pepper & Tomato Pasta

The sweet cherry tomatoes in this recipe add colour and flavour
and are complemented by the black olives and (bell) peppers.

Serves 4
225 g/8 oz/2 cups penne
2 tbsp olive oil
2 tbsp butter
2 garlic cloves, crushed
1 green (bell) pepper, thinly sliced
1 yellow (bell) pepper, thinly sliced
16 cherry tomatoes, halved
1 tbsp chopped oregano
125 ml/4 floz/$^{1}/_{2}$ cup dry white wine
2 tbsp quartered, pitted black olives
75 g/2$^{3}/_{4}$ oz rocket
salt and pepper
fresh oregano sprigs, to garnish

1 Cook the pasta in a saucepan of boiling salted water for 8–10 minutes or until 'al dente'. Drain thoroughly.

2 Heat the oil and butter in a pan until the butter melts. Sauté the garlic for 30 seconds. Add the (bell) peppers and cook for 3–4 minutes, stirring.

3 Stir in the cherry tomatoes, oregano, wine and olives and cook for 3–4 minutes. Season well and stir in the rocket until just wilted.

4 Transfer the pasta to a serving dish and spoon the sauce on top. Toss well to mix, garnish and serve.

COOK'S TIP

Ensure that the saucepan is large enough to prevent the pasta from sticking together during cooking.

Baked Pasta in Tomato Sauce

This pasta dish is baked in a pudding basin and cut into slices for serving.
It looks and tastes terrific and is perfect when you want to impress.

Serves 8

100 g/3½ oz/1 cup pasta shapes,
such as penne or casareccia

1 tbsp olive oil

1 leek, chopped

3 garlic cloves, crushed

1 green (bell) pepper, chopped

400 g/14 oz can chopped tomatoes

2 tbsp chopped, pitted black olives

2 eggs, beaten

1 tbsp chopped basil

TOMATO SAUCE

1 tbsp olive oil

1 onion, chopped

225 g/8 oz can chopped tomatoes

1 tsp caster (superfine) sugar

2 tbsp tomato purée (paste)

150 ml/¼ pint/⅔ cup vegetable stock

salt and pepper

1 Cook the pasta in a saucepan of boiling salted water for 8 minutes. Drain thoroughly.

2 Meanwhile, heat the oil in a saucepan and sauté the leek and garlic for 2 minutes, stirring. Add the (bell) pepper, tomatoes and olives and cook for a further 5 minutes.

3 Remove the pan from the heat and stir in the pasta, beaten eggs and basil. Season well, and spoon into a lightly greased 1 litre/2 pint ovenproof pudding basin.

4 Place the pudding basin in a roasting tin (pan) and half-fill the tin (pan) with boiling water. Cover and

cook in a preheated oven, 180°C/
350°F/Gas Mark 6, for 40 minutes
until set.

5 To make the sauce, heat the oil in a pan and sauté the onion for 2 minutes. Add the remaining ingredients and cook for 10 minutes.

Put the sauce in a food processor or blender and blend until smooth. Return to a clean saucepan and heat until hot.

6 Turn the pasta out of the pudding basin on to a warm plate. Slice and serve with the tomato sauce.

Spinach, Mushroom & Pine Nut Pasta

Use any pasta shapes that you have for this recipe,
the tricolore pasta being visually the best to use.

Serves 4
225 g/8 oz pasta shapes or spaghetti
125 ml/4 fl oz/$^1/_2$ cup olive oil
2 garlic cloves, crushed
1 onion, quartered and sliced
3 large flat mushrooms, sliced
225 g/8 oz spinach
2 tbsp pine nuts
85 ml/3 fl oz/6 tbsp dry white wine
salt and pepper
Parmesan shavings, to garnish

1 Cook the pasta in a saucepan of boiling salted water for 8–10 minutes or until 'al dente'. Drain well.

2 Meanwhile, heat the oil in a large saucepan and sauté the garlic and onion for 1 minute.

3 Add the mushrooms and cook for 2 minutes, stirring. Add the spinach and cook for 4–5 minutes or until the spinach has wilted.

4 Stir in the pine nuts and wine, season well and cook for 1 minute.

5 Transfer the pasta to a warm serving bowl and toss the sauce into it, mixing well. Garnish with shavings of Parmesan and serve.

COOK'S TIP

Freshly grate a little nutmeg over the dish for extra flavour as it is particularly good with spinach.

Baked Cheese & Tomato Macaroni

This is a really simple, family dish which is easy
to prepare and cook. Serve with a salad.

Serves 4
225 g/8 oz/2 cups elbow macaroni
175 g/6 oz/1½ cups grated vegetarian cheese
100 g/3½ oz/1 cup grated Parmesan cheese
4 tbsp fresh white breadcrumbs
1 tbsp chopped basil
1 tbsp butter or margarine
TOMATO SAUCE
1 tbsp olive oil
1 shallot, finely chopped
2 garlic cloves, crushed
450 g/1 lb canned chopped tomatoes
1 tbsp chopped basil
salt and pepper

1 To make the tomato sauce, heat the oil in a pan and sauté the shallots and garlic for 1 minute. Add the tomatoes, basil, salt and pepper to taste and cook over a medium heat, stirring, for 10 minutes.

2 Meanwhile, cook the macaroni in a saucepan of boiling salted water for 8 minutes or until just undercooked. Drain well.

3 Mix both of the cheeses together.

4 Grease a deep, ovenproof dish. Spoon a third of the tomato sauce into the base of the dish, top with a third of the macaroni and then a third of the cheeses. Season with salt and pepper. Repeat the layers twice.

5 Mix the breadcrumbs and basil together and sprinkle over the top. Dot with the butter or margarine and cook in a preheated oven, 190°C/ 375°F/Gas Mark 5, for 25 minutes or until the dish is golden brown and bubbling. Serve immediately.

COOK'S TIP

Use other pasta shapes, such as penne, if you have them to hand, instead of the macaroni.

Thai-Style Noodles

This dish is considered the Thai national dish, as it is made and eaten everywhere – a one-dish fast food for eating on the move.

Serves 4
250 g/9 oz dried rice noodles
2 red chillies, deseeded and chopped finely
2 shallots, chopped finely
2 tbsp sugar
2 tbsp tamarind water
1 tbsp lime juice
2 tbsp light soy sauce
1 tbsp sunflower oil
1 tsp sesame oil
175 g/6 oz/$^3/_4$ cup smoked tofu (bean curd), diced
pepper
2 tbsp chopped roasted peanuts, to garnish

1 Cook the rice noodles as directed on the packet, or soak them in a large bowl of boiling water for 5 minutes.

2 Grind together the chillies, shallots, sugar, tamarind water, lime juice, light soy sauce and pepper to taste.

3 Heat both of the oils together in a wok or large, heavy frying pan (skillet) over a high heat. Add the tofu (bean curd) and stir for 1 minute.

4 Add the chilli mixture, bring to the boil and stir for about 2 minutes until thickened.

5 Drain the rice noodles and add them to the chilli mixture. Use 2 spoons to lift and toss them until they are no longer steaming. Serve immediately, garnished with the chopped roasted peanuts.

Grains & Pulses

Grains are the seeds of cultivated grasses, while pulses (legumes) are the dried seeds of pod-bearing plants of the Leguminosae family. Together they are the most universally important staple foods. Grains include wheat, corn, barley, rye, oats, buckwheat and many varieties of rice, as well as associated flours. Pulses (legumes) include chick-peas (garbanzo beans), yellow and green split peas, a fascinating variety of beans, together with many types of lentil.

Grains and pulses (legumes) form a substantial base to which other ingredients can be added. Each has its own distinctive flavour and texture, so it's worth experimenting with less well-known varieties. An excellent source of protein, iron, calcium and B vitamins, these valuable foods are cheap, highly nutritious, versatile and filling, and are virtually fat-free. With the current emphasis on healthier eating, they are a must for the vegetarian diet.

Vegetable Jambalaya

This dish traditionally contains spicy sausage but it is equally delicious
filled with vegetables in this spicy vegetarian version.

Serves 4
75 g/2³/4 oz/¹/2 cup brown rice
2 tbsp olive oil
2 garlic cloves, crushed
1 red onion, cut into eight
1 aubergine (eggplant), diced
1 green (bell) pepper, diced
50 g/1³/4 oz baby corn cobs, halved lengthwise
50 g/1³/4 oz/¹/2 cup frozen peas
100 g/3¹/2 oz small broccoli florets
150 ml/5 floz/²/3 cup vegetable stock
225 ml/8 fl oz can chopped tomatoes
1 tbsp tomato purée (paste)
1 tsp creole seasoning
¹/2 tsp chilli flakes
salt and pepper

1 Cook the rice in a saucepan of
boiling water for 20 minutes or until
cooked through. Drain thoroughly and
set aside until required.

2 Heat the oil in a heavy-based frying
pan (skillet) and cook the garlic and
onion for 2–3 minutes, stirring.

3 Add the aubergine (eggplant), (bell)
pepper, corn, peas and broccoli to the
pan and cook, stirring occasionally,
for 2–3 minutes.

4 Stir in the stock and canned
tomatoes, tomato purée (paste), creole
seasoning and chilli flakes. Season
with salt and pepper to taste and cook
over a low heat for 15–20 minutes or
until the vegetables are tender.

5 Stir the brown rice into the
vegetable mixture and cook, mixing
well, for 3–4 minutes or until hot.

6 Transfer the vegetable jambalaya to
warm serving dishes and serve
immediately.

COOK'S TIP

Use a mixture of rice, such as wild
or red rice, for colour and texture.
Cook the rice in advance for a
speedier recipe.

Mushroom & Parmesan Risotto

Make this creamy risotto with Italian arborio rice
and freshly grated Parmesan for the best results.

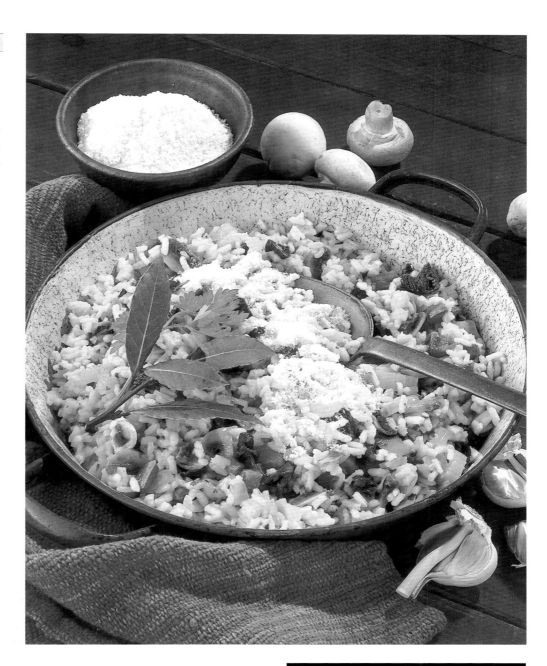

Serves 4

2 tbsp olive or vegetable oil

250 g/9 oz/generous 1 cup
arborio (risotto) rice

2 garlic cloves, crushed

1 onion, chopped

2 celery stalks, chopped

1 red or green (bell) pepper,
deseeded and chopped

250 g/9 oz mushrooms,
sliced

1 tbsp chopped fresh oregano
or 1 tsp dried oregano

1 litre/1³/₄ pints/4 cups Fresh
Vegetable Stock (see page 14)

60 g/2 oz sun-dried
tomatoes in olive oil,
drained and chopped (optional)

60 g/2 oz/¹/₂ cup freshly
grated Parmesan

salt and pepper

TO GARNISH

fresh flat-leaf parsley sprigs

fresh bay leaves

1 Heat the oil in a wok or large frying pan (skillet). Add the rice and cook, stirring, for 5 minutes.

2 Add the garlic, onion, celery and (bell) pepper and cook, stirring, for 5 minutes. Add the mushrooms and cook for a further 3–4 minutes.

3 Stir in the oregano and stock. Heat until just boiling, then reduce the heat, cover and simmer gently for about 20 minutes until the rice is tender and creamy.

4 Add the sun-dried tomatoes, if using, and season with salt and pepper to taste. Stir in half the Parmesan. Top with the remaining cheese, and garnish with flat-leaf parsley and bay leaves. Serve.

COOK'S TIP

Add the stock a little at a time, only adding more when the last addition is fully absorbed.

Lentil Croquettes

These croquettes are ideal served with a crisp salad and a
tahini (sesame seed paste) dip.

Serves 4

225 g/8 oz/1¼ cups split red lentils
1 green (bell) pepper, finely chopped
1 red onion, finely chopped
2 garlic cloves, crushed
1 tsp garam masala
½ tsp chilli powder
1 tsp ground cumin
2 tsp lemon juice
2 tbsp chopped unsalted peanuts
600 ml/1 pint/2½ cups water
1 egg, beaten
3 tbsp plain (all-purpose) flour
1 tsp turmeric
1 tsp chilli powder
4 tbsp vegetable oil
salt and pepper
salad leaves and fresh herbs, to serve

1 Put the lentils in a large saucepan
with the (bell) pepper, onion, garlic,
garam masala, chilli powder, ground
cumin, lemon juice and peanuts.

2 Add the water and bring to the boil.
Reduce the heat and simmer for 30
minutes or until the liquid has been
absorbed, stirring occasionally.

3 Remove the mixture from the heat
and leave to cool slightly. Beat in the
egg and season with salt and pepper
to taste. Leave to cool completely.

4 With floured hands, form the
mixture into eight oblong shapes.

5 Mix the flour, turmeric and chilli
powder together on a small plate. Roll

the croquettes in the spiced flour
mixture to coat.

6 Heat the oil in a large frying pan
(skillet) and cook the croquettes, in
batches, for 10 minutes, turning once,
until crisp on both sides. Serve.

COOK'S TIP

Other lentils could be used, but
they will require soaking and
precooking before use. Red lentils
are used for speed and convenience.

Oriental-style Millet Pilau

Millet makes an interesting alternative to rice, which is the more traditional
ingredient for a pilau. Serve with a crisp salad of oriental vegetables.

Serves 4
300 g/10¹/₂ oz/1¹/₂ cups millet grains
1 tbsp vegetable oil
1 bunch spring onions (scallions), white and green parts, chopped
1 garlic clove, crushed
1 tsp grated ginger root
1 orange (bell) pepper, deseeded and diced
600 ml/1 pint/2¹/₂ cups water
1 orange
125 g/4¹/₂ oz/²/₃ cup chopped pitted dates
2 tsp sesame oil
125 g/4¹/₂ oz/1 cup roasted cashew nuts
2 tbsp pumpkin seeds
salt and pepper
oriental salad vegetables, to serve

1 Place the millet in a large saucepan
and cook over a medium heat for 4–5
minutes to toast, shaking the pan
occasionally, until the grains begin to
crack and pop.

2 Heat the oil in a separate saucepan
and gently fry the spring onions
(scallions), garlic, ginger and (bell)
pepper for 2–3 minutes until just
softened but not browned. Add the
millet and pour in the water.

3 Using a vegetable peeler, pare the
rind from the orange and add the rind
to the pan. Squeeze the juice from the
orange into the pan. Season well.

4 Bring the mixture to the boil,
reduce the heat, cover and cook gently

for 20 minutes or until all of the liquid
has been absorbed. Remove the pan
from the heat, stir in the dates and
sesame oil and leave to stand for
10 minutes.

5 Discard the orange rind and stir in
the cashew nuts. Transfer to a serving
dish, sprinkle with pumpkin seeds
and serve with oriental salad
vegetables.

Brown Rice, Vegetable & Herb Gratin

This is a really filling dish and therefore does not require an accompaniment.
It is very versatile, and could be made with a wide selection of vegetables.

Serves 4
100 g/3½ oz/⅓ cup brown rice
2 tbsp butter or margarine
1 red onion, chopped
2 garlic cloves, crushed
1 carrot, cut into matchsticks
1 courgette (zucchini), sliced
75 g/2¾ oz baby corn cobs, halved lengthwise
2 tbsp sunflower seeds
3 tbsp chopped mixed herbs
100 g/3½ oz/1 cup grated Mozzarella cheese
2 tbsp wholemeal (whole wheat) breadcrumbs
salt and pepper

1 Cook the rice in a saucepan of boiling salted water for 20 minutes or until cooked. Drain well.

2 Lightly grease a 900 ml/1½ pint ovenproof dish.

3 Heat the butter in a frying pan (skillet). Add the onion and cook, stirring, for 2 minutes or until softened.

4 Add the garlic, carrot, courgette (zucchini) and corn cobs and cook for a further 5 minutes, stirring.

5 Mix the rice with the sunflower seeds and mixed herbs and stir into the pan.

6 Stir in half of the Mozzarella cheese and season with salt and pepper to taste.

7 Spoon the mixture into the greased dish and top with the breadcrumbs and remaining cheese. Cook in a preheated oven, 180°C/350°F/Gas Mark 4, for 25–30 minutes or until the cheese begins to turn golden. Serve.

Chatuchak Fried Rice

An excellent way to use up leftover rice. Pop it into the freezer
as soon as it is cool, and it will be ready to reheat at any time.

Serves 4

1 tbsp sunflower oil

2 garlic cloves, crushed

2.5 cm/1 inch piece ginger root,
shredded finely

3 shallots, chopped finely

1 red chilli, deseeded
and chopped finely

$1/2$ green (bell) pepper, deseeded
and sliced finely

150 g/$5^{1}/_{2}$ oz/2–3 baby aubergines
(eggplants), quartered

90 g/3 oz sugar snap peas
or mangetout (snow peas),
trimmed and blanched

90 g/3 oz/6 baby corn cobs, halved
lengthwise and blanched

1 tomato, cut into 8 pieces

90 g/3 oz/$1^{1}/_{2}$ cups bean-sprouts

500 g/1 lb 2 oz/3 cups cooked
Thai jasmine rice

2 tbsp tomato ketchup

2 tbsp light soy sauce

TO GARNISH

fresh coriander (cilantro) leaves

lime wedges

1 Heat the sunflower oil in a wok or
large, heavy frying pan (skillet) over a
high heat. Add the garlic and ginger,
stirring well.

2 Add the shallots, chilli, green
(bell) pepper and baby aubergines
(eggplants) and cook, stirring, until the
shallots have softened. Add the sugar
snap peas or mangetout (snow peas),
corn cobs, tomato and bean-sprouts
and cook, stirring, for 3 minutes.

3 Add the rice, and lift and mix with
two spoons for 4–5 minutes, until no
more steam is released. Stir in the
tomato ketchup and soy sauce.

4 Transfer to serving dishes and serve
immediately, garnished with coriander
(cilantro) leaves and lime wedges to
squeeze over the rice.

Moroccan Vegetable Couscous

Couscous is a semolina grain which is very quick to cook,
and it makes a pleasant change from rice or pasta.

Serves 4

2 tbsp vegetable oil

1 large onion, chopped coarsely

1 carrot, chopped

1 turnip, chopped

600 ml/1 pint/2$\frac{1}{2}$ cups Fresh
Vegetable Stock (see page 14)

175 g/6 oz/1 cup couscous

2 tomatoes, peeled and quartered

2 courgettes (zucchini), chopped

1 red (bell) pepper, deseeded
and chopped

125 g/4$\frac{1}{2}$ oz French (green)
beans, chopped

grated rind of 1 lemon

pinch of ground turmeric (optional)

1 tbsp finely chopped fresh coriander
(cilantro) or parsley

fresh flat-leaf parsley sprigs,
to garnish

1 Heat the oil in a large saucepan and fry the onion, carrot and turnip for 3–4 minutes. Add the vegetable stock and bring to the boil. Cover and simmer gently for about 20 minutes.

2 Meanwhile, put the couscous in a bowl and moisten with a little boiling water, stirring, until the grains have swollen and separated.

3 Add the tomatoes, courgettes (zucchini), (bell) pepper and French (green) beans to the saucepan, mixing well.

4 Stir the lemon rind and turmeric, if using, into the couscous and mix well. Put the couscous in a steamer and position over the vegetables. Simmer the vegetables so that the couscous steams for 8–10 minutes.

5 Transfer the couscous to warmed serving plates. Ladle the vegetables and some of the liquid over the top. Scatter with the coriander (cilantro) or parsley and serve at once, garnished with parsley sprigs.

Green Lentil & Mixed Vegetable Pan-fry

The green lentils used in this recipe require soaking but are worth it for the flavour.
If time is short, use red split peas which do not require soaking.

Serves 4
150 g/5¹/₂ oz/3³/₄ cups green lentils
4 tbsp butter or vegetarian margarine
2 garlic cloves, crushed
2 tbsp olive oil
1 tbsp cider vinegar
1 red onion, cut into eight
50 g/1³/₄ oz baby corn cobs, halved lengthwise
1 yellow (bell) pepper, cut into strips
1 red (bell) pepper, cut into strips
50 g/1³/₄ oz French (green) beans, halved
125 ml/4 fl oz/6 tbsp vegetable stock
2 tbsp clear honey
salt and pepper

1 Soak the lentils in a large saucepan of cold water for 25 minutes. Bring to the boil, reduce the heat and simmer for 20 minutes. Drain thoroughly.

2 Add 1 tablespoon of the butter or margarine, 1 garlic clove, 1 tablespoon of oil and the vinegar to the lentils and mix well.

3 Melt the remaining butter, garlic and oil in a frying pan (skillet) and stir-fry the onion, corn cobs, (bell) peppers and beans for 3–4 minutes.

4 Add the stock and bring to the boil for about 10 minutes or until the liquid has evaporated.

5 Add the honey and season with salt and pepper to taste. Stir in the lentil mixture and cook for 1 minute to heat through. Spoon on to warmed serving plates and serve with crusty bread.

Chick-pea (Garbanzo Bean) & Peanut Balls

These tasty, nutty morsels are delicious served with a fiery,
tangy sauce that counteracts the richness of the peanuts.

Serves 4

3 tbsp groundnut oil

1 onion, chopped finely

1 celery stalk, chopped

1 tsp dried mixed herbs

250 g/9 oz/2 cups roasted unsalted
peanuts, ground

175 g/6 oz/1 cup canned chick-peas
(garbanzo beans), drained and mashed

1 tsp yeast extract

60 g/2 oz/1 cup fresh wholemeal
(whole wheat) breadcrumbs

1 egg yolk

30 g/1 oz/¼ cup plain (all-purpose) flour

strips of fresh red chilli, to garnish

boiled rice and green salad leaves, to serve

HOT CHILLI SAUCE

2 tsp groundnut oil

1 large red chilli, deseeded
and chopped finely

2 spring onions (scallions), chopped finely

2 tbsp red wine vinegar

200 g/7 oz can chopped tomatoes

2 tbsp tomato purée (paste)

2 tsp caster (superfine) sugar

salt and pepper

1 Heat 1 tablespoon of the oil in a
frying pan (skillet) and gently fry the
onion and celery for 3–4 minutes
until softened but not browned.

2 Place all the other ingredients,
except for the remaining oil and the
flour, in a mixing bowl and add the
onion and celery. Mix well.

3 Divide the mixture into 12 portions
and roll into balls. Coat with the flour.

4 Heat the remaining oil in a frying
pan (skillet). Add the chick-pea
(garbanzo bean) balls and cook over a
medium heat for 15 minutes, turning
frequently, until cooked through and
golden. Drain on paper towels.

5 Meanwhile, make the hot chilli
sauce. Heat the oil in a small frying

pan (skillet) and gently fry the chilli
and spring onions (scallions) for
2–3 minutes. Stir in the remaining
ingredients and season. Bring to the
boil and simmer for 5 minutes.

6 Serve the chick-pea (garbanzo bean)
and peanut balls with the hot chilli
sauce, rice and a green salad.

Cashew Nut Paella

Paella traditionally contains chicken and fish, but this recipe is packed with vegetables and nuts for a truly delicious and simple vegetarian dish.

Serves 4
2 tbsp olive oil
1 tbsp butter
1 red onion, chopped
150 g/5½ oz/1 cup arborio rice
1 tsp ground turmeric
1 tsp ground cumin
½ tsp chilli powder
3 garlic cloves, crushed
1 green chilli, sliced
1 green (bell) pepper, diced
1 red (bell) pepper, diced
75 g/2¾ oz baby corn cobs, halved lengthwise
2 tbsp pitted black olives
1 large tomato, seeded and diced
450 ml/¾ pint/2 cups vegetable stock
75 g/2¾ oz/¾ cup unsalted cashew nuts
25 g/1 oz/¼ cup frozen peas
2 tbsp chopped parsley
pinch of cayenne pepper
salt and pepper
fresh herbs, to garnish

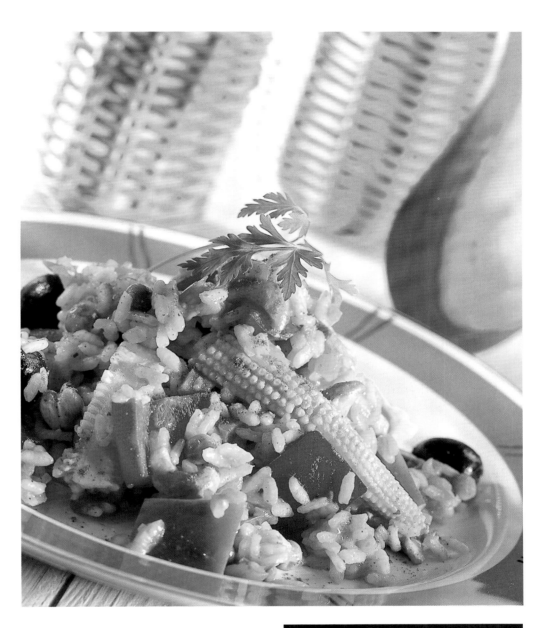

1 Heat the oil and butter in a large frying pan (skillet) or paella pan until the butter has melted.

2 Add the onion to the pan and sauté for 2–3 minutes, stirring.

3 Stir in the rice, turmeric, cumin, chilli powder, garlic, chilli, (bell) peppers, corn cobs, olives and tomato and cook over a medium heat for 1–2 minutes, stirring.

4 Pour in the stock and bring the mixture to the boil. Reduce the heat and cook for 20 minutes, stirring.

5 Add the cashew nuts and peas to the mixture in the pan and cook for a further 5 minutes, stirring occasionally. Season with salt and pepper to taste and sprinkle with parsley and cayenne pepper. Transfer to warm serving plates, garnish and serve immediately.

COOK'S TIP

For authenticity and flavour, use a few saffron strands soaked in a little boiling water instead of the turmeric. Saffron has a lovely, nutty flavour.

Cheesy Semolina Fritters with Apple Relish

Based on a gnocchi recipe, these delicious fritters are
accompanied by a fruity home-made relish.

Serves 4

600 ml/1 pint/2^1/$_2$ cups milk

1 small onion

1 celery stalk

1 bay leaf

2 cloves

125 g/4^1/$_2$ oz/^{2}/$_3$ cup semolina

125 g/4^1/$_2$ oz/1 cup grated mature
(sharp) Cheddar

^{1}/$_2$ tsp dried mustard powder

2 tbsp plain (all-purpose) flour

1 egg, beaten

60 g/2 oz/^{1}/$_2$ cup dried white breadcrumbs

6 tbsp vegetable oil

salt and pepper

celery leaves, to garnish

coleslaw, to serve

RELISH

2 celery stalks, chopped

2 small dessert (eating) apples, cored and
diced finely

90 g/3 oz/^{1}/$_2$ cup sultanas (golden raisins)

90 g/3 oz/^{1}/$_2$ cup no-soak
dried apricots, chopped

6 tbsp cider vinegar

pinch of ground cloves

^{1}/$_2$ tsp ground cinnamon

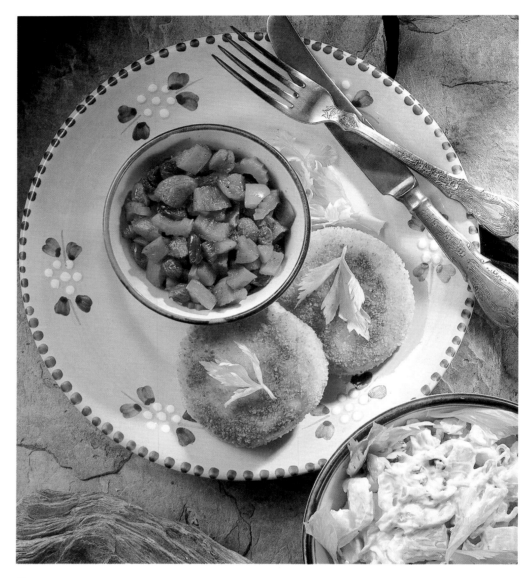

1 Pour the milk into a pan and add
the onion, celery, bay leaf and cloves.
Bring to the boil, remove from the
heat and let stand for 15 minutes.

2 Strain the mixture into another
pan, bring to the boil and sprinkle in
the semolina, stirring constantly.
Reduce the heat and simmer for
5 minutes until very thick, stirring
occasionally to prevent it sticking.

3 Remove from the heat and beat in
the cheese, mustard and seasoning.
Place in a greased bowl and let cool.

4 To make the relish, put all of the
ingredients in a pan, bring to the boil,
cover and simmer for 20 minutes,
until tender. Let cool.

5 Put the flour, egg and breadcrumbs
on to separate plates. Divide the
cooled semolina mixture into eight
and press into 6 cm/2^1/$_2$ inch rounds.
Coat the rounds lightly in the flour,
then in the egg and breadcrumbs. Heat
the oil in a large frying pan (skillet)
and fry the fritters for 3–4 minutes on
each side until golden. Drain on paper
towels. Garnish and serve with the
relish and coleslaw.

Pesto Rice with Garlic Bread

Try this combination of two types of rice with the richness
of pine kernels (nuts), basil, and freshly grated Parmesan.

Serves 4

300 g/10½ oz/1½ cups mixed
long-grain and wild rice

fresh basil sprigs, to garnish

tomato and orange salad, to serve

PESTO DRESSING

15 g/½ oz fresh basil leaves

125 g/4½ oz/1 cup pine kernels (nuts)

2 garlic cloves, crushed

6 tbsp olive oil

60 g/2 oz/½ cup freshly
grated Parmesan

salt and pepper

GARLIC BREAD

2 small granary or wholemeal (whole
wheat) French bread sticks

90 g/3 oz/½ cup butter or
vegetarian margarine, softened

2 garlic cloves, crushed

1 tsp dried mixed herbs

1 Place the rice in a saucepan and
cover with water. Bring to the boil and
cook according to the packet
instructions. Drain thoroughly, set
aside and keep warm.

2 Meanwhile, make the pesto
dressing. Remove the basil leaves
from the stalks and finely chop the
leaves. Reserve 30 g/1 oz/¼ cup of the
pine kernels (nuts) and finely chop
the remainder. Mix with the chopped
basil and the rest of the dressing
ingredients. Alternatively, put all of
the ingredients in a food processor or
blender and blend for a few seconds
until smooth. Set aside.

3 To make the garlic bread, slice the
bread at 2.5 cm/1 inch intervals,
taking care not to slice all the way
through. Mix the butter or margarine
with the garlic, herbs and seasoning.
Spread thickly between each slice.

4 Wrap the bread in foil and bake in a
preheated oven, 200°C/400°F/Gas
Mark 6, for 10–15 minutes.

5 To serve, toast the reserved pine
kernels (nuts) under a preheated
medium grill (broiler) for 2–3 minutes
until golden. Toss the pesto dressing
into the hot rice and transfer to a
warm serving dish. Sprinkle with
toasted pine kernels (nuts) and
garnish with basil sprigs. Serve with
the garlic bread and a tomato and
orange salad.

Lentil & Rice Casserole

This is a really hearty dish, perfect for cold days
when a filling hot dish is just what you need.

Serves 4

225 g/8 oz/1¼ cup red split lentils

50 g/1¾ oz/⅓ cup long-grain white rice

1 litre/1¾ pints/5 cups vegetable stock

150 ml/¼ pint/⅔ cup dry white wine

1 leek, cut into chunks

3 garlic cloves, crushed

400 g/14 oz can chopped tomatoes

1 tsp ground cumin

1 tsp chilli powder

1 tsp garam masala

1 red (bell) pepper, sliced

100 g/3½ oz small broccoli florets

8 baby corn cobs, halved lengthwise

50 g/1¾ oz French (green) beans, halved

1 tbsp fresh basil, shredded

fresh basil sprigs, to garnish

1 Place the lentils, rice, stock and
wine in a flameproof casserole dish
and cook over a gentle heat for 20
minutes, stirring occasionally.

2 Add the leek, garlic, tomatoes,
spices, (bell) pepper, broccoli, corn
cobs and beans. Bring the mixture to
the boil, reduce the heat, cover and
simmer for a further 10–15 minutes
or until the vegetables are tender. Add
the shredded basil and season to
taste. Garnish with fresh basil sprigs
and serve immediately.

COOK'S VARIATION

You can vary the rice in this recipe
– use brown or wild rice, if
you prefer.

Couscous Royale

Serve this stunning dish as a centrepiece for a Moroccan-style feast;
a truly memorable meal.

Serves 4
3 carrots
3 courgettes (zucchini)
350 g/12 oz pumpkin or squash
1.25 litres/2¼ pints/5 cups Fresh Vegetable Stock (see page 14)
2 cinnamon sticks, broken in half
2 tsp ground cumin
1 tsp ground coriander
pinch of saffron strands
2 tbsp olive oil
pared rind and juice of 1 lemon
2 tbsp clear honey
500 g/1 lb 2 oz/2⅔ cups pre-cooked couscous
60 g/2 oz/¼ cup butter or vegetarian margarine, softened
175 g/6 oz/1 cup large seedless raisins
salt and pepper
fresh coriander (cilantro), to garnish

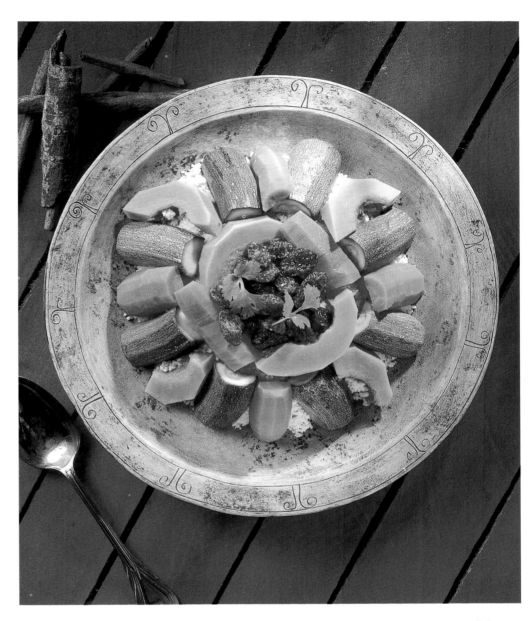

1 Cut the carrots and courgettes (zucchini) into 7 cm/3 inch pieces and cut in half lengthwise.

2 Trim the pumpkin or squash and discard the seeds. Peel and cut into 7 cm/3 inch pieces.

3 Put the stock, spices, saffron and carrots in a large pan. Bring to the boil, skim off any scum and add the oil. Simmer for 15 minutes. Add the lemon rind and juice to the pan with the honey, courgettes (zucchini) and pumpkin or squash. Season. Bring back to the boil and simmer for 10 minutes.

4 Soak the couscous according to the packet instructions. Transfer to a steamer or large sieve (strainer) lined with muslin (cheesecloth) and place over the vegetable pan. Cover and steam as directed. Stir in the butter.

5 Transfer the couscous to a serving plate. Drain the vegetables, reserving the stock, lemon rind and cinnamon. Arrange the vegetables on top of the couscous. Sprinkle the raisins on top and spoon over 6 tbsp of the reserved stock. Keep warm. Return the remaining stock to the heat and boil for 5 minutes to reduce slightly. Discard the lemon rind and cinnamon. Garnish and serve with the sauce.

Vegetable Biryani

The Biryani originated in the North of India, and was a dish reserved for festivals. The main ingredient, the vegetables, are marinated in a yogurt-based marinade and cooked in a casserole dish with the rice and onions.

Serves 4
1 large potato, cubed
100 g/3¹/₂ oz baby carrots
50 g/1³/₄ oz okra, thickly sliced
2 celery sticks, sliced
75 g/2³/₄ oz baby button mushrooms, halved
1 aubergine (eggplant), halved and sliced
300 ml/¹/₂ pint/1¹/₄ cups natural yogurt
1 tbsp grated root ginger
2 large onions, grated
4 garlic cloves, crushed
1 tsp turmeric
1 tbsp curry powder
2 tbsp butter
2 onions, sliced
225 g/8 oz/1¹/₄ cups basmati rice
chopped coriander (cilantro), to garnish

1 Cook the potato cubes, carrots and okra in a pan of boiling salted water for 7–8 minutes. Drain well and place in a large bowl. Mix with the celery, mushrooms and aubergine (eggplant).

2 Mix the yogurt, ginger, grated onions, garlic, turmeric and curry powder and pour over the vegetables. Leave to marinate for at least 2 hours.

3 Heat the butter in a frying pan (skillet) and cook the sliced onions for 5–6 minutes until golden brown. Remove a few onions from the pan and reserve for garnishing.

4 Cook the rice in a pan of boiling water for 7 minutes. Drain well.

5 Add the marinated vegetables to the onions and cook for 10 minutes.

6 Put half of the rice in a 2 litre/3¹/₂ pint casserole dish. Spoon the vegetables on top and cover with the remaining rice. Cover and cook in a preheated oven, 190°C/375°F/Gas Mark 5, for 20–25 minutes or until the rice is tender.

7 Spoon the biryani on to a serving plate, garnish with the reserved onions and chopped coriander (cilantro) and serve immediately.

COOK'S VARIATION

Long-grain white rice or brown rice may be used instead of the basmati rice, if you prefer.

Kofta Kebabs (Kabobs) with Tabbouleh

Traditionally, koftas are made from a spicy meat mixture, but this bean and wheat version makes a tasty vegetarian alternative.

  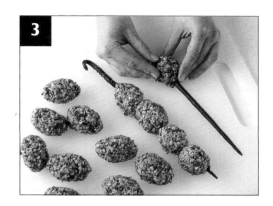

Serves 4

175 g/6 oz/1 cup aduki beans

175 g/6 oz/1 cup bulgar wheat

450 ml/$^3/_4$ pint/scant 2 cups Fresh Vegetable Stock (see page 14)

3 tbsp olive oil

1 onion, chopped finely

2 garlic cloves, crushed

1 tsp ground coriander

1 tsp ground cumin

2 tbsp chopped fresh coriander (cilantro)

3 eggs, beaten

125 g/4$^1/_2$ oz/1 cup dried breadcrumbs

salt and pepper

TABBOULEH

175 g/6 oz/1 cup bulgar wheat

2 tbsp lemon juice

1 tbsp olive oil

6 tbsp chopped fresh parsley

4 spring onions (scallions), chopped finely

60 g/2 oz cucumber, chopped finely

3 tbsp chopped fresh mint

1 extra-large tomato, chopped finely

TO SERVE

Tahini Cream (see page 14)

black olives

pitta bread

1 Cook the aduki beans in a pan of boiling water for 40 minutes or until tender. Drain, rinse and cool. Cook the bulgar wheat in the stock for 10 minutes or until the stock is absorbed.

2 Heat 1 tbsp of the oil in a frying pan (skillet) and fry the onion, garlic and spices for 4–5 minutes. Transfer to a bowl with the beans, coriander

(cilantro), seasoning and eggs and mash with a potato masher or fork. Add the breadcrumbs and bulgar wheat and stir well. Cover and chill for 1 hour, or until firm.

3 To make the tabbouleh, soak the bulgar wheat in 450 ml/$^3/_4$ pint/scant 2 cups of boiling water for 15 minutes.

Combine with the remaining ingredients. Cover and chill. With wet hands, mould the kofta mixture into 32 oval shapes. Press 4 koftas on to each skewer, brush with oil and grill (broil) for 5–6 minutes until golden. Turn, brush with oil, and cook for 5–6 minutes. Drain on paper towels. Serve with the tabbouleh.

Chick-pea (Garbanzo Bean) & Vegetable Casserole

Serve this hearty dish with warm crusty bread to mop up the juices.

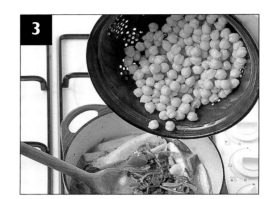

Serves 4

1 tbsp olive oil
1 red onion, halved and sliced
3 garlic cloves, crushed
225 g/8 oz spinach
1 fennel bulb, cut into eight
1 red (bell) pepper, cubed
1 tbsp plain (all-purpose) flour
450 ml/^{3}/$_4$ pint/3^3/$_4$ cups vegetable stock
85 ml/3 fl oz/6 tbsp dry white wine
400 g/14 oz can chick-peas (garbanzo beans), drained
1 bay leaf
1 tsp ground coriander
^{1}/$_2$ tsp paprika
salt and pepper
fennel fronds, to garnish

1 Heat the oil in a large flameproof casserole dish and sauté the onion and garlic for 1 minute, stirring. Add the spinach and cook for 4 minutes or until wilted.

2 Add the fennel and (bell) pepper and cook for 2 minutes, stirring. Stir in the flour and cook for 1 minute.

3 Add the stock, wine, chick-peas (garbanzo beans), bay leaf, coriander and paprika, cover and cook for 30 minutes. Season to taste, garnish with fennel fronds and serve immediately.

COOK'S TIP

Use other canned pulses or mixed beans instead of the chick-peas (garbanzo beans), if you prefer.

Deep South Spiced Rice & Beans

Cajun spices add a flavour of the American Deep South
to this colourful rice and red kidney bean salad.

Serves 4

175 g/6 oz/scant 1 cup
long-grain rice

4 tbsp olive oil

1 small green (bell) pepper,
deseeded and chopped

1 small red (bell) pepper,
deseeded and chopped

1 onion, chopped finely

1 small red or green chilli,
deseeded and chopped finely

2 tomatoes, chopped

125 g/4$^{1}/_{2}$ oz/$^{1}/_{2}$ cup canned red kidney
beans, rinsed and drained

1 tbsp chopped fresh basil

2 tsp chopped fresh thyme
(or 1 tsp dried)

1 tsp Cajun spice

salt and pepper

fresh basil leaves and thyme sprigs, to
garnish

1 Cook the rice in a saucepan of boiling, lightly salted water for 12 minutes, or until tender. Rinse with cold water and drain well. Transfer to a large bowl.

2 Meanwhile, heat the olive oil in a frying pan (skillet). Add the green and red (bell) peppers and the onion and cook gently for about 5 minutes, or until softened.

3 Add the chilli and tomatoes, and cook for a further 2 minutes.

4 Add the vegetable mixture and red kidney beans to the rice. Stir well to combine thoroughly.

5 Stir the chopped herbs and Cajun spice into the rice mixture and season with salt and pepper to taste. Transfer to serving plates, garnish with basil leaves and thyme sprigs and serve.

COOK'S TIP

The fresh red or green chilli can be replaced by 1 tsp chilli powder.

Vegetable Curry

Vegetables are cooked in a mildly spiced curry sauce with yogurt
and fresh coriander (cilantro) stirred in just before serving.

Serves 4

2 tbsp sunflower oil

1 onion, sliced

2 tsp cumin seeds

2 tbsp ground coriander

1 tsp ground turmeric

2 tsp ground ginger

1 tsp chopped fresh red chilli

2 garlic cloves, chopped

400 g/14 oz can chopped tomatoes

3 tbsp powdered coconut mixed with
300 ml/^{1}/$_2$ pint/1^1/$_4$ cups boiling water

1 small cauliflower, broken into florets

2 courgettes (zucchini), sliced

2 carrots, sliced

1 potato, diced

400 g/14 oz can chick-peas (garbanzo
beans), drained and rinsed

150 ml/^{1}/$_4$ pint/^{3}/$_4$ cup thick natural yogurt

2 tbsp mango chutney

3 tbsp chopped fresh coriander (cilantro)

salt and pepper

fresh herbs, to garnish

MINT RAITA

150 ml/^{1}/$_4$ pint/^{2}/$_3$ cup natural yogurt

1 tbsp chopped fresh mint

TO SERVE

onion relish

basmati rice

naan bread

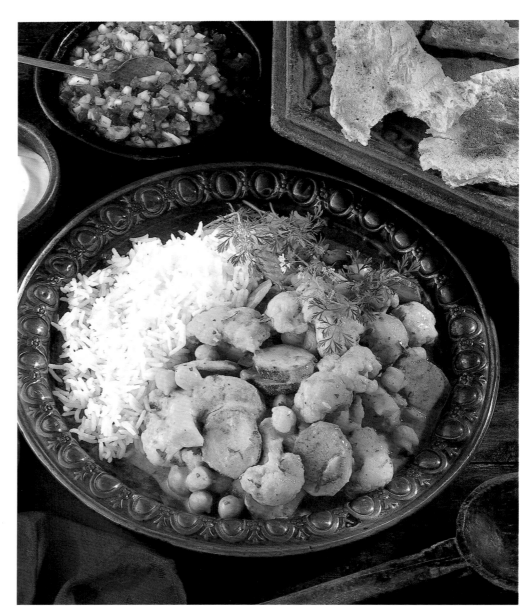

1 Heat the oil in a pan and fry the onion until softened. Add the cumin, ground coriander, turmeric, ginger, chilli and garlic and fry for 1 minute.

2 Add the tomatoes and coconut mixture and mix well.

3 Add the cauliflower, courgettes (zucchini), carrots, potato, chick-peas (garbanzo beans) and seasoning. Cover and simmer for 20 minutes.

4 Stir in the yogurt, mango chutney and fresh coriander (cilantro) and heat through gently, but do not boil.

5 To make the mint raita, mix the yogurt and mint. Transfer to a serving dish, then cover and chill.

6 Transfer the curry to serving plates, garnish with fresh herbs and serve with mint raita, onion relish, basmati rice and naan bread.

Egg & Chick-pea (Garbanzo Bean) Curry

This easy vegetarian curry is always enjoyed. Double the quantities for a great dish if you're cooking for a crowd.

Serves 4

2 tbsp vegetable oil
2 garlic cloves, crushed
1 large onion, chopped
1 large carrot, sliced
1 apple, cored and chopped
2 tbsp medium-hot curry powder
1 tsp finely grated ginger root
2 tsp paprika
850 ml/1^1/$_2$ pints/3^1/$_2$ cups Fresh
Vegetable Stock (see page 14)
2 tbsp tomato purée (paste)
^{1}/$_2$ small cauliflower, broken into florets
475 g/1 lb 1 oz can chick-peas (garbanzo
beans), rinsed and drained
25 g/1 oz/2 tbsp sultanas
(golden raisins) or raisins
2 tbsp cornflour (cornstarch)
2 tbsp water
4 hard-boiled (hard-cooked) eggs,
quartered
salt and pepper
paprika, to garnish

CUCUMBER DIP

7.5 cm/3 inch piece cucumber,
chopped finely
1 tbsp chopped fresh mint
150 ml/^{1}/$_4$ pint/^{2}/$_3$ cup natural yogurt
sprigs of fresh mint, to garnish

1 Heat the oil in a large pan and fry the garlic, onion, carrot and apple for 4–5 minutes, until softened. Add the curry powder, ginger and paprika and fry for 1 minute. Stir in the vegetable stock and tomato purée (paste).

2 Add the cauliflower, chick-peas (garbanzo beans) and sultanas (golden raisins) or raisins. Bring to the boil, reduce the heat and simmer, covered, for 25–30 minutes or until tender.

3 Blend the cornflour (cornstarch) with the water and add to the curry, stirring until thickened. Cook gently for 2 minutes. Season to taste.

4 To make the dip, mix together the cucumber, mint and yogurt. Garnish with fresh mint.

5 Ladle the curry on to 4 serving plates. Arrange the eggs on top and sprinkle with a little paprika. Serve with the cucumber dip.

Risotto Verde

Risotto is an Italian dish which is easy to make and uses arborio rice,
onion and garlic as a base for a range of savoury recipes.

Serves 4
1.75 litres/3 pints/7^1/$_2$ cups vegetable stock
2 tbsp olive oil
2 garlic cloves, crushed
2 leeks, shredded
225 g/8 oz/1^1/$_4$ cups arborio rice
300 ml/^{1}/$_2$ pint/1^1/$_4$ cups dry white wine
4 tbsp mixed chopped herbs
225 g/8 oz baby spinach
3 tbsp natural yogurt
shredded leek, to garnish

1 Pour the stock into a large pan and bring to the boil. Reduce the heat to a simmer. Meanwhile, heat the oil in a separate pan and sauté the garlic and leeks for 2–3 minutes until softened.

2 Stir in the rice and cook for 2 minutes, stirring until well coated.

3 Pour in half of the wine and a little of the hot stock. Cook over a gentle heat until all of the liquid has been absorbed. Add the remaining stock and wine and cook over a low heat for 25 minutes or until the rice is creamy.

4 Stir in the herbs and spinach, season well and cook for 2 minutes. Stir in the yogurt, garnish and serve.

COOK'S TIP

Do not hurry the process of cooking the risotto as the rice must absorb the liquid slowly in order for it to reach the correct consistency.

Fried Rice In Pineapple

This has a mild, pleasant flavour and looks very impressive
as part of a party buffet, so everyone can enjoy it.

Serves 4-6

1 large pineapple

1 tbsp sunflower oil

1 garlic clove, crushed

1 small onion, diced

$^{1}/_{2}$ celery stalk, sliced

1 tsp coriander seeds, ground

1 tsp cumin seeds, ground

150 g/5$^{1}/_{2}$ oz/1$^{1}/_{2}$ cups button
mushrooms, sliced

250 g/9 oz/1$^{1}/_{3}$ cups cooked rice

2 tbsp light soy sauce

$^{1}/_{2}$ tsp sugar

$^{1}/_{2}$ tsp salt

25 g/1 oz/$^{1}/_{4}$ cup cashew nuts

TO GARNISH

1 spring onion (scallion),
sliced finely

fresh coriander
(cilantro) leaves

fresh mint sprig

1 Cut the pineapple in half
lengthwise and scoop out the flesh to
make 2 boat-shaped shells. Cut the
flesh into cubes and reserve 125 g/
4$^{1}/_{2}$ oz/1 cup to use in this recipe.
(Any remaining pineapple cubes can
be served separately.)

2 Heat the oil in a wok or large, heavy
frying pan (skillet).

3 Add the garlic, onion and celery
and cook over a high heat, stirring
constantly, for 2 minutes.

4 Stir in the coriander and cumin
seeds, and the mushrooms.

5 Add the pineapple cubes and
cooked rice to the pan and stir well.
Stir in the soy sauce, sugar, salt and
cashew nuts.

6 Using two spoons, lift and stir the

rice for about 4 minutes until it is
thoroughly heated through.

7 Spoon the rice mixture into the
pineapple boats. Garnish and serve
immediately.

Indonesian Hot Rice Salad

Nutty brown rice combines well with peanuts and a sweet and sour mixture
of fruit and vegetables in this tangy combination.

Serves 4

300 g/10½ oz/1½ cups brown rice

400 g/14 oz can pineapple pieces
in natural juice, drained

1 bunch spring onions
(scallions), chopped

1 red (bell) pepper,
deseeded and chopped

125 g/4½ oz/2 cups bean-sprouts

90 g/3 oz/¾ cup
dry-roasted peanuts

125 g/4½ oz radishes, sliced thinly

DRESSING

2 tbsp crunchy peanut butter

1 tbsp groundnut oil

2 tbsp light soy sauce

2 tbsp white wine vinegar

2 tsp clear honey

1 tsp chilli powder

½ tsp garlic salt

pepper

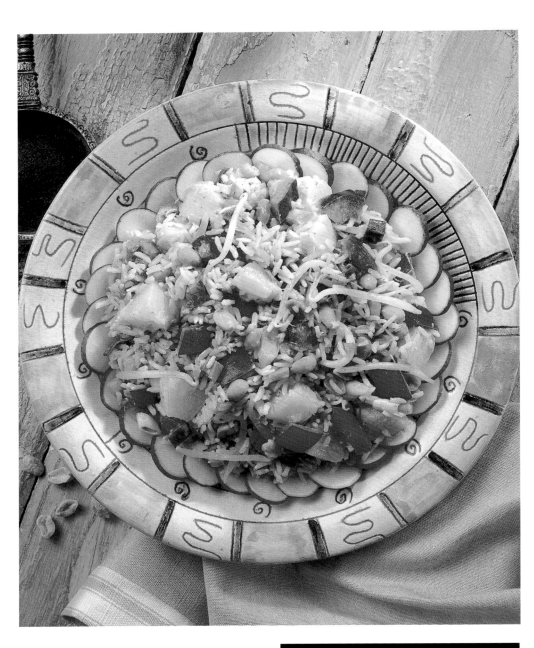

1 Put the rice in a saucepan and cover
with water. Bring to the boil, then
cover and simmer for 30 minutes
until the rice is tender.

2 Meanwhile, make the dressing.
Place all of the ingredients in a small
bowl and whisk for a few seconds
until well combined.

3 Drain the rice and place in a
heatproof bowl. Heat the dressing in a
small saucepan for 1 minute and then
toss into the rice and mix well.

4 Working quickly, stir in the
pineapple, spring onions (scallions),

(bell) pepper, bean-sprouts and
peanuts.

5 Transfer the rice salad to a warmed
serving dish. Arrange the radish
slices around the outside and serve
immediately.

COOK'S TIP

Peanut butter is nutritious and
can be used to flavour and
thicken a wide range of sauces
and dressings.

Red (Bell) Peppers Stuffed with Rice

Stuffed (bell) peppers are a well-known dish, but this
is a new version adapted for the barbecue.

Serves 4
2 red (bell) peppers, halved lengthwise and deseeded
2 tomatoes, halved
2 courgettes (zucchini), sliced thinly lengthwise
1 red onion, cut into 8 sections, each section held together by the root
4 tbsp olive oil
2 tbsp fresh thyme leaves
60 g/2 oz/¹⁄₃ cup mixed basmati and wild rice, cooked
salt and pepper

1 Put the (bell) peppers, tomatoes, courgettes (zucchini) and onion sections on to a baking sheet (cookie sheet). Brush the vegetables with olive oil and sprinkle over the fresh thyme leaves.

2 Cook the (bell) pepper, onion and courgette (zucchini) over a medium hot barbecue for about 6 minutes, turning once. Cook the tomato halves for 2–3 minutes only; remove the tomatoes from the barbecue, set aside and keep warm.

3 When the (bell) peppers are cooked, put a spoonful of the cooked rice into each one. Season with plenty of salt and pepper and serve with the tomatoes, courgettes (zucchini), and onions.

Stir-fries & Sautés

Whether you're cooking a Chinese-style meal or any other kind of dish, stir-frying is one of the most convenient and nutritious ways of cooking vegetarian food. The food is cooked quickly over very high heat in a very little oil. The high heat seals in the natural juices and helps preserve nutrients. The short cooking time makes the vegetables more succulent and preserves texture as well as the natural flavour and colour.

A round-bottomed wok is ideal for stir-frying as it conducts and retains heat evenly. The conical shape requires far less oil and the food always returns to the centre where the heat is most intense, however vigorously you stir.

Sautéeing requires a flat-bottomed pan so that the food can be tossed and stirred without being too crowded. A brisk heat is essential so that the food turns golden and crisp. If you use a non-stick pan you can cut down on the amount of oil required.

Cabbage & Walnut Stir-Fry

This is a really quick, one-pan dish using white
and red cabbage for colour and flavour.

Serves 4
350 g/12 oz white cabbage
350 g/12 oz red cabbage
4 tbsp peanut oil
1 tbsp walnut oil
2 garlic cloves, crushed
8 spring onions (scallions), trimmed
225 g/8 oz firm tofu (bean curd), cubed
2 tbsp lemon juice
100 g/3¹/₂ oz walnut halves
2 tsp Dijon mustard
2 tsp poppy seeds
salt and pepper

1 Using a sharp knife, shred the
white and red cabbages thinly and set
aside until required.

2 Heat the peanut and walnut oils
in a preheated wok. Add the garlic,
cabbage, spring onions (scallions)
and tofu (bean curd) and cook for
5 minutes, stirring.

3 Add the lemon juice, walnuts and
mustard, season with salt and pepper
and cook for a further 5 minutes or
until the cabbage is tender.

4 Transfer the stir-fry to a warm
serving bowl, sprinkle with poppy
seeds and serve.

COOK'S VARIATION

Sesame seeds could be used instead
of the poppy seeds and drizzle
1 teaspoon of sesame oil over the
dish just before serving, if you wish.

Tofu (Bean Curd) & Vegetable Stir-Fry

This is a quick dish to prepare, making it ideal as a mid-week supper dish,
after a busy day at work!

Serves 4
175 g/6 oz/1¼ cups potatoes, cubed
1 tbsp olive oil
1 red onion, sliced
225 g/8 oz firm tofu (bean curd), diced
2 courgettes (zucchini), diced
8 canned artichoke hearts, halved
150 ml/¼ pint/⅔ cup passata (sieved tomatoes)
1 tsp caster (superfine) sugar
2 tbsp chopped basil
salt and pepper

1 Cook the potatoes in a saucepan of boiling water for 10 minutes. Drain thoroughly.

2 Heat the oil in a large frying pan (skillet) and sauté the red onion for 2 minutes, stirring.

3 Stir in the tofu (bean curd) and courgettes (zucchini) and cook for 3–4 minutes until they begin to brown slightly. Add the potatoes, stirring to mix.

4 Stir in the artichoke hearts, passata (sieved tomatoes), sugar and basil, season with salt and pepper and cook for a further 5 minutes, stirring well. Transfer to serving dishes and serve immediately.

COOK'S VARIATION

Aubergines (eggplants) could be used instead of the courgettes (zucchini), if preferred.

Red Curry with Cashew Nuts

This is a wonderfully quick dish to prepare. If you don't have time to prepare the curry paste, it can be bought ready-made (use 3 tablespoons for this recipe).

Serves 4

250 ml/9 fl oz/1 cup coconut milk

1 kaffir lime leaf, mid-rib removed

1/4 tsp light soy sauce

60 g/2 oz/4 baby corn cobs, halved lengthwise

125 g/4 1/2 oz broccoli florets

125 g/4 1/2 oz French (green) beans, cut into 5 cm/2 inch pieces

25 g/1 oz/1/4 cup cashew nuts

15 fresh basil leaves

1 tbsp chopped fresh coriander (cilantro)

1 tbsp chopped roasted peanuts, to garnish

cooked rice, to serve

RED CURRY PASTE

7 fresh red chillies, halved, deseeded and blanched (use dried if fresh are not available)

2 tsp cumin seeds

2 tsp coriander seeds

2.5 cm/1 inch piece galangal, peeled and chopped

1/2 stalk lemon grass, chopped

1 tsp salt

grated rind of 1 lime

4 garlic cloves, chopped

3 shallots, chopped

2 kaffir lime leaves, mid-rib removed, shredded

1 tbsp oil to blend

1 To make the red curry paste, grind the chillies, cumin, coriander, galangal, lemon grass, salt, lime, garlic, shallots and lime leaves in a pestle and mortar, food processor or grinder. Blend with the oil. The paste will keep for up to 3 weeks in a sealed jar in the refrigerator.

2 Preheat a wok or large, heavy frying pan (skillet), add 3 tablespoons of the red curry paste and cook over a high heat, stirring, until fragrant.

3 Reduce the heat and add the coconut milk, lime leaf, light soy sauce, corn cobs, broccoli, beans and cashew nuts. Bring to the boil and simmer for about 10 minutes until the vegetables are cooked, but still firm.

4 Remove the lime leaf and stir in the basil leaves and coriander (cilantro). Garnish with peanuts and serve with cooked rice.

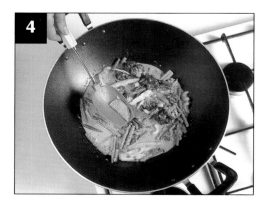

Three Mushrooms in Coconut Milk

A filling and tasty main course dish served over rice or noodles.

Serves 4
2 lemon grass stalks, sliced thinly
2 green chillies, deseeded and chopped finely
1 tbsp light soy sauce
2 garlic cloves, crushed
2 tbsp chopped fresh coriander (cilantro)
2 tbsp chopped fresh parsley
6 slices galangal, peeled
3 tbsp sunflower oil
1 aubergine (eggplant), cubed
60 g/2 oz/²/₃ cup oyster mushrooms
60 g/2 oz/²/₃ cup chestnut (crimini) mushrooms
60 g/2 oz/²/₃ cup field mushrooms, quartered if large
125 g/4¹/₂ oz French (green) beans, cut into 5 cm/2 inch lengths, blanched
300 ml/¹/₂ pint/1¹/₄ cups coconut milk
1 tbsp lemon juice
fresh coriander (cilantro) sprigs, to garnish
cooked rice, to serve

1 Grind the lemon grass, chillies, soy sauce, garlic, coriander (cilantro), parsley and galangal in a large pestle and mortar or a food processor. Set aside until required.

2 Heat the sunflower oil in a preheated wok or large, heavy frying pan (skillet). Add the aubergine (eggplant) and stir over a high heat for 3 minutes. Stir in the mushrooms and beans and cook for 3 minutes, stirring constantly. Add the ground spice paste, stirring to mix.

3 Add the coconut milk and lemon juice to the pan, bring to the boil and simmer for 2 minutes.

4 Serve immediately with rice, and garnish with fresh coriander (cilantro).

COOK'S TIP

Any mixture of tasty mushrooms can be used in this recipe. You can even use dried mushrooms.

Cantonese Garden Vegetable Stir-Fry

This dish tastes as fresh as it looks. Try to get hold of baby vegetables as
they look and taste so much better in this dish.

Serves 4
2 tbsp peanut oil
1 tsp Chinese five spice powder
75 g/2³/₄ oz baby carrots, halved
2 celery sticks, sliced
2 baby leeks, sliced
50 g/1³/₄ oz mangetout (snow peas)
4 baby courgettes (zucchini), halved lengthwise
8 baby corn cobs
225 g/8 oz firm marinated tofu (bean curd), cubed
4 tbsp fresh orange juice
1 tbsp clear honey
celery leaves and orange zest, to garnish
cooked rice or noodles, to serve

1 Heat the oil in a preheated wok until almost smoking. Add the Chinese five spice powder, carrots, celery, leeks, mangetout (snow peas), courgettes (zucchini) and corn cobs and stir-fry for 3–4 minutes.

2 Add the tofu (bean curd) and cook for a further 2 minutes, stirring.

3 Stir in the orange juice and honey, reduce the heat and cook for 1–2 minutes. Garnish with celery leaves and orange zest and serve with rice or noodles.

COOK'S VARIATION

Lemon juice would be just as delicious as the orange juice in this recipe, but use 3 tablespoons instead of 4 tablespoons.

Stir-Fried Greens

This is an easy recipe to make as a quick accompaniment to a main course.
The water chestnuts give a delicious crunch to the greens.

Serves4
1 tbsp sunflower oil
1 garlic clove, halved
2 spring onions (scallions), sliced finely
200 g/7 oz can water chestnuts, drained and sliced finely (optional)
500 g/1 lb 2 oz spinach, tough stalks removed
1 tsp sherry vinegar
1 tsp light soy sauce
pepper

1 Heat the oil in a preheated wok or large, heavy frying pan (skillet) over a high heat.

2 Add the garlic and cook, stirring, for 1 minute. Be careful not to let the garlic burn on the bottom of the wok or pan.

3 Add the spring onions (scallions) and water chestnuts, if using, and stir for 2–3 minutes.

4 Stir in the spinach. Add the sherry vinegar, soy sauce and a sprinkling of pepper and cook, stirring, until the spinach is tender. Remove the garlic.

5 Transfer the stir-fried greens to a warmed serving dish, using a slotted spoon in order to drain off the excess liquid. Serve immediately.

Sweet & Sour Vegetables & Tofu (Bean Curd)

This dish is ideal served with plain noodles for a filling, Oriental meal.

Serves 4
1 tbsp peanut oil
2 garlic cloves, crushed
1 tsp grated root ginger
50 g/1³/₄ oz baby corn cobs
50 g/1³/₄ oz mangetout (snow peas)
1 carrot, cut into matchsticks
1 green (bell) pepper, cut into matchsticks
8 spring onions (scallions), trimmed
50 g/1³/₄ oz canned bamboo shoots
225 g/8 oz marinated firm tofu (bean curd), cubed
2 tbsp dry sherry
2 tbsp rice vinegar
2 tbsp clear honey
1 tbsp light soy sauce
150 ml/¹/₄ pint/²/₃ cup vegetable stock
1 tbsp cornflour (cornstarch)

1 Heat the oil in a preheated wok until almost smoking. Add the garlic and ginger and cook for 30 seconds.

2 Add the corn cobs, mangetout (snow peas), carrot and (bell) pepper and stir-fry for 5 minutes or until the vegetables are tender.

3 Add the spring onions (scallions), bamboo shoots and tofu (bean curd) and cook for a further 2 minutes.

4 Stir in the sherry, rice vinegar, honey, soy sauce, vegetable stock and cornflour (cornstarch) and bring to the boil. Reduce the heat and simmer for 2 minutes. Transfer to serving dishes and serve.

Stir-Fried Winter Vegetables with Coriander (Cilantro)

Ordinary winter vegetables are given extraordinary treatment in this lively stir-fry, just the thing for perking up jaded palates.

4 Add the chopped coriander (cilantro), soy sauce, seasoning and almonds to the mixture, stirring gently. Serve the vegetables, garnished with a few of sprigs of fresh coriander (cilantro).

COOK'S TIP

Pumpkin or poppy seeds can be used instead of the sesame seeds. Pumpkin seeds are a good source of zinc.

Serves 4
3 tbsp sesame oil
25 g/1 oz/$^1/_4$ cup blanched almonds
1 large carrot, cut into thin strips
1 large turnip, cut into thin strips
1 onion, sliced finely
1 garlic clove, crushed
3 celery sticks, sliced finely
125 g/4$^1/_2$ oz Brussels sprouts, trimmed and halved
125 g/4$^1/_2$ oz cauliflower, broken into florets
125 g/4$^1/_2$ oz/2 cups white cabbage, shredded
2 tsp sesame seeds
1 tsp grated fresh root ginger
$^1/_2$ tsp medium chilli powder
1 tbsp chopped fresh coriander (cilantro)
1 tbsp light soy sauce
salt and pepper
sprigs of fresh coriander (cilantro), to garnish

1 Heat the sesame oil in a preheated wok or large frying pan (skillet). Add the almonds and stir-fry until lightly browned. Remove the almonds with a slotted spoon and drain well on paper towels.

2 Add all the vegetables to the wok or frying pan (skillet), except for the cabbage. Stir-fry briskly for 3–4 minutes.

3 Add the cabbage, sesame seeds, ginger and chilli powder to the vegetables and cook, stirring, for 2 minutes.

Green Curry with Tempeh

Green curry paste will keep for up to 3 weeks in the refrigerator. If you don't have time to make the green curry paste, it can be bought ready-made (use 6 tablespoons for this recipe).

Serves 4

1 tbsp sunflower oil

175 g/6 oz marinated or plain tempeh, cut into diamonds

6 spring onions (scallions), cut into 2.5 cm/1 inch pieces

150 ml/1/4 pint/2/3 cup coconut milk

grated rind of 1 lime

15 g/1/2 oz/1/4 cup fresh basil leaves

1/4 tsp liquid seasoning, such as Maggi

GREEN CURRY PASTE

2 tsp coriander seeds

1 tsp cumin seeds

1 tsp black peppercorns

4 large green chillies, deseeded and chopped

2 shallots, quartered

2 garlic cloves, peeled

2 tbsp chopped fresh coriander (cilantro), including root and stalk

grated rind of 1 lime

1 tbsp roughly chopped galangal

1 tsp ground turmeric

salt

2 tbsp oil

TO GARNISH

fresh coriander (cilantro) leaves

2 green chillies, sliced thinly

1 To make the curry paste, grind the coriander, cumin seeds and the peppercorns in a food processor or pestle and mortar. Blend the remaining ingredients together and add to the ground spice mixture.

2 Heat the oil in a wok or frying pan (skillet). Add the tempeh and stir-fry

over a high heat for about 2 minutes or until sealed on all sides. Add the spring onions (scallions) and stir-fry for 1 minute. Remove the tempeh and spring onions (scallions) and reserve.

3 Put half of the coconut milk into the wok or pan (skillet) and bring to the

boil. Add 6 tbsp of the curry paste and the lime rind, and cook for 1 minute. Add the reserved tempeh and spring onions (scallions). Add the remaining coconut milk and simmer for 7–8 minutes. Stir in the basil leaves and liquid seasoning and simmer for 1 minute. Garnish and serve.

Indonesian Chestnut & Vegetable Stir-Fry with Peanut Sauce

This colourful, spicy stir-fry has an Indonesian influence,
with the shallots, chillies, ginger, fresh coriander (cilantro) and lime.

Serves 4

PEANUT SAUCE

125 g/4¹/₂ oz/1 cup unsalted
roasted peanuts

2 tsp hot chilli sauce

175 ml/6 fl oz/³/₄ cup coconut milk

2 tbsp soy sauce

1 tbsp ground coriander

pinch of ground turmeric

1 tbsp dark muscovado sugar

STIR-FRY

3 tbsp sesame oil

3–4 shallots, finely sliced

1 garlic clove, finely sliced

1–2 red chillies, deseeded and
finely chopped

1 large carrot, cut into fine strips

1 yellow and 1 red (bell) pepper, sliced

1 courgette (zucchini),
cut into fine strips

125 g/4¹/₂ oz sugar-snap peas, trimmed

7.5 cm/3 inch piece of cucumber,
cut into strips

250 g/9 oz oyster mushrooms

250 g/9 oz canned chestnuts, drained

2 tsp grated ginger root

finely grated rind and juice of 1 lime

1 tbsp chopped fresh coriander (cilantro)

salt and pepper

1 To make the sauce, grind the peanuts in a blender, or chop very finely. Put into a small pan with the remaining ingredients. Heat gently and simmer for 3–4 minutes.

2 Heat the oil in a wok or frying pan (skillet). Add the shallots, garlic and chillies and stir-fry for 2 minutes.

3 Add the carrot, (bell) peppers, courgette (zucchini) and sugar-snap peas to the wok or pan (skillet) and stir-fry for 2 minutes.

4 Add the cucumber, mushrooms, chestnuts, ginger, lime rind and juice, coriander (cilantro) and salt and pepper to taste to the wok or pan (skillet) and stir-fry briskly for about 5 minutes, or until the vegetables are crisp, yet crunchy.

5 Divide the stir-fry between 4 warmed serving plates and serve with the peanut sauce.

Cauliflower with Oriental Greens

This is a delicious way to cook cauliflower – even without the greens.

Serves 4
175 g/6 oz cauliflower, cut into florets
1 garlic clove
1/2 tsp turmeric
1 tbsp coriander (cilantro) root or stem
1 tbsp sunflower oil
2 spring onions (scallions), cut into 2.5 cm/1 inch pieces
125 g/4 1/2 oz oriental greens, such as Thai spinach, bok choy or mustard greens, tough stalks removed
1 tsp yellow mustard seeds

1 Blanch the cauliflower, rinse in cold running water and drain thoroughly. Set aside until required.

2 Grind the garlic, turmeric and coriander (cilantro) root or stem together in a pestle and mortar or spice grinder.

3 Heat the oil in a wok or large, heavy frying pan (skillet). Add the spring onions (scallions) and stir-fry over a high heat for 2 minutes. Add the greens and stir-fry for 1 minute. Remove and set aside.

4 Return the wok or frying pan (skillet) to the heat. Add the mustard seeds and stir-fry until they start to pop. Add the turmeric mixture and the cauliflower and stir-fry until the cauliflower is coated.

5 Transfer to a warmed serving plate and serve with the greens.

Kidney Bean Kiev

This is a vegetarian version of chicken kiev, the bean patties taking the place of the chicken.
Topped with garlic and herb butter and coated in breadcrumbs, this version is just as delicious.

Serves 4

GARLIC BUTTER

100 g/3½ oz/ 8 tbsp butter

3 garlic cloves, crushed

1 tbsp chopped parsley

BEAN PATTIES

650 g/1 lb 7 oz canned red kidney beans

150 g/5½ oz/1¼ cups fresh white breadcrumbs

25 g/1 oz/2 tbsp butter

1 leek, chopped

1 celery stick, chopped

1 tbsp chopped parsley

1 egg, beaten

salt and pepper

vegetable oil, for shallow frying

1 To make the garlic butter, put the butter,garlic and parsley in a bowl and blend together with a wooden spoon. Place the garlic butter mixture on to a sheet of greaseproof paper, roll into a cigar shape and wrap in the greaseproof paper. Leave to chill in the refrigerator.

2 Using a potato masher, mash the beans in a mixing bowl and stir in 75 g/2¾ oz/¾ cup of the breadcrumbs.

3 Melt the butter in a frying pan (skillet) and sauté the leek and celery for 3–4 minutes, stirring.

4 Add the bean mixture to the pan together with the parsley, season with salt and pepper to taste and mix well. Remove from the heat and leave to cool slightly.

5 Shape the bean mixture into 4 equal sized ovals.

6 Slice the garlic butter into 4 and place a slice in the centre of each bean patty. Mould the bean mixture around the garlic butter to encase it completely.

7 Dip each bean patty into the beaten egg to coat and then roll in the remaining breadcrumbs.

8 Heat a little oil in a frying pan (skillet) and fry the patties, turning once, for 7–10 minutes or until golden. Serve.

Vegetable Chop Suey

A classic Chinese dish found on all take-away menus,
this recipe is quick to prepare and makes a tasty meal.

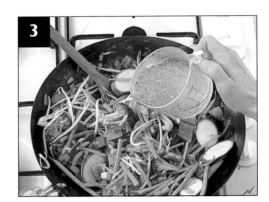

Serves 4
2 tbsp peanut oil
1 onion, chopped
3 garlic cloves, chopped
1 green (bell) pepper, diced
1 red (bell) pepper, diced
75 g/2³/₄ oz broccoli florets
1 courgette (zucchini), sliced
25 g/1 oz French (green) beans
1 carrot, cut into matchsticks
100 g/3¹/₂ oz bean-sprouts
2 tsp light brown sugar
2 tbsp light soy sauce
125 ml/4 fl oz/¹/₂ cup vegetable stock
salt and pepper

1 Heat the oil in a preheated wok
until almost smoking. Add the onion
and garlic and stir-fry for 30 seconds.

2 Stir in the (bell) peppers, broccoli,
courgette (zucchini), beans and carrot
and stir-fry for a further 2–3 minutes.

3 Add the bean-sprouts, sugar, soy
sauce, vegetable stock and salt and
pepper to taste and cook for about
2 minutes.

4 Transfer to serving plates and serve
immediately with noodles.

COOK'S TIP

Ensure that the vegetable pieces are
of the same size in order that they
all cook in the stated time.

Vegetable & Feta Cheese Patties

Grated carrots, courgettes (zucchini) and Feta cheese are combined with cumin seeds, poppy seeds, curry powder and chopped fresh parsley.

Serves 4
2 large carrots
1 large courgette (zucchini)
1 small onion
60 g/2 oz Feta cheese
25 g/1 oz/¼ cup plain (all-purpose) flour
¼ tsp cumin seeds
½ tsp poppy seeds
1 tsp medium curry powder
1 tbsp chopped fresh parsley
1 egg, beaten
25 g/1 oz/2 tbsp butter
2 tbsp vegetable oil
salt and pepper
sprigs of fresh herbs, to garnish

1 Grate the carrots, courgette (zucchini), onion and Feta cheese coarsely, either by hand or in a food processor.

2 Mix together the flour, cumin seeds, poppy seeds, curry powder and parsley in a large bowl. Season well with salt and pepper.

3 Add the vegetable and Feta cheese mixture to the seasoned flour, tossing well to combine. Stir in the beaten egg and mix well.

4 Heat the butter and oil in a large frying pan (skillet). Place heaped tablespoonfuls of the vegetable and cheese mixture in the pan, flattening them slightly with the back of the spoon. Fry gently for about 2 minutes on each side, until crisp and golden brown. Drain on paper towels and keep warm.

5 Garnish with sprigs of fresh herbs and serve.

COOK'S VARIATION

Omit the cumin and curry powder; use 1 tbsp oregano for the parsley.

Sweetcorn & Potato Fritters

An ideal supper dish for two, or for one if you halve the quantities.
You can use the remaining sweetcorn in another recipe.

· Serves 2
2 tbsp oil
1 small onion, sliced thinly
1 garlic clove, crushed
350 g/12 oz potatoes
200 g/7 oz can sweetcorn, drained ·
$^{1}/_{2}$ tsp dried oregano
1 egg, beaten
60 g/2 oz/$^{1}/_{2}$ cup Edam or Gouda cheese, grated
2–4 eggs
2–4 tomatoes, sliced
salt and pepper
fresh parsley sprigs, to garnish

1 Heat 1 tablespoon of the oil in a non-stick frying pan (skillet). Add the onion and garlic and fry very gently, stirring frequently, until soft, but only lightly coloured. Remove the pan from the heat.

2 Grate the potatoes coarsely into a bowl and mix in the sweetcorn, oregano, beaten egg and seasoning. Add the fried onion and garlic and mix well.

3 Heat the remaining oil in the frying pan (skillet). Divide the potato mixture in half to make two oval-shaped fritters. Add the fritters to the pan, levelling and shaping the fritters with a palette knife (spatula). Sauté the fritters gently, turning once (making sure that they do not stick to the bottom of the pan), for about 10 minutes or until browned underneath and almost cooked through. Remove the fritters from the pan.

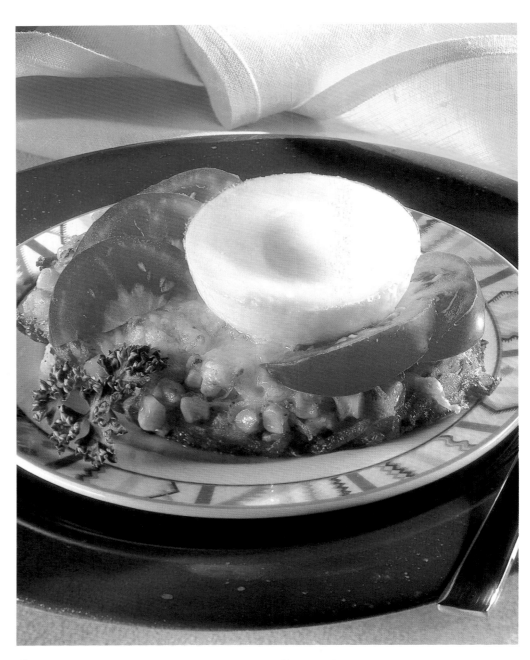

4 Sprinkle each fritter with the cheese and place under a preheated medium hot grill (broiler) until golden.

5 Meanwhile, poach either one or two eggs for each person until just cooked.

6 Transfer the sweetcorn and potato fritters to warmed plates and top each with the eggs and sliced tomatoes.

7 Garnish with fresh parsley and serve at once.

Golden Cheese, Leek & Potato Cakes

Make these tasty potato cakes for a quick and simple supper dish.
Serve them with scrambled eggs if you're very hungry.

Serves 4
1 kg/2 lb 4 oz potatoes
4 tbsp milk
60 g/2 oz/¼ cup butter or vegetarian margarine
2 leeks, chopped finely
1 onion, chopped finely
175 g/6 oz/1½ cups grated mature (sharp) Cheddar
1 tbsp chopped fresh parsley or chives
1 egg, beaten
2 tbsp water
90 g/3 oz/1½ cups fresh white or brown breadcrumbs
vegetable oil, for shallow frying
salt and pepper
fresh flat-leaf parsley sprigs, to garnish
tomato salad and cucumber and sweetcorn relish, to serve

1 Cook the potatoes in a saucepan of lightly salted boiling water until tender. Drain thoroughly. Mash the potatoes with the milk and the butter or margarine.

2 Cook the leeks and onion in a small amount of salted boiling water for about 10 minutes until tender. Drain.

3 In a large mixing bowl, combine the leeks and onion with the mashed potato, cheese and parsley or chives. Season to taste.

4 Beat the egg and water together in a bowl. Sprinkle the breadcrumbs into a separate bowl.

5 Shape the potato mixture into 12 cakes. Brush each cake with the egg mixture, then coat in the breadcrumbs.

6 Heat the oil in a large frying pan (skillet) and fry the potato cakes gently, in batches, for 2–3 minutes on each side or until light golden brown. Garnish with flat-leaf parsley and serve with a tomato salad and relish.

Sauté of Summer Vegetables with Tarragon Dressing

The freshness of lightly cooked summer vegetables is enhanced by the aromatic flavour of a tarragon and white wine dressing.

Serves 4
250 g/9 oz baby carrots, scrubbed
125 g/4^1/$_2$ oz runner (green) beans
2 courgettes (zucchini), trimmed
1 bunch large spring onions (scallions), trimmed
1 bunch radishes, trimmed
60 g/2 oz/^{1}/$_2$ cup butter
2 tbsp light olive oil
2 tbsp white wine vinegar
4 tbsp dry white wine
1 tsp caster (superfine) sugar
1 tbsp chopped fresh tarragon
salt and pepper
sprigs of fresh tarragon, to garnish

1 Trim and halve the carrots, slice the beans and courgettes (zucchini), and halve the spring onions (scallions) and radishes, so that all of the vegetables are cut to even-sized pieces.

2 Melt the butter in a large frying pan (skillet) or wok. Add all of the vegetables and stir-fry over a medium heat, stirring frequently.

3 Heat the olive oil, vinegar, white wine, sugar and salt and pepper to taste in a small saucepan. Remove from the heat and add the tarragon.

4 When the vegetables are just cooked, but still retain their crunchiness, pour over the 'dressing'. Stir through, and then transfer to a warmed serving dish. Garnish with sprigs of fresh tarragon and serve at once.

Sweetcorn Patties

These are a delicious addition to any party buffet, and are very simple to prepare.
Serve with a sweet chilli sauce.

Makes 12
325 g/11¹/₂ oz can sweetcorn, drained
1 onion, chopped finely
1 tsp curry powder
1 garlic clove, crushed
1 tsp ground coriander
2 spring onions (scallions), chopped
3 tbsp plain (all-purpose) flour
¹/₂ tsp baking powder
salt
1 large egg
4 tbsp sunflower oil
spring onions (scallions), sliced diagonally, to garnish

1 Mash the drained sweetcorn lightly in a medium-sized bowl.

2 Add all the remaining ingredients, except for the oil, one at a time, stirring after each addition.

3 Heat the sunflower oil in a frying pan (skillet). Drop tablespoonfuls of the mixture carefully into the hot oil, far enough apart for them not to run into each other as they cook. Alternatively, cook the patties one at a time. Cook the patties for 4–5 minutes, turning each patty once, until golden brown and firm. Take care not to turn them too soon, or they will break up in the pan.

4 Remove the patties from the pan and drain on paper towels. Serve quickly while still warm.

Bakes & Roasts

Anyone who ever thought that vegetarian meals were dull will be proved very wrong by the rich variety of dishes in this chapter. You'll recognize influences from all over the world, but there are also traditional stews and casseroles as well as hearty bakes and roasts. They all make exciting eating at any time of year, and for virtually any occasion. There are lots of ideas for mid-week meals or for entertaining, some traditional and some more unusual.

Some of the ingredients may be unfamiliar but you should have no difficulty in buying them from health food stores or large supermarkets. Don't be afraid to substitute ingredients where appropriate. There is no reason why you cannot enjoy experimenting and adding your own touch to these imaginative ideas.

Chick-pea (Garbanzo Bean) Roast with Sherry Sauce

This is a vegetarian version of the classic 'Beef Wellington', and just as delicious.
Served with a sherry sauce and roast vegetables it makes a tasty and impressive main dish.

Serves 4

450 g/1 lb can chick-peas (garbanzo beans), drained

1 tsp marmite (yeast extract)

150 g/5^1/$_2$ oz/1^1/$_4$ cups chopped walnuts

150 g/5^1/$_2$ oz/1^1/$_4$ cups fresh white breadcrumbs

1 onion, finely chopped

100 g/3^1/$_2$ oz/1^1/$_4$ cups mushrooms, sliced

50 g/1^3/$_4$ oz canned sweetcorn, drained

2 garlic cloves, crushed

2 tbsp dry sherry

2 tbsp vegetable stock

1 tbsp chopped coriander (cilantro)

225 g/8 oz prepared puff pastry

1 egg, beaten

2 tbsp milk

salt and pepper

SAUCE

1 tbsp vegetable oil

1 leek, thinly sliced

4 tbsp dry sherry

150 ml/^{1}/$_4$ pint/^{2}/$_3$ cup vegetable stock

1 Put the chick-peas (garbanzo beans), marmite, nuts, and breadcrumbs in a food processor and blend for 30 seconds. Put the onion and mushrooms in a large frying pan (skillet) and sauté in their own juices for 3–4 minutes.

2 Stir the chick-pea (garbanzo bean) mixture into the pan with the sweetcorn and garlic. Stir in the sherry, stock, coriander (cilantro) and seasoning and bind the mixture together. Remove from the heat and allow to cool.

3 Roll the pastry out on to a lightly floured surface to form a 35.5 cm/ 14 inch × 30 cm/12 inch rectangle.

4 Shape the chick-pea (garbanzo bean) mixture into a loaf shape and wrap the pastry around it, sealing the edges. Place seam-side down on a dampened baking sheet (cookie sheet) and score the top in a criss-cross pattern. Mix the egg and milk and brush over the pastry to glaze. Cook in a preheated oven, 200°C/400°F/Gas Mark 6, for 25–30 minutes or until risen and golden. Heat the oil for the sauce in a pan and sauté the leek for 5 minutes, stirring. Add the remaining ingredients and bring to the boil. Simmer for 5 minutes and serve with the roast.

Savoury Bread & Butter Pudding

Quick, simple and nutritious – what more could
you ask for an inexpensive mid-week meal?

Serves 4

60 g/2 oz/¼ cup butter or
vegetarian margarine

1 bunch spring onions
(scallions), sliced

6 slices white or brown bread,
crusts removed

175g/6 oz/1½ cups grated mature
(sharp) Cheddar

2 eggs

425 ml/¾ pint/scant 2 cups milk

salt and pepper

sprigs of fresh flat-leaf parsley,
to garnish

1 Grease a 1.5 litre/2¾ pint baking
dish with a little of the butter or
margarine. Melt the remaining butter
or margarine in a small saucepan and
fry the spring onions (scallions) until
softened and golden.

2 Cut the bread into triangles and
layer half of them in the baking dish.
Top with the spring onions (scallions)
and half of the cheese.

3 Beat together the eggs and milk and
season with salt and pepper to taste.
Layer the remaining triangles of bread
in the dish and carefully pour over
the milk mixture. Leave to soak for
15–20 minutes.

4 Sprinkle the remaining cheese over
the soaked bread. Bake in a preheated
oven, 190°C/375°F/Gas Mark 5, for
35–40 minutes or until puffed up and
golden brown. Garnish with flat-leaf
parsley and serve at once.

Mushroom & Nut Crumble

A filling, tasty dish that is ideal for a warming family supper.
The crunchy topping is flavoured with three different types of nuts.

Serves 4

350 g/12 oz open-cup mushrooms, sliced

350 g/12 oz chestnut mushrooms, sliced

400 ml/14 fl oz/1³/₄ cups Fresh
Vegetable Stock (see page 14)

60 g/2 oz/¹/₄ cup butter or vegetarian
margarine

1 large onion, chopped finely

1 garlic clove, crushed

60 g/2 oz/¹/₂ cup plain (all-purpose) flour

4 tbsp double (heavy) cream

2 tbsp chopped fresh parsley

salt and pepper

fresh herbs, to garnish

CRUMBLE TOPPING

90 g/3 oz/³/₄ cup medium oatmeal

90 g/3 oz/³/₄ cup wholemeal
(whole wheat) flour

25 g/1 oz/¹/₄ cup ground almonds

25 g/1 oz/¹/₄ cup finely chopped walnuts

60 g/2 oz/¹/₂ cup finely chopped unsalted
shelled pistachio nuts

1 tsp dried thyme

90 g/3 oz/¹/₃ cup butter or vegetarian
margarine, softened

1 tbsp fennel seeds

1 Put the mushrooms and stock in a
large saucepan, bring to the boil, cover
and simmer for 15 minutes until
tender. Drain the mushrooms,
reserving the stock.

2 In another saucepan, melt the
butter or margarine, and gently fry
the onion and garlic for 2–3 minutes
until just softened but not browned.
Stir in the flour and cook for about
1 minute.

3 Remove the pan from the heat and
stir in the reserved stock. Return to
the heat and cook, stirring, until
thickened. Stir in the mushrooms,
seasoning, cream and parsley and
spoon into a shallow ovenproof dish.

4 To make the topping, mix together
the oatmeal, flour, nuts, thyme and
plenty of seasoning.

5 Using a fork, mix in the butter or
margarine until the topping resembles
coarse breadcrumbs.

6 Sprinkle the mixture over the
mushrooms, sprinkle with fennel
seeds and bake in a preheated oven,
190°C/375°F/Gas Mark 5, for 25–30
minutes until golden and crisp.
Garnish with herbs and serve.

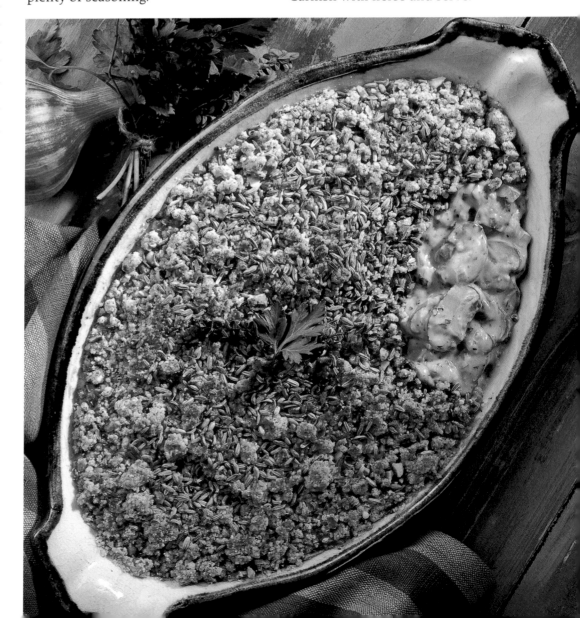

Spicy Potato & Lemon Casserole

This is based on a Moroccan dish in which potatoes are spiced
with coriander (cilantro) and cumin and cooked in a lemon sauce.

Serves 4
100 ml/3¹/₂ fl oz/¹/₂ cup olive oil
2 red onions, cut into eight
3 garlic cloves, crushed
2 tsp ground cumin
2 tsp ground coriander
pinch of cayenne pepper
1 carrot, thickly sliced
2 small turnips, quartered
1 courgette (zucchini), sliced
450 g/1 lb potatoes, thickly sliced
juice and rind of 2 large lemons
300 ml/¹/₂ pint/1¹/₄ cups vegetable stock
2 tbsp chopped coriander (cilantro)
salt and pepper

1 Heat the olive oil in a flameproof casserole.

2 Add the red onion and sauté for 3 minutes, stirring.

3 Add the garlic and cook for 30 seconds. Mix in the cumin, ground coriander and cayenne pepper and cook for 1 minute, stirring.

4 Add the carrot, turnips, courgette (zucchini) and potatoes and stir to coat in the oil.

5 Add the lemon juice and rind, stock and salt and pepper to taste, cover and cook over a medium heat for 20–30 minutes, stirring occasionally.

6 Remove the lid, sprinkle in the coriander (cilantro) and stir well. Serve immediately.

COOK'S TIP

A selection of spices and herbs is important for adding variety to your cooking – add to your range each time you try a new recipe.

COOK'S TIP

Check the vegetables whilst cooking as they may begin to stick to the pan. Add a little more boiling water or stock if necessary.

Lentil Roast

The perfect dish to serve for an alternative Sunday lunch.
Roasted vegetables make a succulent accompaniment.

Serves 6
250 g/9 oz/1 cup red lentils
500 ml/18 fl oz/2 cups Fresh Vegetable Stock (see page 14)
1 bay leaf
15 g/½ oz/1 tbsp butter or vegetarian margarine, softened
2 tbsp dried wholemeal (whole wheat) breadcrumbs
250 g/9 oz/2 cups grated mature (sharp) Cheddar
1 leek, chopped finely
125 g/4½ oz button mushrooms, chopped finely
90 g/3 oz/1½ cups fresh wholemeal (whole wheat) breadcrumbs
2 tbsp chopped fresh parsley
1 tbsp lemon juice
2 eggs, beaten lightly
salt and pepper
sprigs of fresh flat-leaf parsley, to garnish
mixed roasted vegetables, to serve

1 Put the lentils, stock and bay leaf in a saucepan. Bring to the boil, cover and simmer gently for 15–20 minutes or until all of the liquid is absorbed and the lentils have softened. Discard the bay leaf.

2 Line the base of a 1 kg/2 lb 4 oz loaf tin (pan) with baking parchment. Grease the tin (pan) with the butter or margarine and sprinkle with the dried breadcrumbs.

3 Stir the cheese, leek, mushrooms, fresh breadcrumbs and parsley into the lentils and season to taste. Bind the mixture together with the lemon juice and eggs.

4 Spoon the mixture into the prepared loaf tin (pan) and smooth the top. Bake in a preheated oven, 190°C/375°F/Gas Mark 5, for 1 hour until golden. Loosen the loaf with a palette knife (spatula) and turn out on to a warmed serving plate. Garnish with parsley and serve sliced with a selection of roasted vegetables.

Vegetable Hot Pot

In this recipe, a variety of vegetables are cooked under a layer of potatoes,
topped with cheese and cooked until golden brown for a filling and tasty meal.

Serves 4

2 large potatoes, thinly sliced

2 tbsp vegetable oil

1 red onion, halved and sliced

1 leek, sliced

2 garlic cloves, crushed

1 carrot, cut into chunks

100 g/3¹⁄₂ oz broccoli florets

100 g/3¹⁄₂ oz cauliflower florets

2 small turnips, quartered

1 tbsp plain (all-purpose) flour

700 ml/1¹⁄₄ pints/3¹⁄₂ cups vegetable stock

150 ml/¹⁄₄ pint/²⁄₃ cup dry cider

1 dessert (eating) apple, sliced

2 tbsp chopped sage

pinch of cayenne pepper

50 g/1³⁄₄ oz/¹⁄₂ cup vegetarian Cheddar
cheese, grated

salt and pepper

1 Cook the potato slices in a
saucepan of boiling water for 10
minutes. Drain well and reserve.

2 Heat the oil in a flameproof
casserole dish and sauté the onion,
leek and garlic for 2–3 minutes. Add
the remaining vegetables and cook for
a further 3–4 minutes, stirring.

3 Stir in the flour and cook for
1 minute. Gradually add the stock
and cider and bring the mixture to the
boil. Add the apple, sage and cayenne
pepper and season well. Remove the
dish from the heat. Transfer the
vegetables to an ovenproof dish.

4 Arrange the potato slices on top
of the vegetable mixture to cover.

5 Sprinkle the cheese on top of the
potato slices and cook in a preheated
oven, 190°C/375°F/Gas Mark 5, for
30–35 minutes or until the potato is
golden brown and beginning to
crispen slightly around the edges.
Serve immediately.

COOK'S TIP

If the potato begins to brown too
quickly, cover with foil for the last
10 minutes of cooking time to
prevent the top from burning.

Winter Vegetable Cobbler

Seasonal fresh vegetables are casseroled with lentils then topped with
a ring of fresh cheese scones (biscuits) to make this tasty cobbler.

Serves 4
1 tbsp olive oil
1 garlic clove, crushed
8 small onions, halved
2 celery stalks, sliced
250 g/9 oz swede, chopped
2 carrots, sliced
1/2 small cauliflower, broken into florets
250 g/9 oz mushrooms, sliced
400 g/14 oz can chopped tomatoes
60 g/2 oz/1/4 cup red lentils
2 tbsp cornflour (cornstarch)
3–4 tbsp water
300 ml/1/2 pint/1 1/4 cups Fresh Vegetable Stock (see page 14)
2 tsp Tabasco sauce
2 tsp chopped fresh oregano or parsley
sprigs of oregano, to garnish

COBBLER TOPPING

250 g/9 oz/2 cups self-raising flour
60 g/2 oz/1/4 cup butter
125 g/4 1/2 oz/1 cup grated Cheddar
2 tsp chopped fresh oregano or parsley
1 egg, beaten
150 ml/1/4 pint/2/3 cup skimmed milk
salt

1 Heat the oil in a large pan and fry
the garlic and onions for 5 minutes.
Add the celery, swede, carrots and
cauliflower and fry for 2–3 minutes.

2 Remove the pan from the heat and
add the mushrooms, tomatoes and
lentils. Mix the cornflour (cornstarch)
with the water and add to the pan
with the stock, Tabasco sauce and
oregano or parsley. Bring to the boil,
stirring, until thickened. Transfer to

an ovenproof dish, cover and bake in
a preheated oven, 180°C/350°F/Gas
Mark 4, for 20 minutes.

3 To make the topping, sift the flour
and a pinch of salt into a bowl. Rub in
the butter, then stir in most of the
cheese and the herbs. Beat the egg and
milk and add enough to the dry

ingredients to make a dough. Knead
and roll out to 1 cm/1/2 inch thick. Cut
into 5 cm/2 inch rounds. Remove the
dish from the oven and increase the
temperature to 200°C/400°F/Gas Mark
6. Arrange the rounds around the edge
of the dish, brush with the egg and milk
and sprinkle with the cheese. Cook for
10–12 minutes. Garnish and serve.

Roast (Bell) Pepper Tart

This tastes truly delicious, the flavour of roasted vegetables being entirely different from that of boiled or fried.

Serves 8
PASTRY
175 g/6 oz/1¼ cups plain (all-purpose) flour
pinch of salt
75 g/2¾ oz/6 tbsp butter or vegetarian margarine
2 tbsp green pitted olives, finely chopped
3 tbsp cold water
FILLING
1 red (bell) pepper
1 green (bell) pepper
1 yellow (bell) pepper
2 garlic cloves, crushed
2 tbsp olive oil
100 g/3½ oz/1 cup Mozzarella cheese, grated
2 eggs
150 ml/5 fl oz/⅔ cup milk
1 tbsp chopped basil
salt and pepper

1 To make the pastry, sieve the flour and a pinch of salt into a mixing bowl. Rub in the butter or margarine until the mixture resembles breadcrumbs. Add the olives and cold water, bringing the mixture together to form a dough.

2 Roll the dough out on to a floured surface and use to line a 20 cm/8 inch loose-bottomed flan tin (pan). Prick the base with a fork and leave to chill.

3 Cut the (bell) peppers in half lengthwise and lay skin-side uppermost on a baking sheet (cookie sheet). Mix the garlic and oil and brush over the (bell) peppers. Cook in a preheated oven, 200°C/400°F/ Gas Mark 6, for 20 minutes or until beginning to char slightly. Let cool slightly and thinly slice. Arrange in the base of the pastry case, layering with the Mozzarella cheese. Beat the egg and milk and add the basil. Season and pour over the (bell) peppers. Put the tart on a baking sheet (cookie sheet) and return to the oven for 20–25 minutes or until set. Serve hot or cold.

COOK'S TIP

Make sure that the olives are very finely chopped, otherwise they will make holes in the pastry. They should be almost paste–like in consistency and could be chopped in a food processor for ease and speed.

Creamy Baked Fennel

Fennel tastes fabulous in this creamy sauce, flavoured with caraway seeds.
A crunchy breadcrumb topping gives an interesting change of texture.

Serves 4
2 tbsp lemon juice
2 fennel bulbs, trimmed
125 g/4¹/₂ oz/¹/₄ cup low-fat soft cheese
150 ml/¹/₄ pint/²/₃ cup single (light) cream
150 ml/¹/₄ pint/²/₃ cup milk
1 egg, beaten
60 g/2 oz/¹/₄ cup butter
2 tsp caraway seeds
60 g/2 oz/1 cup fresh white breadcrumbs
salt and pepper
sprigs of flat-leaf parsley, to garnish

1 Bring a large saucepan of water to the boil and add the lemon juice. Slice the bulbs of fennel thinly and add them to the saucepan. Cook for 2–3 minutes to blanch, and then drain.

2 Arrange the slices of fennel in a buttered ovenproof baking dish.

3 Beat the soft cheese in a bowl until smooth. Add the cream, milk and beaten egg and whisk together until combined. Season with salt and pepper to taste and pour the mixture over the fennel.

4 Melt 15 g/¹/₂ oz of the butter in a small frying pan (skillet) and fry the caraway seeds gently for 1–2 minutes, to release their flavour and aroma. Sprinkle them over the fennel.

5 Melt the remaining butter in a frying pan (skillet).

6 Add the breadcrumbs to the frying pan (skillet) and fry gently until lightly browned. Sprinkle the breadcrumbs evenly over the surface of the fennel.

7 Cook in a preheated oven, 180°C/350°F/Gas Mark 4, for 25–30 minutes, or until the fennel is tender. Transfer to serving plates, garnish with sprigs of parsley and serve.

Mexican Chilli Corn Pie

This bake of sweetcorn and kidney beans, flavoured with chilli and fresh coriander (cilantro), is topped with crispy cheese cornbread.

Serves 4

1 tbsp corn oil

2 garlic cloves, crushed

1 red (bell) pepper, deseeded and diced

1 green (bell) pepper, deseeded and diced

1 celery stalk, diced

1 tsp hot chilli powder

400 g/14 oz can chopped tomatoes

325 g/11½ oz can sweetcorn, drained

215 g/7½ oz can kidney beans, drained and rinsed

2 tbsp chopped fresh coriander (cilantro)

salt and pepper

sprigs of fresh coriander (cilantro), to garnish

tomato and avocado salad, to serve

TOPPING

125 g/4½ oz/⅔ cup cornmeal

1 tbsp plain (all-purpose) flour

½ tsp salt

2 tsp baking powder

1 egg, beaten

100 ml/3½ fl oz/6 tbsp milk

1 tbsp corn oil

125 g/4½ oz/1 cup grated mature (sharp) Cheddar

1 Heat the oil in a large frying pan (skillet) and gently fry the garlic, (bell) peppers and celery for 5–6 minutes or until just softened.

2 Stir in the chilli powder, tomatoes, sweetcorn, kidney beans and seasoning. Bring to the boil and simmer for 10 minutes. Stir in the coriander (cilantro) and spoon into an ovenproof dish.

3 To make the topping, mix together the cornmeal, flour, salt and baking powder. Make a well in the centre, add the egg, milk and oil and beat until a smooth batter is formed.

4 Spoon over the (bell) pepper and sweetcorn mixture and sprinkle with the cheese. Bake in a preheated oven, 220°C/425°F/Gas Mark 7, for 25–30 minutes until golden and firm.

5 Garnish with fresh coriander (cilantro) sprigs and serve immediately with a tomato and avocado salad.

Cauliflower, Broccoli & Cheese Flan

This really is a tasty flan, the pastry case for which may
be made in advance and frozen until required.

Serves 8

PASTRY

175 g/6 oz/1¼ cups plain (all-purpose)
flour

pinch of salt

½ tsp paprika

1 tsp dried thyme

75 g/2¾ oz/6 tbsp vegetarian margarine

3 tbsp water

FILLING

100 g/3½ oz cauliflower florets

100 g/3½ oz broccoli florets

1 onion, cut into eight

2 tbsp butter or vegetarian margarine

1 tbsp plain (all-purpose) flour

85 ml/3 fl oz/6 tbsp vegetable stock

125 ml/4 fl oz/8 tbsp milk

75 g/2¾ oz/¾ cup vegetarian Cheddar
cheese, grated

salt and pepper

paprika and thyme, to garnish

1 To make the pastry, sieve the flour
and salt into a bowl. Add the paprika
and thyme and rub the margarine
into the mixture until it resembles
breadcrumbs. Stir in the water and
bring together to form a dough.

2 Roll the pastry out on a floured
surface and use to line an 18cm/7 inch
loose-bottomed flan tin (pan). Prick
the base with a fork and line with
baking parchment. Fill with ceramic
baking beans and bake blind in a
preheated oven, at 190°C/375°F/Gas
Mark 5, for 15 minutes. Remove the
parchment and beans and return the
pastry case to the oven for 5 minutes.

3 To make the filling, cook the
cauliflower, broccoli and onion in a
pan of boiling water for 10–12 minutes
until tender. Drain and reserve.

4 Melt the butter in a pan. Add the
flour and cook, stirring, for 1 minute.
Remove from the heat, stir in the
stock and milk and return to the heat.

Bring to the boil, stirring, and add 50g/
1¾ oz/½ cup of the cheese. Season.

5 Spoon the cauliflower, broccoli and
onion into the pastry case. Pour over
the sauce and sprinkle with the cheese.
Return to the oven for 10 minutes until
the cheese is bubbling. Dust with
paprika and garnish with thyme. Serve.

Vegetable Jalousie

This is a really easy dish to make, but looks impressive.
The mixture of vegetables gives the dish a wonderful colour and flavour.

Serves 4
450 g/1 lb prepared puff pastry
1 egg, beaten
FILLING
2 tbsp butter or vegetarian margarine
1 leek, shredded
2 garlic cloves, crushed
1 red (bell) pepper, sliced
1 yellow (bell) pepper, sliced
50 g/1¾ oz mushrooms, sliced
75 g/2¾ oz small asparagus spears
2 tbsp flour
85 ml/3 fl oz/6 tbsp vegetable stock
85 ml/3 fl oz/6 tbsp milk
4 tbsp dry white wine
1 tbsp chopped oregano
salt and pepper

1 Melt the butter or margarine in a saucepan and sauté the leek and garlic for 2 minutes, stirring. Add the remaining vegetables and cook, stirring for 3–4 minutes.

2 Add the flour and cook for 1 minute. Remove the pan from the heat and stir in the stock, milk and wine. Return the pan to the heat and bring to the boil, stirring, until thickened. Stir in the oregano and season with salt and pepper to taste.

3 Roll half of the pastry out on a lightly floured surface to form a rectangle 42.5 cm/15 inches × 15 cm/ 6 inches. Roll out the other half of the pastry to the same shape, but a little larger. Put the smaller rectangle on a baking sheet (cookie sheet) lined with dampened baking parchment.

4 Spoon the filling on top of the smaller rectangle, leaving a 1.25 cm/ ½ inch clean edge.

5 Cut parallel slits across the larger rectangle to within 2.5 cm/1 inch of each edge.

6 Brush the edge of the smaller rectangle with egg and place the larger rectangle on top, sealing the edges well.

7 Brush the whole jalousie with egg and cook in a preheated oven, 200°C/400°F/Gas Mark 6, for 30–35 minutes until risen and golden. Serve immediately.

Spinach Pancake Layer

Nutty-tasting buckwheat pancakes are combined with a cheesy spinach mixture and baked with a crispy topping.

Serves 4
125 g/4$^{1}/_{2}$ oz/1 cup buckwheat flour
1 egg, beaten
1 tbsp walnut oil
300 ml/$^{1}/_{2}$ pint/1$^{1}/_{4}$ cups milk
2 tsp vegetable oil

FILLING

1 kg/2 lb 4 oz young spinach leaves
2 tbsp water
1 bunch spring onions (scallions), white and green parts, chopped
2 tsp walnut oil
1 egg, beaten
1 egg yolk
250 g/9 oz/1 cup cottage cheese
$^{1}/_{2}$ tsp grated nutmeg
25 g/1 oz/$^{1}/_{4}$ cup grated Cheddar cheese
25 g/1 oz/$^{1}/_{4}$ cup walnut pieces
salt and pepper

1 Sift the flour into a bowl and add any husks that remain behind in the sieve (strainer). Make a well in the centre and add the egg and walnut oil. Whisk in the milk to make a smooth batter. Leave to stand for 30 minutes.

2 To make the filling, wash the spinach and pack into a pan with the water. Cover tightly and cook on a high heat for 5–6 minutes until soft. Drain well and leave to cool. Fry the spring onions (scallions) in the walnut oil for 2–3 minutes until just soft. Drain and set aside.

3 Whisk the batter. Brush a crêpe pan with vegetable oil, heat until hot and pour in enough batter to lightly cover the base. Cook for 1–2 minutes until set, turn and cook for 1 minute until golden. Repeat to make 8–10 pancakes, layering them with parchment. Chop the spinach and pat dry with paper towels. Mix with the spring onions (scallions), beaten egg, egg yolk, cottage cheese, nutmeg and seasoning.

4 Layer the spinach mixture between the pancakes on a baking sheet (cookie sheet) lined with baking parchment, finishing with a pancake. Sprinkle with Cheddar. Bake in a preheated oven, 190°C/375°F/Gas Mark 5, for 20–25 minutes until firm and golden. Sprinkle with the walnuts and serve.

Cauliflower Bake

The red of the tomatoes is a great contrast to the cauliflower and herbs, making this dish appealing to both the eye and the palate.

Serves 4

450 g/1 lb cauliflower, broken into florets

2 large potatoes, cubed

100 g/3¹/₂ oz cherry tomatoes

SAUCE

25 g/1 oz/2 tbsp butter or vegetarian margarine

1 leek, sliced

1 garlic clove, crushed

25 g/1 oz/3 tbsp plain (all-purpose) flour

300 ml/¹/₂ pint/1¹/₄ cups milk

75 g/2³/₄ oz/³/₄ cup mixed grated cheese, such as Cheddar, Parmesan and Gruyère

¹/₂ tsp paprika

2 tbsp chopped flat-leaf parsley

salt and pepper

chopped fresh parsley, to garnish

1 Cook the cauliflower in a saucepan of boiling water for 10 minutes. Drain well and reserve. Meanwhile, cook the potatoes in a pan of boiling water for 10 minutes, drain and reserve.

2 To make the sauce, melt the butter or margarine in a pan and sauté the leek and garlic for 1 minute. Add the flour and cook for 1 minute. Remove the pan from the heat and gradually stir in the milk, 50 g/1³/₄ oz/ ¹/₂ cup of the cheese, the paprika and parsley. Return the pan to the heat and bring to the boil, stirring. Season.

3 Spoon the cauliflower into a deep ovenproof dish. Add the cherry tomatoes and top with the potatoes. Pour the sauce over the potatoes and sprinkle on the remaining cheese.

4 Cook in a preheated oven, 180°C/350°F/Gas Mark 4, for 20 minutes or until the vegetables are cooked through and the cheese is golden brown and bubbling. Garnish and serve immediately.

COOK'S VARIATION

This dish could be made with broccoli instead of the cauliflower as an alternative.

Root Croustades with Sunshine (Bell) Peppers

This colourful combination of grated root vegetables and mixed (bell) peppers would make a stunning dinner-party dish.

Serves 4
1 orange (bell) pepper
1 red (bell) pepper
1 yellow (bell) pepper
3 tbsp olive oil
2 tbsp red wine vinegar
1 tsp French mustard
1 tsp clear honey
salt and pepper
sprigs of fresh flat-leaf parsley, to garnish
green vegetables, to serve

CROUSTADES

250 g/9 oz potatoes, grated
250 g/9 oz carrots, grated
350 g/12 oz celeriac (celery root), grated
1 garlic clove, crushed
1 tbsp lemon juice
25 g/1 oz/2 tbsp butter or vegetarian margarine, melted
1 egg, beaten
1 tbsp vegetable oil

1 Place the (bell) peppers on a baking sheet (cookie sheet). Bake in a preheated oven, 190°C/375°F/Gas Mark 5, for 35 minutes, turning after 20 minutes. Remove the (bell) peppers from the oven, cover with a tea towel (dish cloth) and let cool for 10 minutes. Peel the skin from the cooked (bell) peppers; cut in half and discard the seeds. Thinly slice the flesh into strips and place in a shallow dish.

2 Put the oil, vinegar, mustard, honey and seasoning in a screw-top jar and shake to mix. Pour over the (bell) pepper strips, toss to mix and leave to marinate for 2 hours.

3 To make the croustades, mix the potatoes, carrots and celeriac (celery root); toss in the garlic and lemon juice. Mix in the butter or margarine and the egg. Season. Divide the mixture into 8 and pile on to 2 baking sheets (cookie sheets) lined with baking parchment,

forming each into a 10 cm/ 4 inch round. Brush with oil. Bake in a preheated oven, 220°C/ 425°F/Gas Mark 7, for 30–35 minutes until crisp and golden. Heat the (bell) peppers and the marinade for 2–3 minutes, then spoon over the croustades, garnish and serve.

Leek & Herb Soufflé

Hot soufflés look very impressive if served as soon as they
come out of the oven, otherwise they will sink quite quickly.

Serves 4
350 g/12 oz baby leeks
1 tbsp olive oil
125 ml/4 fl oz/$^{1}/_{2}$ cup vegetable stock
50 g/1$^{3}/_{4}$ oz/$^{1}/_{2}$ cup walnuts
2 eggs, separated
2 tbsp chopped mixed herbs
2 tbsp natural yogurt
salt and pepper

1 Using a sharp knife, chop the
leeks finely.

2 Heat the oil in a frying pan (skillet)
and sauté the leeks for 2–3 minutes.

3 Add the stock to the pan and
cook over a gentle heat for a further
5 minutes.

4 Place the walnuts in a food
processor and blend until finely
chopped.

5 Add the leek mixture to the nuts
and blend to form a purée. Transfer
the leek purée to a large mixing bowl.

6 Mix the egg yolks, herbs and yogurt
together and pour into the bowl
containing the leek purée. Season
with salt and pepper to taste and
mix well.

7 In a separate mixing bowl, whisk
the egg whites until firm peaks form.

8 Fold the egg whites into the leek
mixture. Spoon the mixture into a
lightly greased 900 ml/1$^{1}/_{2}$ pint

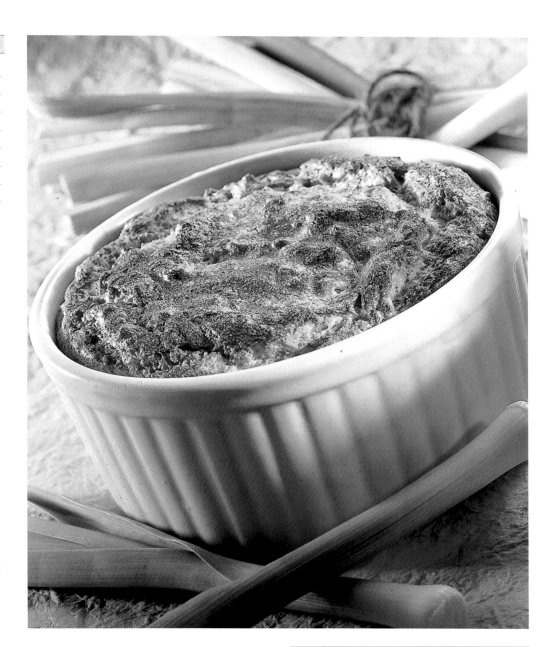

ramekin dish and place on a warmed
baking sheet (cookie sheet).

9 Cook in a preheated oven, 180°C/
350°F/Gas Mark 4, for 35–40 minutes
or until set. Serve the soufflé
immediately.

COOK'S TIP

Placing the ramekin on to a warm
baking sheet (cookie sheet) helps to
cook the soufflé from the bottom,
thus aiding its cooking.

Spicy Stuffed Chinese Leaves

Mushrooms, spring onions (scallions), celery and rice are flavoured
with five-spice powder and wrapped in Chinese leaves.

Serves 4
8 large Chinese leaves
60 g/2 oz/^{1}/$_3$ cup long-grain rice
^{1}/$_2$ vegetable stock (bouillon) cube
60 g/2 oz/^{1}/$_4$ cup butter
1 bunch spring onions (scallions), trimmed and chopped finely
1 celery stalk, chopped finely
125 g/4^1/$_2$ oz/1^1/$_4$ cups button mushrooms, sliced
1 tsp Chinese five-spice powder
300 ml/^{1}/$_2$ pint/1^1/$_4$ cups passata (sieved tomatoes)
salt and pepper
fresh chives, to garnish

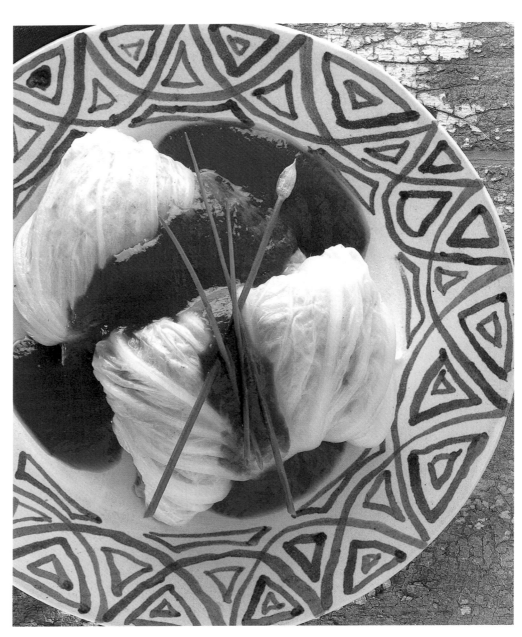

1 Blanch the Chinese leaves in a saucepan of boiling water for about 1 minute. Refresh under cold running water and drain well. Be careful not to tear the leaves.

2 Cook the rice in a saucepan of boiling water, with the stock (bouillon) cube, for 15–20 minutes or until just tender. Drain well.

3 Meanwhile, melt the butter in a frying pan (skillet) and fry the spring onions (scallions) and celery gently for 3–4 minutes until softened, but not browned. Add the mushrooms and cook for a further 3–4 minutes, stirring frequently.

4 Add the cooked rice and Chinese five-spice powder to the frying pan (skillet). Season with salt and pepper to taste and stir well to combine the ingredients.

5 Lay out the Chinese leaves on a chopping board and divide the rice mixture between them. Roll each leaf into a neat parcel to enclose the stuffing. Place the Chinese leaves, seam-side down, in a greased ovenproof dish.

6 Pour the passata (sieved tomatoes) over them and cover with foil.

7 Bake in a preheated oven, 190°C/375°F/Gas Mark 5, for 25–30 minutes. Serve immediately, garnished with fresh chives.

Artichoke & Cheese Flan

Artichoke hearts are delicious to eat, being very delicate in flavour and appearance.
They are ideal for cooking in a cheese-flavoured pastry case.

Serves 8

175 g/6 oz/1¼ cups wholemeal (whole wheat) flour

2 garlic cloves, crushed

75 g/2¾ oz/6 tbsp butter or vegetarian margarine

salt and pepper

FILLING

2 tbsp olive oil

1 red onion, halved and sliced

10 canned or fresh artichoke hearts

100 g/3½ oz/1 cup vegetarian Cheddar, grated

50 g/1¾ oz/½ cup Gorgonzola cheese, crumbled

2 eggs, beaten

1 tbsp chopped fresh rosemary

150 ml/¼ pint/⅔ cup milk

1 To make the pastry, sieve the flour into a mixing bowl, add a pinch of salt and the garlic. Rub in the butter or margarine until the mixture resembles breadcrumbs. Stir in 3 tablespoons of water and bring the mixture together to form a dough.

2 Roll the pastry out on a lightly floured surface to fit a 20cm/8 inch flan tin (pan). Prick the pastry with a fork.

3 Heat the oil in a frying pan (skillet) and sauté the onion for 3 minutes. Add the artichoke hearts and cook for a further 2 minutes.

4 Mix the cheeses with the beaten eggs, rosemary and milk. Stir in the

drained artichoke mixture and season with salt and pepper to taste.

5 Spoon the artichoke and cheese mixture into the pastry case and cook in a preheated oven, 200°C/400°F/ Gas Mark 6, for 25 minutes or until cooked and set. Serve the flan hot or cold.

COOK'S TIP

Gently press the centre of the flan with your fingertip to test if it is cooked through. It should feel fairly firm, but not solid. If overcooked the flan will begin to 'weep'.

Mushroom & Spinach Puff Pastry Parcels

These puff parcels are easy to make and delicious to eat. Filled with garlic, mushrooms and spinach they are ideal with a fresh tomato or cheese sauce.

Serves 4
2 tbsp butter
1 red onion, halved and sliced
2 garlic cloves, crushed
225 g/8 oz/3 cups open-cup mushrooms, sliced
175 g/6 oz baby spinach
pinch of nutmeg
4 tbsp double (heavy) cream
225 g/8 oz prepared puff pastry
1 egg, beaten
salt and pepper
2 tsp poppy seeds

1 Melt the butter in a frying pan (skillet). Add the onion and garlic to the pan and sauté for 3–4 minutes, stirring well.

2 Add the mushrooms, spinach and nutmeg and cook for a further 2–3 minutes.

3 Stir in the cream, mixing well. Season with salt and pepper to taste and remove the pan from the heat.

4 Roll the pastry out on a lightly floured surface and cut into four 15 cm/6 inch circles.

5 Spoon a quarter of the filling on to one half of each circle and fold the pastry over to encase the filling. Seal the edges of the pastry and brush with the beaten egg. Sprinkle with the poppy seeds.

6 Place the parcels on to a dampened baking sheet (cookie sheet) and cook

in a preheated oven, 200°C/400°F/Gas Mark 6, for 20 minutes until risen and golden brown.

7 Transfer the mushroom and spinach puff pastry parcels to serving plates and serve immediately.

COOK'S TIP

The baking sheet (cookie sheet) is dampened so that steam forms with the heat of the oven and helps the pastry to rise and set.

Vegetable & Tofu (Bean Curd) Strudels

These strudels look really impressive and are perfect if friends are coming
round or for a more formal dinner party dish.

Serves 4
FILLING
2 tbsp vegetable oil
2 tbsp butter or vegetarian margarine
150 g/5¹/₂ oz/¹/₃ cup potatoes finely diced
1 leek, shredded
2 garlic cloves, crushed
1 tsp garam masala
¹/₂ tsp chilli powder
¹/₂ tsp turmeric
50 g/1³/₄ oz okra, sliced
100 g/3¹/₂ oz/1¹/₄ cups button mushrooms, sliced
2 tomatoes, diced
225 g/8 oz firm tofu (bean curd), diced
12 sheets filo pastry
2 tbsp butter or vegetarian margarine, melted
salt and pepper

1 To make the filling, heat the oil and
butter in a frying pan (skillet). Add the
potatoes and leek and cook for 2–3
minutes, stirring.

2 Add the garlic and spices, okra,
mushrooms, tomatoes, tofu (bean
curd) and seasoning and cook, stirring,
for 5–7 minutes or until tender.

3 Lay the pastry out on a chopping
board and brush each individual sheet
with butter. Place 3 sheets on top of
one another; repeat to make 4 stacks.

4 Spoon a quarter of the filling along
the centre of each stack and brush the
edges with butter. Fold the short
edges in and roll up lengthwise to
form a cigar shape; brush the outside

with butter. Place the strudels on a
greased baking sheet (cookie sheet).

5 Cook in a preheated oven, 190°C/
375°F/Gas Mark 5, and cook the
strudels for 20 minutes or until
golden brown. Serve immediately.

COOK'S TIP

Decorate the outside of the
strudels with crumpled pastry
trimmings before cooking for a
really impressive effect.

Vegetable Toad-in-the-hole

This dish can be made in one large dish or in
individual Yorkshire pudding tins (pans).

Serves 4
BATTER
100 g/3½ oz/¾ cup plain (all-purpose) flour
2 eggs, beaten
200 ml/7 fl oz/¾ cup milk
2 tbsp wholegrain mustard
2 tbsp vegetable oil
FILLING
2 tbsp butter
2 garlic cloves, crushed
1 onion, cut into eight
75 g/2¾ oz baby carrots, halved lengthwise
50 g/1¾ oz French (green) beans
50 g/1¾ oz canned sweetcorn, drained
2 tomatoes, seeded and cut into chunks
1 tsp wholegrain mustard
1 tbsp chopped mixed herbs
salt and pepper

1 To make the batter, sieve the flour
and a pinch of salt into a large bowl.
Make a well in the centre and beat in
the eggs and milk to make a batter.
Stir in the mustard and leave to stand.

2 Pour the vegetable oil into a
shallow ovenproof dish and heat in
a preheated oven, 200°C/400°F/Gas
Mark 6, for 10 minutes.

3 Meanwhile, make the filling. Melt
the butter in a frying pan (skillet) and
sauté the garlic and onion for 2
minutes, stirring. Cook the carrots
and beans in a saucepan of boiling
water for 7 minutes or until tender.
Drain well.

4 Add the sweetcorn and tomato
to the frying pan (skillet) with the
mustard and herbs. Season well and
add the carrots and beans.

5 Remove the dish from the oven
and pour in the batter. Spoon the
vegetables into the centre, return to
the oven and cook for 30–35 minutes
until the batter has risen and set.

6 Serve the vegetable toad-in-the-hole
immediately.

COOK'S TIP

It is important that the oil is hot
before adding the batter so that
the batter begins to cook and
rise immediately.

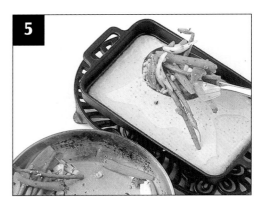

Almond & Sesame Nut Roast

Toasted almonds are combined with sesame seeds, rice and vegetables in this tasty vegetarian roast. Serve with a delicious onion and mushroom sauce.

Serves 4
2 tbsp sesame or olive oil
1 small onion, chopped finely
60 g/2 oz/scant ¼ cup risotto rice
300 ml/½ pint/1¼ cups Fresh Vegetable Stock (see page 14)
1 large carrot, grated
1 large leek, trimmed and chopped finely
2 tsp sesame seeds, toasted
90 g/3 oz/¾ cup chopped almonds, toasted
60 g/2 oz/½ cup ground almonds
90 g/3 oz/¾ cup mature (sharp) Cheddar, grated
2 eggs, beaten
1 tsp dried mixed herbs
salt and pepper
sprigs of flat-leaf parsley, to garnish
fresh vegetables, to serve

SAUCE
25 g/1 oz/2 tbsp butter
1 small onion, chopped finely
125 g/4½ oz/1¼ cup mushrooms, chopped finely
25 g/1 oz/¼ cup plain (all-purpose) flour
300 ml/½ pint/1¼ cups Fresh Vegetable Stock (see page 14)

1 Heat the oil in a frying pan (skillet) and fry the onion gently for 2–3 minutes. Add the rice and cook gently for 5–6 minutes, stirring frequently.

2 Add the vegetable stock, bring to the boil and then simmer for about 15 minutes, or until the rice is tender. Add a little extra water if necessary. Remove the pan from the heat and transfer the rice to a large bowl.

3 Add the carrot, leek, sesame seeds, almonds, cheese, beaten eggs and herbs to the mixture. Mix well and season. Transfer the mixture to a greased 500 g/1 lb 2 oz loaf tin (pan), levelling the surface. Bake in a preheated oven, 180°C/350°F/Gas Mark 4, for about 1 hour, or until set and firm. Leave in the tin (pan) for 10 minutes.

4 To make the sauce, melt the butter in a small saucepan and fry the onion until dark golden brown. Add the mushrooms and cook for a further 2 minutes. Stir in the flour, cook gently for 1 minute and then gradually add the stock. Bring to the boil, stirring constantly, until thickened and blended. Season to taste.

5 Turn out the nut roast, slice and serve on warmed plates with fresh vegetables, accompanied by the sauce. Garnish with sprigs of flat-leaf parsley.

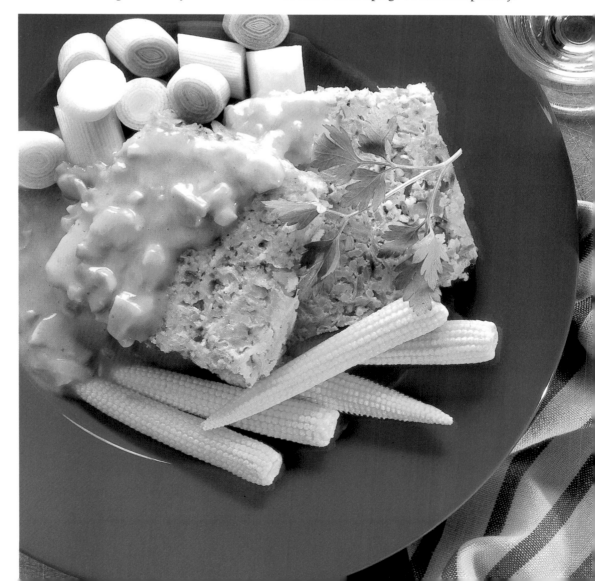

Green Vegetable Gougère

A tasty, simple supper dish of choux pastry and crisp green vegetables.
You can vary the vegetables according to taste.

Serves 4
150 g/5½ oz/1¼ cups plain (all-purpose) flour
125 g/4½ oz/½ cup butter or vegetarian margarine
300 ml/½ pint/1¼ cups water
4 eggs, beaten
90 g/3 oz/¾ cup grated Gruyère cheese
1 tbsp milk
salt and pepper
FILLING
25 g/1 oz/2 tbsp garlic and herb butter or margarine
2 tsp olive oil
2 leeks, shredded
250 g/9 oz green cabbage, shredded finely
125 g/4½ oz/2 cups bean sprouts
½ tsp grated lime rind
1 tbsp lime juice
celery salt and pepper
lime slices, to garnish

1 Sift the flour on to a piece of baking parchment and set aside. Cut the butter or margarine into dice and put in a saucepan with the water. Heat until the butter has melted.

2 Bring the butter and water to the boil, then using the parchment as a funnel, shoot in the flour all at once. Beat until the mixture becomes thick. Remove from the heat and beat until the mixture is glossy and comes away from the sides of the saucepan.

3 Transfer to a bowl and cool for 10 minutes. Beat in the eggs, a little at a time, ensuring they are incorporated after each addition. Stir in 60 g/2 oz/½ cup of the cheese and season.

4 Dampen a baking sheet (cookie sheet). Place spoonfuls of the mixture in a 23 cm/9 inch circle on the baking sheet (cookie sheet). Brush with milk and sprinkle with the cheese. Bake in a preheated oven, 220°C/425°F/Gas Mark 7, for 30–35 minutes until golden and crisp. Transfer to a serving plate.

5 Make the filling about 5 minutes before the end of cooking time. Heat the garlic butter or margarine and the oil in a frying pan (skillet) and stir-fry the leeks and cabbage for 2 minutes.

6 Add the bean sprouts, lime rind and juice and cook for 1 minute, stirring. Season with celery salt and pepper to taste, then pile into the centre of the cooked pastry ring. Garnish with lime slices and serve.

Filled Jacket Potatoes

Cook these potatoes conventionally, wrap them in foil and keep warm
at the edge of the barbecue, ready to fill with inspired mixtures.

Serves 4

4 large or 8 medium baking potatoes
paprika or chilli powder, or chopped
fresh herbs, to garnish

MEXICAN SWEETCORN RELISH

250 g/9 oz can sweetcorn, drained
$^1/_2$ red (bell) pepper deseeded
and chopped finely
5 cm/2 inch piece cucumber,
chopped finely
$^1/_2$ tsp chilli powder
salt and pepper

BLUE CHEESE, CELERY & CHIVE FILLING

125 g/4$^1/_2$ oz/$^1/_2$ cup full-fat soft cheese
125 g/4$^1/_2$ oz/$^1/_2$ cup natural fromage frais
125 g/4$^1/_2$ oz blue cheese, cut into cubes
1 celery stalk, chopped finely
2 tsp snipped fresh chives
celery salt and pepper

MUSHROOMS IN SPICY TOMATO SAUCE

25 g/1 oz/2 tbsp butter or vegetarian
margarine
250 g/9 oz button mushrooms
150 g/5$^1/_2$ oz/$^2/_3$ cup natural yogurt
1 tbsp tomato purée (paste)
2 tsp mild curry powder
salt and pepper

1 Scrub the potatoes and prick them
with a fork. Bake in a preheated oven,
200°C/400°F/Gas Mark 6, for about 1
hour, or until just tender.

2 To make the Mexican Sweetcorn
Relish, put half of the sweetcorn
into a bowl. Put the remainder into
a blender or food processor for

10–15 seconds, or chop and mash
roughly by hand. Add the puréed
sweetcorn to the sweetcorn kernels
with the (bell) pepper, cucumber and
chilli powder. Season to taste.

3 To make the Blue Cheese, Celery &
Chive Filling, mix the soft cheese and
fromage frais together until smooth.
Add the blue cheese, celery and
chives. Season to taste with celery
salt and pepper.

4 To make the Mushrooms in Spicy
Tomato Sauce, melt the butter or
margarine in a small frying pan (skillet).
Add the mushrooms and cook gently
for 3–4 minutes. Remove from the heat
and stir in the yogurt, tomato purée
(paste) and curry powder. Season.

5 Wrap the cooked potatoes in foil
and keep warm at the edge of the
barbecue. Serve the fillings sprinkled
with paprika or chilli powder or herbs.

Side Dishes & Salads

An ideal accompaniment complements the main dish both visually and nutritionally. Many of the main dishes contained in this book will be rich in protein, therefore the side dishes in this chapter have been designed to be a little lighter in texture, while containing other important nutrients and lots of flavour and colour. The recipes contained within this chapter are perfect accompaniments for all occasions. A salad also makes a refreshing accompaniment to the main course. You could even serve two or three salads together as a complete meal – they are a good source of vitamins and minerals. Always use the freshest possible ingredients for maximum flavour and texture.

Pepperonata

A delicious mixture of (bell) peppers and onions, cooked
with tomatoes and herbs for a rich side dish.

Serves 4
4 tbsp olive oil
1 onion, halved and finely sliced
2 red (bell) peppers, cut into strips
2 green (bell) peppers, cut into strips
2 yellow (bell) peppers, cut into strips
2 garlic cloves, crushed
2 x 400 g/14 oz cans chopped tomatoes, drained
2 tbsp chopped coriander (cilantro)
2 tbsp chopped pitted black olives
salt and pepper

1 Heat the oil in a large frying pan (skillet). Add the onion and sauté for 5 minutes, stirring until just beginning to colour.

2 Add the (bell) peppers and garlic to the pan and cook for a further 3–4 minutes. Stir in the tomatoes and coriander (cilantro) and season well. Cover the pan and cook the vegetables gently for about 30 minutes or until the mixture is dry.

3 Stir in the olives and serve immediately.

COOK'S TIP

Stir the vegetables occasionally during the 30 minutes cooking time to prevent them sticking to the bottom of the pan. If the liquid has not evaporated by the end of the cooking time, remove the lid and boil rapidly until the dish is dry.

Cheese & Potato Layer Bake

This really is a great side dish, perfect for serving
with main meals cooked in the oven.

Serves 4
450 g/1 lb potatoes
1 leek, sliced
3 garlic cloves, crushed
50 g/1^3/$_4$ oz/^{1}/$_2$ cup Cheddar, grated
50 g/1^3/$_4$ oz/^{1}/$_2$ cup Mozzarella, grated
25 g/1 oz/^{1}/$_4$ cup Parmesan cheese, grated
2 tbsp chopped parsley
150 ml/^{1}/$_4$ pint/^{2}/$_3$ cup single (light) cream
150 ml/^{1}/$_4$ pint/^{2}/$_3$ cup milk
salt and pepper
freshly chopped flat-leaf parsley, to garnish

1 Cook the potatoes in a saucepan of boiling salted water for 10 minutes. Drain well. Cut the potatoes into thin slices. Arrange a layer of potatoes in the base of an ovenproof dish. Layer with a little of the leek, garlic, cheese and parsley. Season well.

2 Repeat the layers until all of the ingredients have been used, finishing with a layer of cheese on top.

3 Mix the cream and milk together, season and pour over the potato layers. Cook in a preheated oven, 160°C/325°F/Gas Mark 3, for 1–1¼ hours or until golden brown and bubbling and the potatoes are cooked through. Garnish and serve.

COOK'S TIP

Prepare the dish in advance, cover and chill for up to 12 hours until required.

Greek Green Beans

This dish contains many Greek flavours such as lemon, garlic, oregano and olives, for a really flavourful recipe.

Serves 4

400 g/14 oz can haricot (navy) beans, drained
1 tbsp olive oil
3 garlic cloves, crushed
450 ml/³/₄ pint/2 cups vegetable stock
1 bay leaf
2 sprigs oregano
1 tbsp tomato purée (paste)
juice of 1 lemon
1 small red onion, chopped
25 g/1 oz pitted black olives, halved
salt and pepper

1 Put the haricot (navy) beans in a flameproof casserole dish.

2 Add the olive oil and garlic and cook over a gentle heat, stirring occasionally, for 4–5 minutes.

3 Add the stock, bay leaf, oregano, tomato purée (paste), lemon juice and red onion, cover and simmer for about 1 hour or until the sauce has thickened.

4 Stir in the olives, season with salt and pepper to taste and serve.

COOK'S TIP

This dish may be made in advance and served cold with crusty bread, if preferred.

Cauliflower & Broccoli with Herb Sauce

Whole baby cauliflowers are used in this recipe. Try to find them if you can, if not use large bunches of florets.

Serves 4
2 baby cauliflowers
225 g/8 oz broccoli
salt and pepper
SAUCE
8 tbsp olive oil
4 tbsp butter or vegetarian margarine
2 tsp grated root ginger
juice and rind of 2 lemons
5 tbsp chopped coriander (cilantro)
5 tbsp grated Cheddar

1 Cut the cauliflowers in half and the broccoli into very large florets. Cook the cauliflower and broccoli in a saucepan of boiling salted water for 10 minutes. Drain well and transfer to a shallow ovenproof dish.

2 To make the sauce, put the oil and butter or margarine in a pan and heat gently until the butter melts. Add the ginger, lemon juice and rind and coriander (cilantro) and simmer for 2–3 minutes.

3 Pour the sauce over the vegetables in the dish and sprinkle the cheese on top. Cook under a hot grill (broiler) for 2–3 minutes or until the cheese is bubbling and serve immediately.

COOK'S VARIATION

Lime or orange could be used instead of the lemon for a fruity and refreshing sauce.

Pesto Potatoes

Pesto sauce is more commonly used as a pasta sauce but is delicious served over potatoes as well.

Serves 4
900 g/2 lb small new potatoes
75 g/2³/₄ oz fresh basil
2 tbsp pine nuts
3 garlic cloves, crushed
100 ml/3¹/₂ fl oz/¹/₂ cup olive oil
75 g/2³/₄ oz/³/₄ cup freshly grated Parmesan cheese and Pecorino cheese, mixed
salt and pepper
fresh basil sprigs, to garnish

1 Cook the potatoes in a saucepan of boiling salted water for 15 minutes or until tender. Drain well, transfer to a warm serving dish and keep warm.

2 Meanwhile, put the basil, pine nuts, garlic and a little salt and pepper to taste in a food processor. Blend for 30 seconds, adding the oil gradually, until smooth.

3 Remove the mixture from the food processor and stir in the cheeses.

4 Spoon the pesto sauce over the potatoes and mix well. Garnish with fresh basil sprigs and serve immediately.

COOK'S TIP

This sauce would also make a great salad dressing for a crisp green salad.

Sweet & Sour Aubergines (Eggplants)

This is a dish of Persian origin, not Chinese as it sounds. Aubergines (eggplants) are fried and mixed with tomatoes, mint, sugar and vinegar for a really intense flavour.

Serves 4
2 large aubergines (eggplant), cubed
6 tbsp olive oil
4 garlic cloves, crushed
1 onion, cut into eight
4 large tomatoes, seeded and chopped
3 tbsp chopped mint
150 ml/¼ pint/²⁄₃ cup vegetable stock
4 tsp brown sugar
2 tbsp red wine vinegar
1 tsp chilli flakes
salt and pepper
fresh mint sprigs, to garnish

1 Put the aubergines (eggplants) in a colander, sprinkle with salt and leave to stand for 30 minutes. Rinse under cold running water and drain well. Pat dry with absorbent kitchen paper.

2 Heat the oil in a large frying pan (skillet) and sauté the aubergine (eggplant), stirring constantly for 1–2 minutes.

3 Stir in the garlic and onion and cook for a further 2–3 minutes.

4 Stir in the tomatoes, mint and stock, cover and cook for 15–20 minutes or until the vegetables are tender.

5 Stir in the sugar, vinegar and chilli, season with salt and pepper to taste and cook for 2–3 minutes. Garnish with fresh mint sprigs and serve.

Spicy Lentils & Spinach

This is quite a filling dish, and should be served with a light main course.
Green split peas are a type of lentil (legume).

Serves 4
225 g/8 oz/1¼ cups green split peas
900 g/2 lb spinach
4 tbsp vegetable oil
1 onion, halved and sliced
1 tsp grated root ginger
1 tsp ground cumin
½ tsp chilli powder
½ tsp ground coriander
2 garlic cloves, crushed
300 ml/½ pint/1¼ cups vegetable stock
salt and pepper
fresh coriander (cilantro) sprigs and lime wedges, to garnish

1 Rinse the peas under cold running water. Transfer to a mixing bowl, cover with cold water and leave to soak for 2 hours. Drain well.

2 Meanwhile, cook the spinach in a large saucepan for 5 minutes until wilted. Drain well and roughly chop.

3 Heat the oil in a large saucepan and sauté the onion, spices and garlic for 2–3 minutes, stirring well.

4 Add the lentils and spinach and stir in the stock. Cover and simmer for 10–15 minutes or until the lentils are cooked and the liquid has been absorbed. Season, garnish and serve.

COOK'S TIP

Once the lentils have been added, stir occasionally to prevent them from sticking to the pan.

Mini Vegetable Puff Pastry Cases

These are ideal with a more formal meal as they take
a little time to prepare and look really impressive.

Serves 4
450 g/1 lb puff pastry
1 egg, beaten

FILLING

225 g/8 oz sweet potato, cubed
100 g/3^1/$_2$ oz baby asparagus spears
2 tbsp butter or vegetarian margarine
1 leek, sliced
2 small open-cup mushrooms, sliced
1 tsp lime juice
1 tsp chopped thyme
pinch of dried mustard
salt and pepper

1 Cut the pastry into 4 equal pieces. Roll each piece out on a lightly floured surface to form a 12.5 cm/ 5 inch square. Place on a dampened baking sheet (cookie sheet) and score a smaller 7.5 cm/2.5 inch square inside. Brush with beaten egg and cook in a preheated oven, 200°C/ 400°F/Gas Mark 6, for 20 minutes or until risen and golden brown.

2 Remove from the oven, then carefully cut out the central square of pastry, lift out and reserve.

3 To make the filling, cook the sweet potato in a saucepan of boiling water for 15 minutes, then drain well. Blanch the asparagus in a saucepan of boiling water for 10 minutes or until tender. Drain and reserve.

4 Melt the butter or margarine in a saucepan and sauté the leek and mushrooms for 2–3 minutes. Add the lime juice, thyme and mustard, season well and stir in the sweet potatoes and asparagus. Spoon into the pastry cases, top with the reserved pastry squares and serve immediately.

COOK'S TIP

Use a colourful selection of any vegetables you have to hand for this recipe.

Steamed Vegetables with Vermouth

Serve these vegetables in their paper parcels to retain the juices.
The result is truly delicious.

Serves 4
1 carrot, cut into batons
1 fennel bulb, sliced
100 g/3¹/₂ oz courgettes (zucchini), sliced
1 red (bell) pepper, sliced
4 small onions, halved
8 tbsp vermouth
4 tbsp lime juice
zest of 1 lime
pinch of paprika
4 sprigs tarragon
salt and pepper
fresh tarragon sprigs, to garnish

1 Place all of the vegetables in a large bowl and mix well.

2 Cut 4 large squares of greaseproof paper and place a quarter of the vegetables in the centre of each. Bring the sides of the paper up and pinch together to make an open parcel.

3 Mix the vermouth, lime juice, lime zest and paprika and pour a quarter of the mixture into each parcel. Season and add a tarragon sprig to each. Pinch the tops of the parcels together to seal.

4 Place the vegetable parcels in a steamer, cover and cook for 15–20 minutes or until the vegetables are tender. Garnish and serve.

COOK'S TIP

Seal the parcels well to prevent them opening during cooking and causing the juices to evaporate.

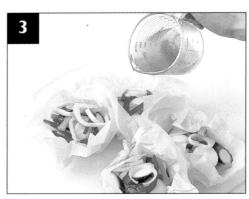

Curried Cauliflower & Spinach

The contrast in colour in this recipe makes it very appealing to the eye, especially as the cauliflower is lightly coloured with yellow turmeric.

Serves 4
1 medium cauliflower
6 tbsp vegetable oil
1 tsp mustard seeds
1 tsp ground cumin
1 tsp garam masala
1 tsp turmeric
2 garlic cloves, crushed
1 onion, halved and sliced
1 green chilli, sliced
450 g/1 lb spinach
85 ml/3 fl oz/6 tbsp vegetable stock
1 tbsp chopped coriander (cilantro)
salt and pepper
coriander (cilantro) sprigs, to garnish

1 Break the cauliflower into small florets.

2 Heat the oil in a deep flameproof casserole dish. Add the mustard seeds and cook until they begin to pop. Stir in the remaining spices, the garlic, onion and chilli and cook for 2–3 minutes, stirring.

3 Add the cauliflower, spinach, stock, coriander (cilantro) and seasoning, cover and cook over a gentle heat for 15 minutes or until the cauliflower is tender. Uncover the dish and boil for 1 minute to thicken the juices. Garnish with fresh coriander (cilantro) and serve.

COOK'S VARIATION

Broccoli may be used instead of the cauliflower, if preferred.

Soufﬂéd Cheesy Potato Fries

These small potato chunks are mixed in a creamy cheese sauce and
fried in oil until deliciously golden brown.

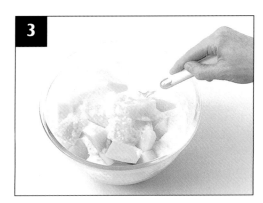

Serves 4

900 g/2 lb potatoes, cut into chunks
150 ml/¼ pint/⅔ cup double (heavy) cream
75 g/2¾ oz/¾ cup Gruyère cheese, grated
pinch of cayenne pepper
2 egg whites
oil, for deep-frying
salt and pepper
chopped flat-leaf parsley and grated
vegetarian cheese, to garnish

1 Cook the potatoes in a saucepan of
boiling salted water for 10 minutes.
Drain well and pat dry with absorbent
kitchen paper.

2 Mix the cream and cheese in a large
bowl. Stir in the cayenne pepper and
season to taste.

3 Whisk the egg whites until stiff
peaks form. Fold into the cheese
mixture until fully incorporated. Add
the potatoes, turning to coat.

4 Heat the oil for deep-frying to
180°C/350°F or until a cube of bread
browns in 30 seconds. Remove the
potatoes from the cheese mixture
with a slotted spoon and cook in the
oil, in batches, for 3–4 minutes or
until golden. Transfer to a serving
dish, garnish and serve.

COOK'S VARIATION

Add other flavourings, such as
grated nutmeg or curry powder, to
the cream and cheese.

Baked Celery with Cream & Pecans

This dish is topped with breadcrumbs for a crunchy topping, underneath
which is hidden a creamy celery and pecan mixture.

Serves 4
1 head of celery
$^1/_2$ tsp ground cumin
$^1/_2$ tsp ground coriander
1 garlic clove, crushed
1 red onion, thinly sliced
50 g/1$^3/_4$ oz/$^1/_2$ cup pecan nut halves
150 ml/$^1/_4$ pint/$^2/_3$ cup vegetable stock
150 ml/$^1/_4$ pint/$^2/_3$ cup single (light) cream
50 g/1$^3/_4$ oz fresh wholemeal (whole wheat) breadcrumbs
25 g/1 oz/$^1/_4$ cup Parmesan cheese, grated
salt and pepper
celery leaves, to garnish

1 Trim the celery and cut into matchsticks. Place the celery in an ovenproof dish with the ground cumin, coriander, garlic, onion and pecan nuts.

2 Mix the stock and cream together and pour over the vegetables. Season with salt and pepper to taste.

3 Mix the breadcrumbs and cheese together and sprinkle over the top to cover the vegetables. Cook in a preheated oven, 200°C/400°F/Gas Mark 6, for 40 minutes or until the vegetables are tender and the top crispy. Garnish with celery leaves and serve at once.

COOK'S VARIATION

You could use carrots or courgettes (zucchini) instead of the celery, if you prefer.

Beans in Lemon & Herb Sauce

Use a variety of beans if possible, although this recipe is
perfectly acceptable with just one type of bean.

Serves 4

900 g/2 lb mixed green beans,
such as broad (fava) beans,
French (green) beans, runner beans

65 g/2¹/₂ oz/¹/₂ cup butter or
vegetarian margarine

4 tsp plain (all-purpose) flour

300 ml/¹/₂ pint/1¹/₄ cups vegetable stock

85 ml/3 fl oz dry white wine

6 tbsp single (light) cream

3 tbsp chopped mixed herbs

2 tbsp lemon juice

zest of 1 lemon

salt and pepper

1 Cook the beans in a saucepan of
boiling salted water for 10 minutes or
until tender. Drain and place in a
warm serving dish.

2 Meanwhile, melt the butter in a
saucepan. Add the flour and cook for
1 minute. Remove the pan from the
heat and gradually stir in the stock
and wine. Return the pan to the heat
and bring to the boil.

3 Remove the pan from the heat once
again and stir in the cream, herbs,
lemon juice and rind. Season to taste.
Pour the sauce over the beans, mixing
well. Serve.

COOK'S TIP

Use a wide variety of herbs for
flavour, such as rosemary, thyme,
tarragon and sage.

Indian Spiced Potatoes & Spinach

This is a classic Indian accompaniment for
curries or plainer main vegetable dishes.

Serves 4
3 tbsp vegetable oil
1 red onion, sliced
2 garlic cloves, crushed
$^1/_2$ tsp chilli powder
2 tsp ground coriander
1 tsp ground cumin
150 ml/$^1/_4$ pint/$^2/_3$ cup vegetable stock
300 g/10$^1/_2$ oz/$^2/_3$ cup potatoes, cubed
450 g/1 lb baby spinach
1 red chilli, sliced
salt and pepper

1 Heat the oil in a frying pan (skillet)
and sauté the onion and garlic for
2–3 minutes, stirring. Stir in the chilli
powder, ground coriander and cumin
and cook for a further 30 seconds.

2 Add the stock, potato and spinach
and bring to the boil. Reduce the
heat, cover and simmer for about
10 minutes or until the potatoes are
cooked through.

3 Uncover, season, add the chilli and
cook for a further 2–3 minutes. Serve.

COOK'S VARIATION

Add other vegetables,
such as chopped tomatoes, for
colour and flavour.

Bulgar Pilau

Bulgar wheat is very easy to use and is a delicious alternative to rice, having a distinctive nutty flavour.

Serves 4

75 g/2¾ oz/6 tbsp butter or vegetarian margarine

1 red onion, halved and sliced

2 garlic cloves, crushed

350 g/12 oz/2 cups bulgar wheat

175 g/6 oz tomatoes, seeded and chopped

50 g/1¾ oz baby corn cobs, halved lengthwise

75 g/2¾ oz small broccoli florets

850 ml/1½ pints/3¾ cups vegetable stock

2 tbsp clear honey

50 g/1¾ oz sultanas (golden raisins)

50 g/1¾ oz pine nuts

½ tsp ground cinnamon

½ tsp ground cumin

salt and pepper

sliced spring onions (scallions), to garnish

1 Melt the butter or margarine in a large flameproof casserole dish.

2 Add the onion and garlic and sauté for 2–3 minutes, stirring occasionally.

3 Add the bulgar wheat, tomatoes, corn cobs, broccoli and stock and bring to the boil. Reduce the heat, cover and cook for 15–20 minutes, stirring occasionally.

4 Stir in the honey, sultanas (golden raisins), nuts, ground cinnamon, cumin and salt and pepper to taste, mixing well. Remove the casserole from the heat, cover and leave for 10 minutes.

5 Spoon the bulgar pilau into a warm serving dish.

6 Garnish the bulgar pilau with sliced spring onions (scallions) and serve immediately.

COOK'S TIP

The dish is left to stand for 10 minutes in order for the bulgar to finish cooking and the flavours to mingle.

Carrot, Orange & Poppy Seed Bake

The poppy seeds add texture and flavour to this recipe,
and counteract the slightly sweet flavour of the carrots.

Serves 4
675 g/1 lb 8 oz carrots, cut into thin strips
1 leek, sliced
300 ml/½ pint/1¼ cups fresh orange juice
2 tbsp clear honey
1 garlic clove, crushed
1 tsp mixed spice
2 tsp chopped thyme
1 tbsp poppy seeds
salt and pepper
fresh thyme sprigs and orange zest, to garnish

1 Cook the carrots and leek in a saucepan of boiling salted water for 5–6 minutes. Drain well and transfer to a shallow baking dish.

2 Mix together the orange juice, honey, garlic, mixed spice and thyme and pour the mixture over the vegetables. Season to taste with salt and pepper.

3 Cover and cook in a preheated oven, 180°C/350°F/Gas Mark 4, for 30 minutes or until the vegetables are tender. Remove the lid and sprinkle with poppy seeds. Garnish and serve.

COOK'S TIP

Lemon or lime juice could be used instead of the orange juice if you prefer. Garnish with lemon or lime zest.

Aubergine (Eggplant) & Courgette (Zucchini) Galette

This is a dish of aubergine (eggplant) and courgettes (zucchini) layered with a quick tomato sauce and melted cheese.

Serves 4
2 large aubergines (eggplants), sliced
4 courgettes (zucchini)
2 x 400 g/14 oz cans chopped tomatoes, drained
2 tbsp tomato purée (paste)
2 garlic cloves, crushed
50 ml/2 fl oz/4 tbsp olive oil
1 tsp caster (superfine) sugar
2 tbsp chopped basil
olive oil, for frying
225 g/8 oz Mozzarella cheese, sliced
salt and pepper
fresh basil leaves, to garnish

1 Put the aubergine (eggplant) slices in a colander and sprinkle with salt. Leave to stand for 30 minutes, then rinse well under cold water and drain. Thinly slice the courgettes (zucchini).

2 Meanwhile, put the tomatoes, tomato purée (paste), garlic, olive oil, sugar and chopped basil into a pan and simmer for 20 minutes or until reduced by half. Season well.

3 Heat 2 tablespoons of olive oil in a large frying pan (skillet) and cook the aubergine (eggplant) slices for 2–3 minutes until just beginning to brown. Remove from the pan.

4 Add a further 2 tablespoons of oil to the pan and fry the courgette (zucchini) slices until browned.

5 Lay half of the aubergine (eggplant) slices in the base of an ovenproof dish. Top with half of the tomato sauce and the courgettes (zucchini) and then half of the Mozzarella. Repeat the layers and bake in a preheated oven, 180°C/350°F/Gas Mark 4, for 45–50 minutes or until the vegetables are tender. Garnish with basil leaves and serve.

COOK'S TIP

Add a little more oil when frying the vegetables, if required and fry in batches to brown all of the slices evenly. The aubergine (eggplant) will absorb the oil quickly.

Red Onion, Cherry Tomato & Pasta Salad

Pasta tastes perfect in this lively salad, dressed with
red wine vinegar, lemon juice, basil and olive oil.

Serves 4

175 g/6 oz/1½ cups pasta shapes

1 yellow (bell) pepper, halved and
deseeded

2 small courgettes
(zucchini), sliced

1 red onion, sliced thinly

125 g/4½ oz cherry tomatoes, halved

salt

sprigs of fresh basil, to garnish

DRESSING

4 tbsp olive oil

2 tbsp red wine vinegar

2 tsp lemon juice

1 tsp Dijon mustard

½ tsp caster (superfine) sugar

handful of fresh basil leaves,
torn into small pieces

salt and pepper

1 Cook the pasta in a saucepan of
lightly salted boiling water for about
8 minutes, or until just tender.

2 Meanwhile, place the (bell) pepper
halves, skin-side uppermost, under a
preheated grill (broiler) until they just
begin to char. Leave them to cool,
then peel and slice them into strips.

3 Cook the courgettes (zucchini)
in a small amount of lightly salted
boiling water for 3–4 minutes, until
cooked, yet still crunchy. Drain and
refresh under cold running water to
cool quickly.

4 To make the dressing, mix together
the olive oil, red wine vinegar, lemon
juice, mustard and sugar. Season
well with salt and pepper to taste.
Add the basil leaves and mix well.

5 Drain the pasta well and transfer it
to a large serving bowl. Add the
dressing and toss well. Add the (bell)
pepper, courgettes (zucchini), onion
and cherry tomatoes, stirring to
combine. Cover and leave at room
temperature for about 30 minutes to
allow the flavours to develop.

6 Garnish the red onion, cherry
tomato and pasta salad with sprigs of
fresh basil and serve.

Courgette (Zucchini) & Mint Salad

This salad uses lots of green-coloured ingredients which look and taste
wonderful with the minty yogurt dressing.

Serves 4

2 courgettes (zucchini), cut into sticks

100 g/3¹/₂ oz French (green) beans,
cut into three

1 green (bell) pepper, cut into strips

2 celery sticks, sliced

1 bunch watercress

DRESSING

200 ml/7 fl oz/³/₄ cup natural yogurt

1 garlic clove, crushed

2 tbsp chopped mint

pepper

1 Cook the courgettes (zucchini) and
beans in a saucepan of salted boiling
water for 7–8 minutes. Drain and
leave to cool completely.

2 Mix the vegetables with the (bell)
pepper, celery and watercress in a
large bowl.

3 To make the dressing, mix the
yogurt, garlic, mint and pepper to
taste in a bowl.

4 Spoon the dressing on to the salad
and serve immediately.

COOK'S TIP

The salad must be served as soon as
the yogurt dressing has been added
– the dressing will start to separate
if kept for any length of time.

Goat's Cheese Salad

A delicious hot salad of melting goat's cheese over sliced
tomato and basil on a base of hot ciabatta bread.

Serves 4
3 tbsp olive oil
1 tbsp white wine vinegar
1 tsp black olive paste
1 garlic clove, crushed
1 tsp chopped fresh thyme
1 ciabatta loaf
4 small tomatoes
12 fresh basil leaves
2 × 125 g/4¹/₂ oz logs goat's cheese

TO SERVE

mixed salad leaves (greens), including
rocket (arugula) and radicchio

1 Mix the oil, vinegar, olive paste,
garlic and thyme together in a screw-
top jar and shake vigorously.

2 Cut the ciabatta in half horizontally,
then in half vertically to make
4 pieces.

3 Drizzle some of the dressing over
the bread then arrange the tomatoes
and basil leaves on top.

4 Cut each roll of goat's cheese into
6 slices and lay 3 slices on each piece
of ciabatta.

5 Brush with some of the dressing
and place in a preheated oven,
230°C/450°F/Gas Mark 8, for
5–6 minutes until just turning
brown at the edges.

6 Pour the remaining dressing over
the salad leaves (greens) and serve
with the baked bread.

Alfalfa, Beetroot & Spinach Salad

This is a really refreshing salad that must be assembled just before serving
to prevent all of the ingredients being tainted pink by the beetroot.

Serves 4
100 g/3$\frac{1}{2}$ oz baby spinach
75 g/2$\frac{3}{4}$ oz alfalfa sprouts
2 celery sticks, sliced
4 cooked beetroot, cut into eight
DRESSING
4 tbsp olive oil
1$\frac{1}{2}$ tbsp garlic wine vinegar
1 garlic clove, crushed
2 tsp clear honey
1 tbsp chopped chives

1 Place the spinach and alfalfa sprouts in a large bowl and mix together.

2 Add the celery and mix well.

3 Toss in the beetroot and mix well.

4 To make the dressing, mix the oil, wine vinegar, garlic, honey and chopped chives.

5 Pour the dressing over the salad, toss well and serve immediately.

COOK'S TIP

Alfalfa sprouts should be available from most supermarkets, if not, use beansprouts instead.

Moroccan Orange & Couscous Salad

Couscous is a type of semolina made from durum wheat. It is wonderful
in salads as it readily absorbs the flavour of the dressing.

Serves 4-6

175 g/6 oz/2 cups couscous

1 bunch spring onions (scallions),
trimmed and chopped finely

1 small green (bell) pepper, deseeded
and chopped

10 cm/4 inch piece cucumber,
chopped

175 g/6 oz can chick-peas (garbanzo
beans), rinsed and drained

60 g/2 oz/²/₃ cup sultanas
(golden raisins) or raisins

2 oranges

salt and pepper

mixed salad leaves, to serve

sprigs of fresh mint, to garnish

DRESSING

finely grated rind of 1 orange

1 tbsp chopped fresh mint

150 ml/¹/₄ pint/²/₃ cup
natural yogurt

1 Place the couscous in a large bowl,
cover with boiling water and leave
to soak for about 15 minutes or until
the grains have swelled. Stir with a
fork to separate the grains.

2 Add the spring onions (scallions),
green (bell) pepper, cucumber, chick-
peas (garbanzo beans) and sultanas
(golden raisins) or raisins to the
couscous, stirring to combine. Season
well with salt and pepper.

3 To make the dressing, mix the
orange rind, mint and yogurt. Pour
over the couscous mixture and
stir well.

4 Using a sharp serrated knife,
remove the peel and pith from the
oranges.

5 Cut the orange flesh into segments,
removing all the membrane.

6 Arrange the lettuce leaves on
4 serving plates. Divide the couscous
mixture between the plates and
arrange the orange segments on top.
Garnish with sprigs of fresh mint
and serve.

Aubergine (Eggplant) Salad

This salad uses tahini paste (sesame seed paste) as a flavouring for the dressing, which complements the aubergine (eggplant).

Serves 4
1 large aubergine (eggplant)
3 tbsp tahini paste (sesame seed paste)
juice and rind of 1 lemon
1 garlic clove, crushed
pinch of paprika
1 tbsp chopped coriander (cilantro)
salt and pepper
Little Gem lettuce leaves

DRESSING

strips of pimiento
lemon wedges
toasted sesame seeds

1 Cut the aubergine (eggplant) in half and place, skin-side uppermost, on an oiled baking sheet (cookie sheet). Cook in a preheated oven, 230°C/ 450°F/Gas Mark 8, for 10–15 minutes. Remove from the oven and let cool.

2 Cut the aubergine (eggplant) into cubes and reserve. Mix the tahini paste (sesame seed paste), lemon juice and rind, garlic, paprika and coriander (cilantro) together. Season and stir in the aubergine (eggplant).

3 Line a serving dish with lettuce leaves and spoon the salad into the centre. Top with the dressing, garnish with pimiento slices, lemon wedges and toasted sesame seeds and serve.

COOK'S TIP

Tahini (sesame seed) paste is available from most health food shops.

Carrot & Cashew Nut Coleslaw

This simple salad has a dressing made from poppy seeds
pan-fried in sesame oil to bring out their flavour.

Serves 4
1 large carrot, grated
1 small onion, chopped finely
2 celery stalks, chopped
$^1/_4$ small, hard white cabbage, shredded
1 tbsp chopped fresh parsley
4 tbsp sesame oil
$^1/_2$ tsp poppy seeds
60 g/2 oz/$^1/_2$ cup cashew nuts
2 tbsp white wine or cider vinegar
salt and pepper
chopped parsley, to garnish

1 In a large salad bowl, mix together the carrot, onion, celery and cabbage. Stir in the chopped parsley and season with salt and pepper.

2 Heat the sesame oil in a saucepan with a lid. Add the poppy seeds and cover the pan. Cook over a medium-high heat until the seeds start to make a popping sound. Remove from the heat and leave to cool.

3 Scatter the cashew nuts on to a baking sheet (cookie sheet). Place them under a medium-hot grill (broiler) and toast until lightly browned, being careful not to burn them. Leave to cool.

4 Add the vinegar to the oil and poppy seeds, mix well then pour over the carrot mixture. Add the cooled cashew nuts and toss together to coat with the dressing. Garnish the salad with sprigs of parsley and serve immediately.

Gado Gado

This is a very well known Indonesian salad of mixed
vegetables with a peanut dressing.

Serves 4
100 g/3½ oz/1 cup white cabbage, shredded
100 g/3½ oz French (green) beans, cut into 3
100 g/3½ oz carrots, cut into matchsticks
100 g/3½ oz cauliflower florets
100 g/3½ oz beansprouts
DRESSING
100 ml/3½ fl oz/½ cup vegetable oil
100 g/3½ oz/1 cup unsalted peanuts
2 garlic cloves, crushed
1 small onion, finely chopped
½ tsp chilli powder
⅓ tsp light brown sugar
425 ml/¾ pint/2 cups water
juice of ½ lemon
salt
sliced spring onions (scallions), to garnish

1 Cook the vegetables separately in a
saucepan of salted boiling water for
4–5 minutes, drain well and chill.

2 To make the dressing, heat the oil
in a frying pan (skillet) and fry the
peanuts for 3–4 minutes, turning.
Remove from the pan with a slotted
spoon and leave to drain on absorbent
kitchen paper. Grind the peanuts in a
blender or crush with a rolling pin
until a fine mixture is formed.

3 Pour all but 1 tablespoon of oil
from the pan and fry the garlic and
onions for 1 minute. Add the chilli
powder, sugar, a pinch of salt and the
water and bring to the boil.

4 Stir in the peanuts. Reduce the heat
and simmer for 4–5 minutes until the
sauce thickens. Add the lemon juice
and leave to cool.

5 Arrange the vegetables in a serving
dish and spoon the peanut dressing
into the centre. Garnish and serve.

COOK'S TIP

If necessary, you can prepare
the peanut dressing in advance
and then store it in the
refrigerator for up to 12 hours
before serving.

Salad with Garlic Yogurt Dressing

This is a very quick and refreshing salad using a whole range of colourful ingredients which make it look as good as it tastes.

Serves 4

75 g/2¾ oz cucumber,
cut into sticks

6 spring onions (scallions), halved

2 tomatoes, seeded
and cut into eight

1 yellow (bell) pepper, cut into strips

2 celery sticks, cut into strips

4 radishes, quartered

75 g/2¾ oz rocket

1 tbsp chopped mint, to serve

DRESSING

2 tbsp lemon juice

1 garlic clove, crushed

150 ml/¼ pint/⅔ cup natural yogurt

2 tbsp olive oil

salt and pepper

1 Mix the cucumber, spring onions (scallions), tomatoes, (bell) pepper, celery, radishes and rocket together in a large serving bowl.

2 To make the dressing, stir the lemon juice, garlic, yogurt and oil together and season well.

3 Spoon the dressing over the salad and toss to mix. Sprinkle with chopped mint and serve.

COOK'S TIP

Do not toss the dressing into the salad until just before serving, otherwise it will turn soggy.

Three-Way Potato Salad

There's nothing to beat the flavour of new potatoes,
served just warm in a delicious dressing.

Serves 4
450 g/1 lb new potatoes, for each dressing
fresh herbs, to garnish
salt and pepper

LIGHT CURRY DRESSING

1 tbsp vegetable oil
1 tbsp medium curry paste
1 small onion, chopped
1 tbsp mango chutney, chopped
6 tbsp natural yogurt
3 tbsp single (light) cream
2 tbsp mayonnaise
1 tbsp single (light) cream, to garnish

VINAIGRETTE DRESSING

6 tbsp hazelnut oil
3 tbsp cider vinegar
1 tsp wholegrain mustard
1 tsp caster (superfine) sugar
few basil leaves, torn into shreds

PARSLEY, SPRING ONION (SCALLION) & SOURED CREAM DRESSING

150 ml/¼ pint/⅔ cup soured cream
3 tbsp light mayonnaise
4 spring onions (scallions), trimmed and chopped finely
1 tbsp chopped fresh parsley

1 To make the Light Curry Dressing, heat the vegetable oil in a frying pan (skillet). Add the curry paste and onion and fry together, stirring frequently, until the onion is soft. Remove the pan from the heat and leave to cool slightly.

2 Mix together the mango chutney, yogurt, cream and mayonnaise. Add the curry mixture and blend together. Season with salt and pepper.

3 To make the Vinaigrette Dressing, whisk the hazelnut oil, cider vinegar, mustard, sugar and basil together in a small jug or bowl. Season with salt and pepper to taste.

4 To make the Parsley, Spring Onion (Scallion) and Soured Cream Dressing, combine all the ingredients, mixing well. Season with salt and pepper.

5 Cook the potatoes in a pan of lightly salted boiling water until just tender. Drain and leave to cool for 5 minutes. Add the chosen dressing, tossing to coat. Serve, garnished with fresh herbs, spooning a little single (light) cream on to the potatoes if you have used the curry dressing.

Bean, Avocado & Tomato Salad

This is a colourful salad with a Mexican theme, using beans, tomatoes and avocado.
The chilli dressing adds a little kick.

Serves 4

lollo rosso lettuce

2 ripe avocados

2 tsp lemon juice

4 medium tomatoes

1 onion

175 g/6 oz/2 cups mixed canned beans,
drained

DRESSING

4 tbsp olive oil

drop of chilli oil

2 tbsp garlic wine vinegar

pinch of caster (superfine) sugar

pinch of chilli powder

1 tbsp chopped parsley

1 Line a serving bowl with the
lettuce. Thinly slice the avocados and
sprinkle with lemon juice.

2 Thinly slice the tomato and onion.
Arrange the avocado, tomatoes and
onion around the salad bowl, leaving
a space in the centre.

3 Spoon the beans into the centre of
the salad and whisk the dressing
ingredients together. Pour the
dressing over the salad and serve.

COOK'S TIP

The lemon juice is sprinkled on
to the avocados to prevent
discoloration when in contact with
the air. For this reason the salad
should be prepared, assembled and
served quite quickly.

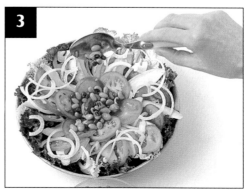

Grilled Vegetables with Mustard Dressing

The vegetables for this dish are best prepared well in advance and chilled before serving.

Serves 4

1 courgette (zucchini), sliced
1 yellow (bell) pepper, sliced
1 aubergine (eggplant), sliced
1 fennel bulb, cut into eight
1 red onion, cut into eight
16 cherry tomatoes
3 tbsp olive oil
1 garlic clove, crushed
fresh rosemary sprigs, to garnish

DRESSING

4 tbsp olive oil
2 tbsp balsamic vinegar
2 tsp chopped rosemary
1 tsp Dijon mustard
1 tsp clear honey
2 tsp lemon juice

1 Put all of the vegetables except for the cherry tomatoes on to a baking sheet (cookie sheet).

2 Mix the oil and garlic and brush over the vegetables. Cook under a medium-hot grill (broiler) for 10 minutes until tender and beginning to char. Leave to cool. Spoon the vegetables into a serving bowl.

3 Mix the dressing ingredients and pour over the vegetables. Cover and chill for 1 hour. Garnish and serve.

COOK'S TIP

This dish could also be served warm – heat the dressing in a pan and then toss into the vegetables.

Red Cabbage & Pear Salad

Red cabbage is much underused – it is a colourful and tasty ingredient which is perfect with fruits, such as pears or apples.

Serves 4

350 g/12 oz/4 cups red cabbage, finely shredded

2 Conference pears, thinly sliced

4 spring onions (scallions), sliced

1 carrot, grated

fresh chives, to garnish

lollo biondo leaves, to serve

DRESSING

4 tbsp pear juice

1 tsp wholegrain mustard

3 tbsp olive oil

1 tbsp garlic wine vinegar

1 tbsp chopped chives

1 Toss the cabbage, pears and spring onions (scallions) together.

2 Line a serving dish with lettuce leaves and spoon the cabbage and pear mixture into the centre.

3 Sprinkle the carrot into the centre of the cabbage to form a domed pile.

4 To make the dressing, mix the pear juice, mustard, oil, wine vinegar and chives together. Pour the dressing over the salad, garnish and serve immediately.

COOK'S TIP

Mix the salad just before serving to prevent the colour from the red cabbage bleeding into the other ingredients.

Three Bean Salad

Fresh dwarf (thin) green beans are combined with soya beans and
red kidney beans in a chive and tomato dressing to make a tasty salad.

Serves 4–6
3 tbsp olive oil
1 tbsp lemon juice
1 tbsp tomato purée (paste)
1 tbsp light malt vinegar
1 tbsp chopped fresh chives
175 g/6 oz dwarf (thin) green beans
400 g/14 oz can soya beans, rinsed and drained
400 g/14 oz can red kidney beans, rinsed and drained
2 tomatoes, chopped
4 spring onions (scallions), trimmed and chopped
125 g/4^1/$_2$ oz Feta cheese, cut into cubes
salt and pepper
mixed salad leaves (greens), to serve
chopped fresh chives, to garnish

1 Put the olive oil, lemon juice,
tomato purée (paste), vinegar and
chives into a large bowl and whisk
together until thoroughly combined.

2 Cook the dwarf (thin) green beans
in a little boiling, lightly salted water
until just cooked, about 4–5 minutes.
Drain, refresh under cold running
water and drain again. Pat dry with
paper towels.

COOK'S VARIATION

Try haricot (navy) beans or black-
eye beans (peas) instead of the soya
beans and red kidney beans.

3 Add the green beans, soya beans
and red kidney beans to the dressing,
stirring to mix.

4 Add the tomatoes, spring onions
(scallions) and Feta cheese to the bean
mixture, tossing gently to coat in the

dressing. Season well with salt and
pepper to taste.

5 Arrange the mixed salad leaves on
4 serving plates. Transfer the bean
salad to serving plates and garnish
with chopped chives.

Marinated Vegetable Salad

Lightly steamed vegetables taste superb served slightly warm in a marinade
of olive oil, white wine, vinegar and fresh herbs.

Serves 4–6

175 g/6 oz baby carrots, trimmed

2 celery hearts, cut into 4 pieces

125g/4$^{1}/_{2}$ oz sugar snap peas
or mangetout (snow peas)

1 fennel bulb, sliced

175 g/6 oz small asparagus spears

15 g/$^{1}/_{2}$ oz/1$^{1}/_{2}$ tbsp
sunflower seeds

sprigs of fresh dill, to garnish

DRESSING

4 tbsp olive oil

4 tbsp dry white wine

2 tbsp white wine vinegar

1 tbsp chopped fresh dill

1 tbsp chopped fresh parsley

salt and pepper

1 Steam the carrots, celery, sugar
snap peas or mangetout (snow peas),
fennel and asparagus over a pan of
gently boiling water until just tender.
It is important that they retain a
little 'bite'.

2 Meanwhile, make the dressing. Mix
together the olive oil, wine, vinegar
and chopped herbs. Season well with
salt and pepper.

3 When the vegetables are cooked,
transfer to a serving dish and pour
over the dressing at once. The hot
vegetables will absorb the flavour of
the dressing as they cool.

4 Scatter the sunflower seeds on to a
baking sheet (cookie sheet) and toast
them under a preheated grill (broiler)

until lightly browned. Sprinkle them
over the vegetables.

5 Serve the salad while the vegetables
are still slightly warm, garnished with
sprigs of fresh dill.

Goat's Cheese with Walnuts in Oil & Vinegar Dressing

This delicious salad combines soft goat's cheese with walnut halves, served on a bed of mixed salad leaves (greens).

Serves 4
90 g/3 oz/1 cup walnut halves
mixed salad leaves (greens)
125 g/4$\frac{1}{2}$ oz soft goat's cheese
snipped fresh chives, to garnish

DRESSING

6 tbsp walnut oil
3 tbsp white wine vinegar
1 tbsp clear honey
1 tsp Dijon mustard
pinch of ground ginger
salt and pepper

1 To make the dressing, whisk together the walnut oil, wine vinegar, honey, mustard and ginger in a small saucepan. Season to taste.

2 Heat the dressing gently, stirring occasionally, until warm. Add the walnut halves and continue to heat for 3–4 minutes.

3 Arrange the salad leaves on 4 serving plates and place spoonfuls of goat's cheese on top. Lift the walnut halves from the dressing with a perforated spoon, and scatter them over the salad.

4 Transfer the warm dressing to a small jug. Sprinkle chives over the salads and serve with the dressing.

COOK'S VARIATION

Use hazelnut oil and hazelnuts rather than walnut oil and walnuts.

Grilled Haloumi with Tomato & Red Onion Salad

Haloumi is a type of Cypriot cheese which remains firm and takes on a marvellous flavour when quickly barbecued.

Serves 4

500 g/1 lb 2 oz Haloumi, thickly sliced
fresh basil leaves, to garnish

ORANGE MARINADE

$^1/_2$ orange
50 ml/2 fl oz/$^1/_4$ cup olive oil
2 tbsp dry white wine
2 tbsp white wine vinegar
$^1/_2$ tbsp snipped fresh chives
$^1/_2$ tbsp chopped fresh marjoram
salt and pepper

SALAD

250 g/9 oz plum tomatoes
1 small red onion
4 tbsp olive oil
2 tbsp cider vinegar
1 tsp lemon juice
pinch of ground coriander
2 tsp chopped fresh coriander
(cilantro)
salt and pepper

1 To make the orange marinade, remove the rind from the orange with a zester, or grate it finely, then squeeze the juice. Mix the orange rind and juice with all the remaining ingredients in a small bowl, whisking together to combine.

2 Place the Haloumi in a shallow dish and pour the marinade over. Cover and chill for at least 30 minutes.

3 To make the salad, slice the tomatoes and arrange them on a serving plate. Slice the onion thinly and scatter over the tomatoes.

4 Whisk together the olive oil, vinegar, lemon juice, ground coriander and fresh coriander (cilantro). Season to taste with salt and pepper, then drizzle the dressing over the tomatoes and onions. Cover and chill.

5 Drain the marinade from the Haloumi. Cook the Haloumi over a hot barbecue for 2 minutes, turning once.

6 Transfer to plates, garnish and serve with the salad.

Desserts

Vegetarian or not, confirmed pudding lovers feel disappointed if there isn't a tempting dessert to finish off a good meal. Desserts help satisfy a deep-seated desire for something sweet, but they are often loaded with fat and sugar which are notorious for piling on the calories.

The recipes in this chapter offer the ideal solution. They are light but full of flavour, so you can still enjoy that sweet treat without the bulging waistline and distended feeling at the end of a meal. This is

particularly important after a vegetarian meal as the food can often be quite filling.

A lot of the recipes are based on fruit, which is the perfect ingredient for healthy desserts that are every bit as tempting as those based on lavish amounts of cream and butter. We've also included one or two indulgences such as Boston Chocolate Pie and Chocolate Chip Ice Cream.

Berry Cheesecake

Use a mixture of berries, such as blueberries, blackberries, raspberries and strawberries, for a really fruity cheesecake.

Serves 8
BASE
75 g/2³/₄ oz/6 tbsp vegetarian margarine
175 g/6 oz oatmeal biscuits
50 g/1³/₄ oz/³/₄ cup desiccated (shredded) coconut
TOPPING
1¹/₂ tsp gelozone
9 tbsp cold water
125 ml/4 fl oz/¹/₂ cup evaporated milk
1 egg
6 tbsp light brown sugar
450 g/1 lb/2 cups soft cream cheese
350 g/12 oz/1³/₄ cups mixed berries
2 tbsp clear honey

1 Put the margarine in a saucepan and heat until melted. Put the biscuits in a food processor and blend until smooth or crush finely with a rolling pin. Stir into the margarine with the coconut. Press the mixture into a base-lined 20 cm/8 inch spring-form tin and chill whilst preparing the filling.

2 To make the topping, sprinkle the gelozone over the water and stir to dissolve. Bring to the boil and boil for 2 minutes. Let cool slightly.

3 Put the milk, egg, sugar and soft cream cheese in a bowl and beat until smooth. Stir in 50 g/1³/₄ oz/¹/₄ cup of the berries. Stir in the gelozone in a stream, stirring constantly.

4 Spoon the mixture on to the biscuit base and return to the refrigerator for 2 hours or until set.

5 Remove the cheesecake from the tin (pan) and transfer to a serving plate. Arrange the remaining berries on top of the cheesecake and drizzle the honey over the top. Serve.

Apricot Brûlée

Serve this delicious dessert with crisp-baked meringues
for an extra-special occasion.

Serves 4

125 g/4^1/$_2$ oz/^{2}/$_3$ cup unsulphured
dried apricots

150 ml/^{1}/$_4$ pint/^{2}/$_3$ cup
orange juice

4 egg yolks

2 tbsp caster (superfine) sugar

150 ml/^{1}/$_4$ pint/^{2}/$_3$ cup
natural yogurt

150 ml/^{1}/$_4$ pint/^{2}/$_3$ cup double
(heavy) cream

1 tsp vanilla flavouring (extract)

90 g/3 oz/^{1}/$_2$ cup demerara sugar

meringues, to serve (optional)

1 Place the apricots in a bowl. Pour
the orange juice over the apricots and
leave to soak for at least 1 hour. Pour
into a small pan, bring slowly to the
boil and simmer for 20 minutes.
Purée in a blender or food processor,
or chop very finely and push through
a sieve (strainer).

2 Beat together the egg yolks and
sugar until the mixture is light and
fluffy. Place the yogurt in a small pan,
add the cream and vanilla and bring
to the boil over a low heat.

3 Pour the yogurt mixture over the
eggs, beating all the time, then
transfer to the top of a double boiler,
or place the bowl over a pan of
simmering water. Stir until the
custard thickens.

4 Divide the apricot mixture between
6 ramekins and spoon the custard on
top. Cool, then chill in the refrigerator.

5 Preheat the grill (broiler) to high.
Sprinkle the demerara sugar over the
custard and grill (broil) until the sugar
caramelizes. Set aside to cool.

6 To serve the apricot brûlée, crack
the hard caramel topping with the
back of a tablespoon. Serve with the
meringues, if using.

Cherry Pancakes

This dish can be made with either fresh pitted cherries or
canned cherries for speed.

Serves 4
FILLING
400 g/14 oz can pitted cherries, plus juice
¹/₂ tsp almond essence
¹/₂ tsp mixed spice
2 tbsp cornflour (cornstarch)
PANCAKES
100 g/3¹/₂ oz/³/₄ cup plain (all-purpose) flour
pinch of salt
2 tbsp chopped mint
1 egg
300 ml/¹/₂ pint/1¹/₄ cups milk
vegetable oil, for frying
icing (confectioners' sugar) and toasted flaked (slivered) almonds, to decorate

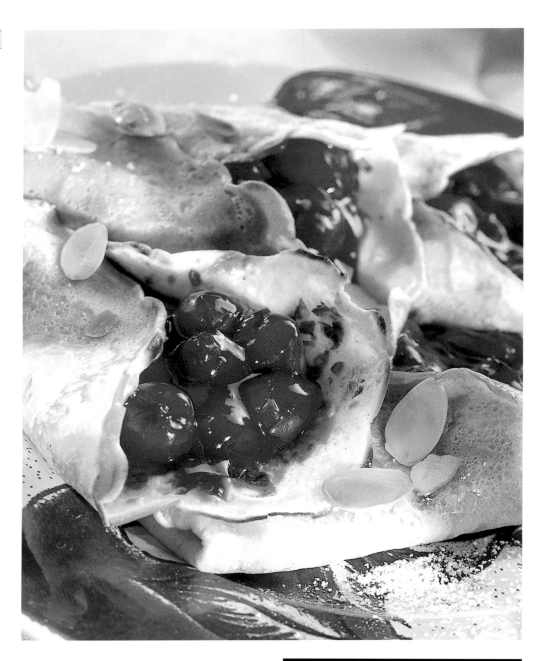

1 Put the cherries and 300 ml/¹/₂ pint/
1¹/₄ cups of the juice in a pan with the
almond essence and mixed spice. Stir
in the cornflour (cornstarch) and bring
to the boil, stirring until thickened
and clear. Set aside.

2 To make the pancakes, sieve the
flour into a bowl with the salt. Add
the chopped mint and make a well in
the centre. Gradually beat in the egg
and milk to make a smooth batter.

3 Heat 1 tbsp of oil in an 18 cm/
7 inch frying pan (skillet); pour off the
oil when hot. Add just enough batter
to coat the base of the frying pan
(skillet) and cook for 1–2 minutes or
until the underside is cooked. Flip the
pancake over and cook for 1 minute.
Remove from the pan and keep warm.
Heat 1 tbsp of the oil in the pan again
and repeat to use up all the batter.

4 Spoon a quarter of the cherry filling
on to a quarter of each pancake and
fold the pancake into a cone shape.
Dust with icing (confectioners') sugar
and sprinkle the flaked (slivered)
almonds over the top. Serve.

COOK'S VARIATION

Use other fillings, such as
gooseberries or blackberries,
as an alternative to the cherries.

Chocolate Chip Ice Cream

This frozen dessert offers the best of both worlds – delicious cookies
and a rich dairy-flavoured ice cream.

Serves 6
300 ml/$\frac{1}{2}$ pint/$1\frac{1}{4}$ cups milk
1 vanilla pod
2 eggs
2 egg yolks
60 g/2 oz/$\frac{1}{4}$ cup caster (superfine) sugar
300 ml/$\frac{1}{2}$ pint/$1\frac{1}{4}$ cups natural yogurt
125 g/4$\frac{1}{2}$ oz chocolate chip cookies, broken into small pieces

6 Remove the ice cream from the
freezer every hour and beat vigorously
to prevent ice crystals forming.
Alternatively, freeze the mixture in an
ice-cream maker, following the
manufacturer's instructions.

7 To serve the chocolate chip ice
cream, transfer it to the main part
of the refrigerator for 1 hour to
soften slightly – this will make it
much easier for serving. Serve
in scoops.

1 Pour the milk into a small pan, add
the vanilla pod and bring slowly to
the boil. Remove the pan from the
heat, cover and leave to cool.

2 Beat the eggs and egg yolks in a
double boiler, or in a bowl set over a
pan of simmering water. Add the
sugar and continue beating until the
mixture is pale and creamy.

3 Reheat the milk to simmering point
and strain it over the egg mixture. Stir
continuously until the custard is thick
enough to coat the back of a spoon.
Remove the custard from the heat and
stand the pan or bowl in cold water to
prevent any further cooking. Wash
and dry the vanilla pod for future use.

4 Stir the yogurt into the cooled
custard and beat until it is well
blended. When the mixture is
thoroughly cold, stir in the broken
chocolate chip cookies.

5 Transfer the mixture to a chilled
metal cake tin (pan) or plastic
container, cover and freeze for 4 hours.

Raspberry Fool

This dish is very easy to make and can be made in advance
and stored in the refrigerator.

Serves 4

300 g/10½ oz fresh raspberries

50 g/1¾ oz/¼ cup icing (confectioners')
sugar

½ tsp vanilla essence

300 ml/½ pint/1¼ cups crème fraîche,
plus extra to decorate

2 egg whites

raspberries and lemon balm leaves,
to decorate

1 Put the raspberries and icing
(confectioners') sugar in a food
processor or blender and blend
until smooth.

2 Put the vanilla essence and crème
fraîche (reserving 1 tablespoon per
portion for decorating) in a bowl and
stir in the raspberry mixture.

3 Whisk the egg whites in a separate
mixing bowl until stiff peaks form
and fold into the raspberry mixture
until fully incorporated.

4 Spoon the raspberry fool into
serving dishes and chill for at least
1 hour. Decorate and serve.

COOK'S VARIATION

This recipe is also delicious made
with strawberries or blackberries.

Steamed Coffee Sponge & Sauce

This sponge pudding is very light and is delicious
with a coffee or chocolate sauce.

Serves 4
2 tbsp vegetarian margarine
2 tbsp soft brown sugar
2 eggs
50 g/1³/₄ oz/¹/₃ cup plain (all-purpose) flour
³/₄ tsp baking powder
6 tbsp milk
1 tsp coffee flavouring (extract)
SAUCE
300 ml/¹/₂ pint/1¹/₄ cups milk
1 tbsp soft brown sugar
1 tsp cocoa powder
2 tbsp cornflour (cornstarch)

1 Lightly grease a 600 ml/1 pint
heatproof pudding basin. Cream the
margarine and sugar until light and
fluffy and beat in the eggs.

2 Gradually stir in the flour and
baking powder and then the milk
and coffee flavouring (extract) to
make a smooth batter.

3 Spoon the mixture into the
prepared pudding basin and cover
with a pleated piece of greaseproof
paper and then a pleated piece of foil,
securing around the bowl with string.
Place in a steamer or large pan and
half fill with boiling water. Cover
and steam for 1–1¹/₄ hours or until
cooked through.

4 To make the sauce, put the milk,
sugar and cocoa powder in a pan
and heat until the sugar dissolves.
Blend the cornflour (cornstarch) with

4 tablespoons of cold water to make a
paste and stir into the pan. Bring to
the boil, stirring until thickened.
Cook over a gentle heat for 1 minute.

5 Turn the pudding out on to a
serving plate and spoon the sauce
over the top. Serve.

Lemon & Lime Syllabub

This dessert is rich but absolutely delicious. It is not, however, for the calorie conscious as it contains a high proportion of cream, but it's well worth blowing the diet for!

Serves 4

50 g/1³/₄ oz/¹/₄ cup caster (superfine) sugar

grated zest and juice of 1 small lemon

grated zest and juice of 1 small lime

50 ml/2 fl oz/4 tbsp Marsala or medium sherry

300 ml/¹/₂ pint/1¹/₄ cups double (heavy) cream

lime and lemon zest, to decorate

1 Put the sugar, fruit juices and zest and sherry in a bowl, mix well and leave to infuse for 2 hours.

2 Add the cream to the mixture and whisk until it just holds its shape.

3 Spoon the mixture into 4 tall serving glasses and chill in the refrigerator for 2 hours before decorating and serving.

COOK'S TIP

Serve with almond biscuits or uncoated florentines. Do not overwhip the cream when adding to the lemon and lime mixture as it may curdle.

Warm Currants in Cassis

Crème de cassis is a blackcurrant-based liqueur which comes
from France and is an excellent flavouring for fruit dishes.

Serves 4
350 g/12 oz blackcurrants
250 g/9 oz redcurrants
4 tbsp caster (superfine) sugar
grated rind and juice of 1 orange
2 tsp arrowroot
2 tbsp crème de cassis
fresh mint leaves, to decorate
whipped cream, to serve

1 Using a fork, strip the currants
from their stalks and place in a
saucepan.

2 Add the sugar and orange rind and
juice, and heat gently until the sugar
has dissolved. Bring to the boil and
simmer gently for 5 minutes.

3 Strain the currants and place in a
bowl. Return the juice to the pan.

4 Blend the arrowroot with a little
water. Mix the arrowroot into the
juice then boil until thickened.

5 Leave to cool slightly, then stir in
the cassis.

6 Serve in individual dishes with
whipped cream.

Cherry Clafoutis

This is a hot dessert that is simple and quick to put together. Try the batter
with other fruits – apricots and plums are particularly delicious.

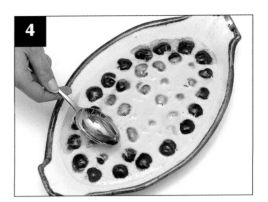

Serves 6
125 g/4$^{1}/_{2}$ oz/1 cup plain (all-purpose) flour
4 eggs, lightly beaten
2 tbsp caster (superfine) sugar
pinch of salt
600 ml/1 pint/2$^{1}/_{2}$ cups milk
butter, for greasing
500 g/1 lb 2 oz black cherries, fresh or canned, pitted
3 tbsp brandy
1 tbsp sugar, to decorate

1 Sift the flour into a large bowl.
Make a well in the centre and add the
eggs, sugar and salt. Draw in the flour
from around the edges and whisk.

2 Pour in the milk and whisk the
batter thoroughly until very smooth.

3 Lightly grease a 1.75 litre/3 pint
ovenproof serving dish and pour in
half of the batter.

4 Spoon in the cherries and pour
the remaining batter over the top.
Sprinkle the brandy over the batter.

5 Bake in a preheated oven, 180°C/
350°F/Gas Mark 4, for 40 minutes.

6 Remove from the oven and sprinkle
with the sugar just before serving.
Serve warm.

Fruit & Nut Loaf

This loaf is like a fruit bread which may be served warm or cold,
perhaps spread with a little vegetarian margarine or butter or topped with jam.

Makes 1 loaf

225 g/8 oz/1¾ cups white
bread flour, plus extra for dusting

½ tsp salt

1 tbsp vegetarian margarine, plus extra
for greasing

2 tbsp soft light
brown sugar

100 g/3½ oz/⅔ cup sultanas (golden
raisins)

50 g/1¾ oz/½ cup no-need to soak dried
apricots, chopped

50 g/1¾ oz/½ cup chopped hazelnuts

2 tsp easy-blend dried yeast

6 tbsp orange juice

6 tbsp natural yogurt

2 tbsp sieved apricot jam

1 Sieve the flour and salt into a
mixing bowl. Rub in the margarine
and stir in the sugar, sultanas
(golden raisins), apricots, nuts
and yeast.

2 Warm the orange juice in a
saucepan but do not allow to boil.

3 Stir the warm orange juice into
the flour mixture with the yogurt
and bring the mixture together to
form a dough.

4 Knead the dough on a lightly
floured surface for 5 minutes until
smooth and elastic. Shape into a
round and place on a lightly greased
baking sheet (cookie sheet). Cover
with a clean tea towel (dish cloth)
and leave to rise in a warm place
until doubled in size.

5 Cook the loaf in a preheated oven,
220°C/425°F/Gas Mark 7, for
35–40 minutes until cooked through.
Transfer to a cooling rack and brush
with the apricot jam. Leave to cool
before serving.

COOK'S TIP

To test if the loaf is cooked through
– tap the base and if it sounds
hollow, it's cooked.

Cinnamon Pears with Maple & Ricotta Cream

These spicy yet sweet pears are accompanied by a delicious melt-in-the-mouth cream, which is relatively low in fat.

Serves 4
1 lemon
4 firm ripe pears
1 cinnamon stick, broken in half
300 ml/$^1/_2$ pint/$1^1/_4$ cups dry cider or unsweetened apple juice
fresh mint leaves, to decorate

MAPLE RICOTTA CREAM

125 g/$4^1/_2$ oz/$^1/_2$ cup medium-fat Ricotta
125 g/$4^1/_2$ oz/$^1/_2$ cup low-fat natural fromage frais
$^1/_2$ tsp ground cinnamon
$^1/_2$ tsp grated lemon rind
1 tbsp maple syrup
grated lemon rind, to decorate

1 Using a vegetable peeler, remove the rind from the lemon and place in a non-stick frying pan (skillet). Squeeze the lemon and pour the juice into a shallow bowl.

2 Peel, halve and core the pears. Place in a bowl and toss in the lemon juice to prevent discoloration. Add to the frying pan (skillet) and pour over the lemon juice remaining in the bowl.

3 Add the cinnamon stick and cider or apple juice. Bring to the boil, then lower the heat and simmer for 10 minutes. Remove the pears using a slotted spoon, reserving the cooking juice.

4 Put the pears in a warm heatproof serving dish, cover with foil and keep warm in a preheated oven at 110°C/ 225°F/Gas Mark $^1/_4$.

5 Return the pan to the heat, bring to the boil, then simmer for 8–10 minutes until reduced by half. Spoon the syrup over the pears.

6 To make the maple Ricotta cream, mix together all the ingredients. Decorate with lemon rind and serve with the pears.

Blackberry, Apple & Fresh Fig Compôte

Elderflower cordial is used in the syrup for this refreshing fruit compôte, giving it a delightfully summery flavour.

Serves 4
1 lemon
60 g/2 oz/¹/₄ cup caster (superfine) sugar
4 tbsp elderflower cordial
300 ml/¹/₂ pint/1¹/₄ cups water
4 dessert (eating) apples
250 g/9 oz/2 cups blackberries
2 fresh figs
SAUCE
150 g/5¹/₂ oz/²/₃ cup thick natural yogurt
2 tbsp clear honey

1 Pare the rind from the lemon, using a potato peeler. Squeeze the juice. Put the lemon rind and juice into a saucepan with the sugar, elderflower cordial and water. Heat gently and simmer, uncovered, for 10 minutes.

2 Core and slice the apples, then add them to the saucepan. Simmer gently for 4–5 minutes or until just tender. Leave to cool.

3 Transfer the apples and syrup to a serving bowl and add the blackberries. Slice the figs and add to the bowl, stirring gently to mix. Cover and chill until ready to serve.

4 To make the sauce, spoon the yogurt into a small serving bowl and drizzle the honey over the top. Cover and chill before serving.

Autumn (Fall) Fruit Bread Pudding

This is like a summer pudding, but it uses fruits which appear later in the year, such as apples, pears and blackberries, as a succulent filling.

Serves 8

900 g/2 lb/4 cups mixed blackberries, chopped apples, chopped pears

150 g/5½ oz/¾ cup soft light brown sugar

1 tsp cinnamon

225 g/8 oz white bread, thinly sliced, crusts removed

1 Place the fruit in a large saucepan with the sugar, cinnamon and 100 ml/ 3½ fl oz of water, stir and bring to the boil. Reduce the heat and simmer for 5–10 minutes so that the fruits soften but still hold their shape.

2 Meanwhile, line the base and sides of a 850 ml/1½ pint pudding basin with the bread slices, ensuring that there are no gaps between the pieces of bread.

3 Spoon the fruit into the centre of the bread-lined bowl and cover the fruit with the remaining bread.

4 Place a saucer on top of the bread and weight it down. Leave to chill in the refrigerator overnight.

5 Turn the pudding out on to a serving plate and serve immediately.

COOK'S TIP

Stand the pudding on a plate when chilling to catch any juices that run down the sides of the basin.

Green Fruit Salad with Mint & Lemon Syrup

This delightful fresh fruit salad is the perfect finale for a summer barbecue.
It has a lovely light syrup made with fresh mint and honey.

Serves 4

1 small Charentais or honeydew melon
2 green apples
2 kiwi fruit
125 g/4¹/₂ oz/1 cup seedless white grapes
fresh mint sprigs, to decorate

SYRUP

1 lemon
150 ml/¹/₄ pint/²/₃ cup white wine
150 ml/¹/₄ pint/²/₃ cup water
4 tbsp clear honey
few sprigs of fresh mint

1 To make the syrup, pare the rind from the lemon, using a potato peeler.

2 Put the lemon rind in a saucepan with the wine, water and honey. Bring to the boil, then simmer gently for 10 minutes. Remove from the heat. Add the sprigs of mint and leave to cool.

3 Slice the melon in half and scoop out the seeds. Using a melon baller or a teaspoon, scoop out melon balls.

4 Core and chop the apples. Peel and slice the kiwi fruit.

5 Strain the cooled syrup into a serving bowl, removing and reserving the lemon rind and discarding the mint sprigs. Add the apple, grapes, kiwi and melon. Stir through gently to mix.

6 Decorate with sprigs of fresh mint and some of the reserved lemon rind and serve.

Chocolate Mousse

This is a light and fluffy, but fruity-tasting mousse which
is delicious with a fresh fruit sauce.

Serves 8
100 g/3¹/₂ oz dark chocolate, melted
300 ml/¹/₂ pint/1¹/₄ cups natural yogurt
150 ml/¹/₄ pint/²/₃ cup quark
4 tbsp caster (superfine) sugar
1 tbsp orange juice
1 tbsp brandy
1¹/₂ tsp gelozone
9 tbsp cold water
2 large egg whites
coarsely grated dark and white chocolate
and orange zest, to decorate

1 Put the chocolate, yogurt, quark,
sugar, orange juice and brandy in a
food processor and blend for 30
seconds. Transfer to a mixing bowl.

2 Sprinkle the gelozone over the
water and stir until dissolved. Bring to
the boil for 2 minutes. Cool slightly,
then stir into the chocolate mixture.

3 Whisk the egg whites until peaking
and fold into the chocolate mixture.

4 Line a 850 ml/1¹/₂ pint loaf tin (pan)
with cling film (plastic wrap). Spoon
the mousse into the tin (pan). Chill
for 2 hours until set. Turn the mousse
out on to a plate, decorate and serve.

COOK'S TIP

For a quick fruit sauce, blend a can
of mandarin segments in natural
juice in a food processor and press
through a sieve. Stir in 1 tbsp clear
honey and serve with the mousse.

Apple Fritters & Almond Sauce

These apple fritters are coated in a light, spiced batter
and deep-fried until crisp and golden. Serve warm.

Serves 4

100 g/3¹⁄₂ oz/³⁄₄ cup plain (all-purpose)
flour

pinch of salt

¹⁄₂ tsp ground cinnamon

12 tbsp warm water

4 tsp vegetable oil

2 egg whites

2 dessert (eating) apples, peeled

vegetable or sunflower oil, for deep-frying

caster (superfine) sugar and cinnamon,
to decorate

SAUCE

150 ml/¹⁄₄ pint/1¹⁄₄ cups natural yogurt

¹⁄₂ tsp almond essence

2 tsp clear honey

1 Sieve the flour and salt into a
mixing bowl.

2 Add the cinnamon and mix well.
Stir in the water and oil to make a
smooth batter.

3 Whisk the egg whites until stiff
peaks form and fold into the batter.

4 Cut the apples into chunks and
dip the pieces of apple into the batter
to coat.

5 Heat the oil for deep-frying to
180°C/350°F or until a cube of bread
browns in 30 seconds. Fry the apple
pieces, in batches, for 3–4 minutes
until golden brown and puffy.
Remove the apple fritters from the oil
with a slotted spoon and leave to
drain on absorbent kitchen paper.

6 Mix the caster (superfine) sugar and
cinnamon and sprinkle over the fritters.

7 Mix the sauce ingredients in a serving
bowl and serve with the fritters.

COOK'S VARIATION

Use pieces of banana or pineapple
instead of the apple, if you prefer.

Mixed Fruit Crumble

I have used tropical fruits in this crumble, flavoured with ginger
and coconut, for something a little different and very tasty.

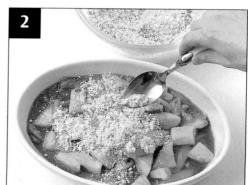

Serves 4

2 mangoes, sliced

1 paw paw, seeded and sliced

225 g/8 oz fresh pineapple, cubed

1½ tsp ground ginger

100 g/3½ oz/8 tbsp vegetarian margarine

100 g/3½ oz/½ cup soft light brown
sugar

175 g/6 oz/1½ cups plain (all-purpose)
flour

50 g/1¾ oz desiccated (shredded)
coconut, plus extra to decorate

1 Place the fruit in a pan with ½ tsp
of the ginger, 25 g/1 oz/2 tbsp of the
margarine and 50 g/1¾ oz/¼ cup of
the sugar. Cook over a gentle heat for
10 minutes until the fruit softens.
Spoon the fruit into the base of a
shallow ovenproof dish.

2 Mix the flour and remaining ginger
together. Rub in the remaining
margarine until the mixture resembles
fine breadcrumbs. Stir in the remaining
sugar and the coconut and spoon over
the fruit to cover completely.

3 Cook the crumble in a preheated
oven at 180°C/350°F/Gas Mark 4
for about 40 minutes or until the top
is crisp. Decorate and serve.

COOK'S VARIATION

Use other fruits, such as plums,
apples or blackberries, as a fruit
base and add chopped nuts to the
topping instead of the coconut.

Boston Chocolate Pie

This lighter version of the popular chocolate cream pie
is made with yogurt and crème fraîche.

Serves 6
250 g/9 oz shortcrust pastry
250 g/9 oz dark chocolate
150 ml/¼ pint/⅔ cup crème fraîche
FILLING
3 eggs
125 g/4½ oz/½ cup caster (superfine) sugar
60 g/2 oz/½ cup flour, plus extra for dusting
1 tbsp icing (confectioners') sugar, plus extra to decorate
pinch of salt
1 tsp vanilla flavouring (extract)
400 ml/14 fl oz/1¾ cups milk
150 ml/¼ pint/⅔ cup natural yogurt
150 g/5½ oz dark chocolate, broken into pieces
2 tbsp kirsch

1 Roll out the pastry and use to line a
23 cm/9 inch loose-bottomed flan tin
(pan). Prick the base with a fork, line
with baking parchment, fill with
baking beans and bake blind in a
preheated oven, 200°C/400°F/Gas Mark
6, for 20 minutes. Remove the beans
and parchment and return to the oven
for 5 minutes. Cool on a wire rack.

2 To make the Chocolate Caraque,
melt the chocolate in a heatproof
bowl set over a pan of simmering
water. Spread on to a cool surface
with a palette knife (spatula). When
cool, scrape it into curls by drawing a
sharp knife firmly across the surface.

3 To make the filling, beat the eggs and
sugar until fluffy. Sieve the flour, icing
(confectioners') sugar and salt over the
beaten eggs and stir until blended. Stir
in the vanilla flavouring (extract). Put
the milk and yogurt in a small pan,
bring slowly to the boil, then strain into
the egg mixture. Pour into the top of a
double boiler, or a bowl set over a pan
of simmering water, and stir until thick
enough to coat the back of a spoon.
Melt the chocolate and kirsch over a

low heat. When it has melted, stir into
the custard. Remove the custard from
the heat and stand the double boiler or
bowl in cold water to prevent further
cooking. Leave to cool.

4 Pour the chocolate filling into the
pastry case. Spread the crème fraîche
over the chocolate, and arrange the
caraque on top.

Fruit Brûlée

This is a cheat's brûlée, in that yogurt is used to cover a base of fruit,
before being sprinkled with sugar and grilled (broiled).

Serves 4
4 plums, stoned and sliced
2 cooking apples, peeled and sliced
1 tsp ground ginger
600 ml/1 pint/2½ cups Greek-style yogurt
2 tbsp icing (confectioners') sugar, sieved
1 tsp almond essence
75 g/2¾ oz/⅓ cup demerara sugar

1 Put the plums and apples in a saucepan with 2 tablespoons of water and cook for 7–10 minutes until tender but not mushy. Leave to cool, then stir in the ginger. Using a slotted spoon, spoon the mixture into the base of a shallow serving dish.

2 Mix the yogurt, icing (confectioners') sugar and almond essence together and spoon on to the fruit.

3 Sprinkle the demerara sugar over the top of the yogurt and cook under a hot grill (broiler) for 3–4 minutes or until the sugar has dissolved and formed a crust. Chill in the refrigerator for 1 hour and serve.

COOK'S TIP

Use any variety of fruit, such as mixed berries or mango pieces, for this dessert, but do not poach them.

Chocolate & Tofu (Bean Curd) Cheesecake

This cheesecake takes a little time to prepare and cook but is well worth the effort. It is quite rich and is good served or decorated with a little fresh fruit, such as sliced strawberries.

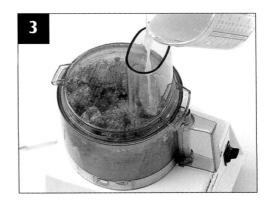

Serves 12
100 g/3½ oz/¾ cup plain (all-purpose) flour
100 g/3½ oz/¾ cup ground almonds
200 g/7 oz/¾ cup demerara sugar
150 g/5½ oz/10 tbsp vegetarian margarine
675 g/1½ lb firm tofu (bean curd)
175 ml/6 fl oz/¾ cup vegetable oil
125 ml/4 fl oz/½ cup orange juice
175 ml/6 fl oz/¾ cup brandy
50 g/1¾ oz/6 tbsp cocoa powder, plus extra to decorate
2 tsp almond essence
icing (confectioners') sugar and Cape gooseberries, to decorate

1 Put the flour, ground almonds and 1 tablespoon of the sugar in a bowl and mix well. Rub the margarine into the mixture to form a dough.

2 Lightly grease and line the base of a 23 cm/9 inch spring-form tin (pan). Press the dough into the base of the tin (pan) to cover.

3 Roughly chop the tofu (bean curd) and put in a food processor with all of the remaining ingredients and blend until smooth and creamy. Pour over the base in the tin (pan) and cook in a preheated oven, 160°C/325°F/Gas Mark 3, for 1–1¼ hours or until set.

4 Leave to cool in the tin (pan) for 5 minutes, then remove from the tin (pan) and chill in the refrigerator. Dust with icing (confectioners') sugar and cocoa powder. Decorate and serve.

Pear Cake

This is a really moist cake, flavoured with chopped pears and cinnamon.

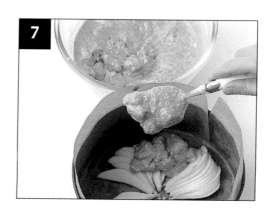

Serves 12
4 pears, peeled and cored
vegetarian margarine, for greasing
2 tbsp water
200 g/7 oz/1½ cups plain (all-purpose) flour
2 tsp baking powder
100 g/3½ oz/½ cup soft light brown sugar
4 tbsp milk
2 tbsp clear honey, plus extra to drizzle
2 tsp ground cinnamon
2 egg whites

1 Grease and line the base of a 20 cm/8 inch cake tin (pan).

2 Put 1 pear in a food processor with the water and blend until almost smooth. Transfer to a mixing bowl.

3 Sieve in the flour and baking powder. Beat in the sugar, milk, honey and cinnamon and mix well.

4 Chop all but one of the remaining pears and add to the mixture.

5 Whisk the egg whites until stiff peaks form and gently fold into the mixture until fully incorporated.

6 Slice the remaining pear and arrange in a fan pattern on the base of the tin (pan).

7 Spoon the cake mixture into the tin (pan) and cook in a preheated oven, 150°C/300°F/Gas Mark 2, for 1¼ – 1½ hours or until cooked through.

8 Remove the cake from the oven and leave to cool in the tin (pan) for 10 minutes.

9 Turn the cake out on to a wire cooling rack and drizzle with honey. Leave to cool completely, then cut into slices to serve.

COOK'S TIP

To test if the cake is cooked through, insert a skewer into the centre – if it comes out clean the cake is cooked. If not, return the cake to the oven and test at frequent intervals.

Banana & Mango Tart

Bananas and mangoes are a great combination of colours and flavours,
especially when topped with toasted coconut chips.

Serves 8
PASTRY
20 cm/8 inch baked pastry case
FILLING
2 small ripe bananas
1 mango, sliced
3½ tbsp cornflour (cornstarch)
50 g/1¾ oz/6 tbsp demerara sugar
300 ml/½ pint/1¼ cups soya milk
150 ml/¼ pint/⅔ cup coconut milk
1 tsp vanilla essence
toasted coconut chips, to decorate

1 Slice the bananas and arrange half in the baked pastry case with half of the mango pieces.

2 Put the cornflour (cornstarch) and sugar in a saucepan and mix together. Slowly stir in the soya and coconut milks until combined and cook over a low heat, stirring until the mixture thickens. Stir in the vanilla essence. Pour the mixture over the fruit.

3 Top with the remaining fruit and toasted coconut chips. Chill in the refrigerator for 1 hour before serving.

COOK'S TIP

Coconut chips are available in some supermarkets and most health food shops. It is worth using them as they look much more attractive and are not as sweet as desiccated (shredded) coconut.

Chocolate Fudge Pudding

This pudding has a hidden surprise when cooked as it separates
to give a rich chocolate sauce at the bottom of the dish.

Serves 4
50 g/1³/₄ oz/4 tbsp vegetarian margarine, plus extra for greasing
75 g/2³/₄ oz/6 tbsp soft light brown sugar
2 eggs, beaten
350 ml/12 fl oz/1¹/₄ cups milk
50 g/1³/₄ oz chopped walnuts
40 g/1¹/₂ oz/¹/₄ cup plain (all-purpose) flour
2 tbsp cocoa powder
icing (confectioners') sugar and cocoa, to dust

1 Lightly grease a 1 litre/1³/₄ pint ovenproof dish.

2 Cream the margarine and sugar until fluffy and beat in the eggs.

3 Gradually stir in the milk and add the walnuts.

4 Sieve the flour and cocoa powder into the mixture and fold in gently until well mixed.

5 Spoon the mixture into the dish and cook in a preheated oven at 180°C/350°F/Gas Mark 4 for 35–40 minutes or until the sponge is cooked. Dust with icing (confectioners') sugar and cocoa powder and serve.

COOK'S VARIATION

Add 1–2 tbsp brandy or rum to the mixture for a slightly alcoholic pudding, or 1–2 tbsp orange juice for a child-friendly version.

Passion Cake

Decorating this moist, rich carrot cake with sugared flowers lifts
it into the celebration class. It is a perfect choice for Easter.

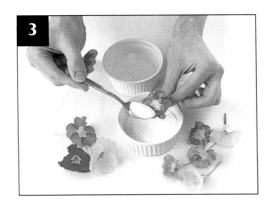

Serves 8–10
150 ml/¼ pint/⅔ cup corn oil
175 g/6 oz/¾ cup golden caster (superfine) sugar
4 tbsp natural yogurt
3 eggs, plus 1 extra yolk
1 tsp vanilla flavouring (extract)
125 g/4½ oz/1 cup walnut pieces, chopped
175 g/6 oz carrots, grated
1 banana, mashed
175 g/6 oz/1½ cups plain (all-purpose) flour
90 g/3 oz/½ cup fine oatmeal
1 tsp bicarbonate of soda (baking soda)
1 tsp baking powder
1 tsp ground cinnamon
½ tsp salt

FROSTING

150 g/5½ oz/generous ½ cup low-fat soft cheese
4 tbsp natural yogurt
90 g/3 oz/¾ cup icing (confectioners') sugar
1 tsp grated lemon rind
2 tsp lemon juice

DECORATION

primroses and violets
1 egg white, lightly beaten
40 g/1½ oz/3 tbsp caster (superfine) sugar

1 Grease and line a 23 cm/9 inch round cake tin (pan). Beat the oil, sugar, yogurt, eggs, egg yolk and vanilla. Beat in the walnuts, carrot and banana. Sift the remaining ingredients and beat into the mixture.

2 Pour the mixture into the tin (pan) and level the surface. Bake in a preheated oven, 180°C/350°F/Gas Mark 4, for 1½ hours or until firm. Insert a skewer into the centre: it should come out clean. Cool in the tin (pan) for 15 minutes, then transfer to a wire rack.

3 To make the frosting, beat together the cheese and yogurt. Sift in the icing (confectioners') sugar and stir in the lemon rind and juice. Spread over the top and sides of the cake. To prepare the decoration, dip the flowers quickly in the beaten egg white, then sprinkle with caster (superfine) sugar to cover. Place well apart on baking parchment. Leave in a warm, dry place for several hours until they are dry and crisp. Arrange the flowers on top of the cake.

Index

Index compiled by Hilary Bird.